A History of the New Testament and Its Times

A
HISTORY
OF THE
NEW
TESTAMENT
AND ITS TIMES

Robert L. Cate

BROADMAN PRESS
NASHVILLE, TENNESSEE

© Copyright 1991 • Broadman Press
All Rights Reserved
4213-25
ISBN: 0-8054-1325-1
Dewey Decimal Classification: 225.9
Subject Heading: BIBLE. N.T. — HISTORY // BIBLE. N.T. — HISTORY OF
BIBLICAL EVENTS
Library of Congress Catalog Card Number: 90-23791
Printed in the United States of America

Unless otherwise noted, all Scripture quotations are from the *Revised Standard Version of the Bible,* copyrighted 1946, 1952, © 1971, 1973.

All Scripture quotations marked (NIV) are from the Holy Bible, *New International Version,* copyright © 1973, 1978, 1984 by International Bible Society.

All Scripture quotations marked (KJV) are from the *King James Version* of the Bible.

Library of Congress Cataloging-in-Publication Data

Cate, Robert L.
     A history of the New Testament and its times / Robert L. Cate
       p.   cm.
     Includes bibliographical references and index.
     ISBN 0-8054-1325-1
     1. Bible. N.T.—History of Biblical events.   2. Bible. N.T.-
-History of contemporary events.   3. Bible. N.T.—Introductions.
I. Title.
BS2407.C38   1991
225.9′5—dc20

                                                                90-23791
                                                                CIP

Like all my labors,
this book is dedicated to Dot,
my wife, companion, sweetheart,
fellow laborer, and friend

CONTENTS

INTRODUCTION

"These are written that you may believe that Jesus is the Christ, the Son of God, and that believing you may have life in his name" (John 20:31). Thus, John set forth his purpose for writing his gospel. Every good book has a purpose—a goal which the author hopes to fulfill by the labors of research and writing invested in its production. This is true, regardless of the subject of the book—history or science, drama or novel, textbook or fiction. So it is with this book. I have had a purpose in mind while searching out the evidence and pondering it. This purpose has guided me as I sought to analyze and synthesize this material into an understandable, connected narrative record. Further, that purpose has guided me in my choices both of what to record and of what to leave out. These choices are frequently involved and seldom easy, yet they have to be made nonetheless.

You have a right to know my purpose from the beginning. In the end, only you can judge how well I have succeeded or failed. Frequently readers are left to determine an author's purposes by deducing them from the text. Rather than leaving that task to you, I will try to state my purpose at the outset. This will allow you to decide whether or not you wish to read any further.

Purpose of the Book

Let me begin by clarifying what I am not trying to do. First, I am not writing a commentary on the New Testament text. Many such commentaries have been written. I have read a large number of these and tried to familiarize myself with their basic approaches. I have also tried to familiarize myself with the approaches made by the commentary authors whose works I have not read. However, I am not trying to interpret the biblical text as such.

Second, I do not intend to write either a geographical or an archaeological atlas for the New Testament. I have tried to keep up with archaeological developments in our understanding of the New Testament and its times. For the reader who wants to focus attention on this subject, I would urge that the books and journal articles on the various subjects be investigated on your own.

In addition, while I do not believe that a person can study the New Testament thoroughly without keeping good Bible maps on hand and referring to them constantly, I am not trying merely to give a summary of the geographical influences which bore upon the developing story of the life of Jesus or the spread of the gospel. However, as in the case of the commentaries, I have sought to become thoroughly familiar with the geographical and archaeological evidence relating to my subject.

Third, I am not writing a biblical theology of the New Testament. Countless numbers of these books are available. I shall make occasional references to the meaning or theological significance of particular words or events. However, these will not be made in any systematic fashion and are being made only where they are significant for the development of my basic purpose.

Putting these negatives aside, *what I am trying to do is to present a history of the New Testament era, showing how the political, economic, social, religious, and geographical influences of the times helped to shape and in turn were shaped by the life and ministry of Jesus of Nazareth and those of His disciples as they carried His message to the extremities of their world and center of the Roman Empire.* This book is written for the beginning student of the New Testament who wants to know more of the world in which Jesus and early Christians lived. It is not written for advanced students, though they may find a review of the subject from this material helpful and perhaps gain an occasional new insight into some event or problem of understanding.

In seeking to accomplish this purpose, I have adopted a specific methodology. I have tried not to burden the new student with excessive technicalities. Therefore, I have sought to keep footnotes to a minimum. Those familiar with the subject will recognize my indebtedness to those many scholars who have gone before. On the other hand, in the hope that this book will serve as the basis for an increasing interest in and for further study for the subjects, I have given a brief bibliography. This will help the enquiring student to find other sources in which to pursue further study.

I am not seeking simply to define or describe what God was doing in these times. The New Testament does that quite well for itself. What I am seeking to do is to investigate and understand those human influences which impinged upon the men and women of the New Testament, shaping their lives while pushing, prodding, and occasionally dragging them along on the human level into the physical and spiritual directions which they took. In so doing, perhaps we gain new insight into how such influences may shape our own lives and ministries within the Christian communities. We shall certainly gain new insights into how the early Christians related to their world.

A final part of the purpose of this book is to complete a story. Every student of the Bible knows that the New Testament is a part of the Bible but not all of it. Our Bible also has the Old Testament as well. In seeking to help make its background more understandable, I have already written a history of that era—*These Sought a Country: A History of Israel in the Old Testament Times.*

In addition, I have also written a history of the interbiblical period—*A History of the Bible Lands in the Interbiblical Period.* It sought to trace the developments in the biblical world following the close of the Old Testament era which had a major impact on the people of Israel and helped to shape the world of the New Testament. This present book will bring to a close the study begun by the first two. Taken together, all three are intended to give the enquiring student a complete introduction to the study of the history of the entire biblical era. It is my hope and intent that these will enable any student to gain a better understanding and appreciation of the whole Bible. It is rooted and grounded in history. It cannot be fully understood apart from a grasp of the world in which its events occurred and its heroes and heroines lived.

Presuppositions of the Author

The presuppositions with which the author approaches the subject are equally as important as identifying an author's purpose for a book. Again, most authors do not generally state these, leaving it to the readers to try to discover them in the process of reading. Yet these basic presuppositions of an author significantly affect the way evidence is gathered and evaluated and how conclusions are drawn and presented.

Not one of us is impartial in the way we deal with any subject. Admittedly, it is highly difficult to be objective about something so subjective as presuppositions. At the same time, if you and I both seek to do this, we will be better able to assess the value of this book for further study.

Therefore, I am going to try to identify the basic presuppositions which I bring to this subject. You need to be aware of them because they determine who I am and the stance from which I will deal with the material.

First of all, I am a Christian. I grew up in a Christian home where Bible reading was a regular and normal part of life. Because of this, I do not remember any time when I did not "love Jesus." On the other hand, I made a personal commitment to Jesus Christ as Lord in my late adolescent years. From that time, I have sought to allow Him to be the Lord of my life, the Guide of my pathways, and the One to whom I always turn for the purpose and goals of my life.

Second, I believe that God is love. Because of this, I believe that He loves everybody. This means that He loves me. It also means that He loves you.

Third, I know that I am a sinner. I have personally rebelled against the will of God. I also believe that all people are sinners. This means that you yourself have chosen to disobey God, choosing to "do your own thing" rather than seeking to do that which pleases Him. Because we have sinned, we live in a state of alienation from God. It is not so much that He has left us but that we have abandoned Him.

Fourth, because we have sinned and been alienated from Him and because He loves us, even in spite of our sin, I believe that God has acted in His infinite mercy and overwhelming grace to deliver us from our sinful condition. To this end, Jesus Christ, the Son of God and Son of Man, has come to save us from our sinful state. Although He wishes to save us, He does not force Himself upon us. Rather, He leaves us free to accept His offer of mercy or reject it. We can choose whether or not we will accept the benefits of His love.

Fifth, God has not left Himself unknown in this world but has chosen to reveal Himself to His human creatures. He has done this both through the world of nature and the Bible, His Word. Further, He has sent His Holy Spirit to guide us in the understanding of His revelation. *In addition, since God reveals Himself both in the world and the Word, these two revelations do not contradict one another*. If there appears to be a contradiction, I believe that it lies in my misunderstanding either of His Word or the world, or else in my ignorance. You or I simply may not know enough to be able to understand the situation fully. It is not easy to say, "I don't know," but it is at least honest.

I believe the Bible is inspired. For me, this is a faith commitment. The word *inspiration* comes from two words which mean "to breath into." Inspiration means that God has breathed into the words. The idea probably derives from the account of God breathing the breath of life into the first man (Gen. 2:7). To say the Scriptures are inspired is to say that they were "God-breathed."

Inspiration is a fact and a process. We are taught that inspiration begins with God's spirit working in the hearts and minds of His people (2 Pet. 1:21). A revelation from God starts with God. A fully developed concept of inspiration must include all these ideas: The process begins with God, moves through the original speakers and writers, fills the very words themselves, and carries on to the contemporary interpreter. Any concept of inspiration which is less than this is less than what the Bible claims for itself.

Inspiration carries elements of faith and mystery. The faith statement is that the Bible is fully inspired, both in its origin and as it comes to us. Yet the ultimate nature of its inspiration belongs to God. We may attempt to explain it, for example, as we explore the nature of biblical history, but such explanations are still only human theories—no more.

Sixth, God has called me to His service and given me the task of trying to make His Word live for people. I perceived this as the God given purpose of my life more than thirty years ago. All the foregoing rests on this call, and it undergirds everything which follows.

Ultimately, then, my specific purpose for this book is to help make the New Testament live for you. The material contained herein is intended to help you understand the background of the lives and ministries of Jesus Christ and those who followed Him in spreading the "good news" from Jerusalem to Rome to the ends of the earth.

The Author's Indebtedness

No work such as this is the result of any one person's labor. I am in great debt to many people. I owe my very life itself to those people who have guided me in my spiritual pilgrimage. They are my parents, my wife, my children, my teachers, the people to whom and with whom I have ministered, and those students and church members who have encouraged me in my pursuit of knowledge. I am also in deep debt to those millions of Southern Baptists whose selfless offerings have made it possible for me to be able to study and probe into the Word of God.

More specifically, I am indebted to those teachers and writers who have forced me to examine both God's Word and their words in my personal search for truth. I learned long ago that a Christian has absolutely nothing to fear from truth. However, each Christian has an inescapable obligation to seek to know what the truth is. To this end, I am indebted to both those with whom I have agreed and those with whom I have disagreed. People from both categories have expanded my mind. Most especially, the disagreements have forced me to a more thorough study and investigation in my search for truth. Both my Lord and my teachers have always driven me never to be satisfied with easy half-truths when the whole truth could be found after enough study and thought.

Facts and Theories

It is also important for a student of any subject to recognize that there is a major difference between facts and theories. Facts stand. They are true regardless of the circumstances. On the other hand, theories are simply human attempts to explain and relate known facts. As we gather new facts or reexamine old ones, we may develop new theories. These may change with the passing years. Further, there may frequently be more than one theory to explain the same facts.

A mother was quite disturbed to note that all of the drawings which her son brought home from kindergarten were done in black. Suspecting some deep psychological problem, she took him to a child psychologist who sought to probe the child's psyche in order to determine what these inner problems were. However, though they were sure he was deeply disturbed, they were never able to find the problem. In exasperation, the mother one day cried out in anguish, "Oh, I wish I knew why you do all of your drawings in black."

At this, her son responded, "I've lost all my other crayons." The facts were clear. The drawings were all done in black. But, the initial theory of some deep psychological problem was quite wrong. It may have made sense, but it was wrong nonetheless.

The same is true of scientific, religious, philosophical, or historical theories. They may be and frequently are wrong, especially when they are based upon limited knowledge and investigation. The historian must always recognize that theories are simply the best attempt to explain known facts.

In writing this book, I have done my best to find all the facts which are available relating to each subject. I am certain that in some instances I have failed. However, when I have determined the facts, I have then sought for the best theories to explain them. At the same time, I have sought to keep clearly distinguished in my mind the difference between the facts and theories. It is imperative, if you are going to profit most fully from this book, that you also seek to keep that distinction clear.

Finally, I wish to say to those who have shaped me and to you who will study with me, I am responsible for the conclusions contained in this book. I will try to deal with the various subjects fairly, present the evidence as I perceive and understand it, and show why I have drawn the conclusions I have. I shall also try to deal fairly with those who disagree with me, holding to other equally valid conclusions. It is my prayer that God will use and bless this book to make you a better and more informed student of the New Testament. I am seeking to make the Bible live for you. I also pray that your study will help you have a richer devotional life and deeper appreciation of those saints who lived through the days we are studying.

Part 1
The World Itself Could Not Contain the Books

1
The New Testament Canon

Most people take for granted the fact that the New Testament contains twenty-seven different books. We seldom, if ever, question why there are not twenty-six or twenty-eight. Neither do we normally question why we have these particular books and not some others written by other Christians of the New Testament era, such as the Gospel of Thomas, the Gospel of Peter, or the Gospel of Philip. In fact, without saying so, we act as if we believe that one day God knocked on the door of the church in Jerusalem, Antioch, or Rome and simply handed the doorkeeper these books with an admonition to preserve, study, teach, and obey them.

However, if we think about the subject at all, we must think otherwise. Luke refers to the existence of other books, writing:

> Inasmuch as *many* have undertaken to compile a narrative of the things which have been accomplished among us, just as they were delivered to us by those who from the beginning were eyewitnesses and ministers of the word, it seemed good to me also, having followed all things closely for some time past, to write an orderly account for you, . . . that you may know the truth concerning the things of which you have been informed (Luke 1:1-4, italics mine).

What were these books to which he referred? Do we have any of them? We need at least to consider these questions and their answers. Paul clearly wrote more than two letters to the church at Corinth because he refers to a letter earlier than 1 Corinthians (1 Cor. 5:9). It also appears that a letter may have been written between the letters we call 1 and 2 Corinthians. There may have been others in addition to these four. Where are they? Furthermore, Paul told the church at Corinth what Jesus said at the last supper (1 Cor. 11:23-25). If they had possessed any of the Gospels at the time he wrote this, that summary would not have been necessary because they already would have known it.

Obviously, the first and primary source for studying the history of the New Testament era is the New Testament itself. However, the New Testament, this collection of twenty-seven diverse books, has a history itself. We must consider how and why these books were collected into the New Testament canon before we actually begin to use them. Until we have actually understood something of the process by which these particular books were collected into a volume revered as authoritative scripture, we shall not be able to use them properly as sources for our study of the history of the New Testament era.

Before we proceed further, however, we need to define what we mean by *canon*. The Greek word from which this English word has been transliterated is *kanon*. It means a reed. As such, it was frequently used by builders and stonemasons to determine if walls were straight and floors and roofs were level. It later came to be applied to any straight rod used for such purposes. From this usage, the term attained a derived meaning defining anything which determined whether something was good, right, or proper. This in turn led to the further idea of defining a collection of laws or rules which establish standards of behavior. In the process of time *kanon* finally came to be applied to collections of books which were established authoritative patterns of behavior or orthodox doctrinal beliefs. With this meaning it came to be applied to the New Testament. The "canon" of the New Testament consists of those books which contain and reveal God's expectations for the lives of His people. This brings us, then, to the New Testament canon itself.

The Nature of the Canon

As we have already noted, the New Testament canon is made up of twenty-seven different books. However, these books are of several different types, clearly distinguishable from one another in literary category and purpose. We find the four Gospels: Matthew, Mark, Luke, and John. The word *gospel* originally meant good news. Then it came to be applied to these four books which told the good news of the life, death, and resurrection of Jesus. These are not biographies of Jesus in any sense of the term because they do not report on most of Jesus' life, focusing primarily upon the years of His ministry. While they give some details of what the early Christians remembered of His life, they obviously leave out a great deal which we would like to know and any modern biography would attempt to record.

Following the Gospels, we next have The Acts of the Apostles, more commonly called Acts. This book has been classified as history. However, as in the case of the Gospels, it is not written like a twentieth-century historian might approach history. (We will return to this subject in much more detail in the following chapter.) In fact, if we read the Book of Acts thoughtfully, we are immediately struck by the fact that the book deals in detail with only two of the apostles—Peter and Paul. Further, from the midpoint of the book even Peter disappears from its pages. Its real emphasis is upon the spread of the gospel message and the Christian movement from Jerusalem to Rome, from the place of its birth to the heart of the Roman Empire.

Next we come to a section of the canon normally called The Epistles. *Epistles* is a term which simply means letters. However, the Epistles may be divided into three or four subsections. First is the Pauline collection, called this because Paul is said to be the author of it. However, these are frequently subdivided as being church epistles (those addressed to a church or churches) and personal (or pastoral) epistles (those addressed to individuals who were followers or friends of Paul). The church epistles are Romans through 2 Thessalonians. The personal epistles are those from 1 Timothy through Philemon.

Following these is the Book of Hebrews. Though it is sometimes attributed to Paul, most biblical students no longer accept his authorship. Anonymous in format, it does not even fit into the form of an epistle. Rather, it appears to be more of a theological essay.

The last group of Epistles extends from James through Jude. These are normally called the General Epistles because they were written by different authors to general audiences, rather than to specific churches or people. They are quite brief and are among the least used and therefore least familiar portions of the New Testament canon.

The final book of the New Testament is The Revelation. It is wholly different from any kind of literature with which most modern writers are familiar. However, it is representative of a class of writing fairly common in the New Testament era which was called apocalyptic. Filled with strange and unusual symbols, it speaks to one era while apparently dealing with great sweeps of human and divine history.

Each of these various kinds of literature which make up the New Testament canon has to be handled differently if we are to understand and interpret them properly. This means that, for our purposes here, in calling the New Testament our primary source for the history of the New Testament era, we must recognize that even within its pages the historical evidence must be dealt with in differing ways.

The Historical Forces Which Demanded a Canon

To the person of faith, from the divine standpoint, the Christian churches have a canon because God intended, inspired, and revealed it. However, from the human standpoint, certain identifiable historical forces were at work which made a canon of Scripture imperative for the developing churches.

At the beginning, the early Christians were also Jews. They therefore already had a canon of authoritative scripture, the Old Testament. Thus they were used to such an idea. It is immaterial that the Hebrew canon may not have been "officially" fixed by that time. The idea was present and the common people had accepted it.

Further, as the apostles and other eyewitnesses of the events surrounding the life of Jesus began to die, the churches needed written records to preserve the memory of the life and teachings of Jesus. In addition, the early churches, like those of our own age, began to have problems because they were made up of humans. These problems needed to be addressed. Yet this could not always be done firsthand. Thus letters were written to help the churches and ministers deal with those issues.

In addition, it also became obvious with the passage of time that the Holy Spirit was continuing the process of revelation begun by Jesus. Jesus had accepted the Hebrew Scriptures, but had also said that He had come to give them new meaning and carry them further (Matt. 5:17-48). The Spirit was clearly doing the same things with the apostles. We should understand in this light Philip's witness to the Ethiopian eunuch, Peter's witness to Cornelius, or the Jerusalem conference itself (Acts 8:26-39; 10:9-48; 15:1-21). In each of these instances, the teaching of the Old Testament Scriptures were expanded and enlarged.

Finally, it is obvious that as the Christian movement spread, it became impossible for those who had known Jesus personally or for their close companions to be present in every new congregation. Thus it became imperative that written materials be provided in order to share with these new churches what they truly needed to know. All of these forces played a part in the thrust to develop a canon of the New Testament.

The Early Period (to A.D. 70)

We do not have a specific historical record of how or when the books of the New Testament were written or of when it was canonized. What we do is study the available materials and make the best deductions based on that evidence.[1] Paul's letters were probably written during this early period, as most likely were some of the gospels. However, during this era the churches still had numerous eyewitnesses and first-generation Christians available to tell the story. Thus the need for a canon of Scripture was not paramount. Not a single reference from this period has been found where any author quoted from any part of what we now call our New Testament ascribing scriptural authority to it.

The Middle Period (A.D. 70 to 150)

A new factor entered Christian experience with the destruction of Jerusalem and its temple in A.D. 70 by the Romans. No longer was Jerusalem the center of the Christian movement. Thus a new source of authority needed to be found. No church rose to the immediate forefront of Christianity. Therefore the Christians' writings began to take on the authority for presenting the Christian faith.

We can demonstrate that by the end of the first century, the letters of Paul had been gathered together into one collection. E. J. Goodspeed thought that Onesimus was responsible for collecting Paul's epistles. Some scholars have suggested that the event which gave impetus to the collection of these books was the publication of Acts by Luke. This book caused the broader Christian community to become aware that Paul had established other churches. Other theories exist about how Paul's letters were gathered. By whatever means it came about, it is almost certain that such a collection had been made by the time that Revelation was written. While Revelation is a typical apocalypse, its one unique feature is the seven letters addressed to the churches in its first three chapters. The human author may have had before him a collection of Paul's letters which served as his pattern.

To this collection, it appears that the general letters and Hebrews were added shortly thereafter. References from some of the early church writers (usually called apostolic fathers) show that by the end of this era that they knew of such a collection. However, when they quoted from these new writings, they did not use the same frame of reference which they did when they quoted from the Old Testament. Thus it appears that they did not yet accept them as Scriptures, even though they were clearly accepted as important.

When we consider the Gospels, we are on even less firm footing. The *Didache,* a book from the late first or early second century, quotes from Matthew in terms which express reverence but again does not use the same terms that were reserved for the Old Testament Scriptures. Most New Testament scholars believe that Mark was the first Gospel written and that it was used as a pattern by both Luke and Matthew. If this is true, then Mark also must have been in circulation by the time of the *Didache*. Further, it seems certain that Luke must also have been in circulation by then if Acts, the second volume of his work, served as the impetus for the beginning of a collection of Pauline correspondence. However, we have no evidence at this time of any collection of the four Gospels as a group being circulated among the churches.

The Final Period (A.D. 150 to 200)

Beginning about A.D. 150, affairs began to move more rapidly. The movement toward a canon was accelerated by the rise of heretics and their false teachings. One of these, Marcion, denied that the God of the New Testament and the God of the Old Testament were the same. He insisted that the churches were to reject the Old Testament and to accept as a canon of Scriptures the books which he collected from among the Christian writings of the era. He rejected anything which came either directly or indirectly from the original twelve apostles, since they were Jews and accepted the Old Testament. He accepted only the writings of Paul (with severe modifications where he had quoted from the Old Testament) and Luke's Gospel, since Luke had been a follower of Paul.

The Gnostics had also challenged the Christian movement at least from the time of Paul. He had been in conflict with them on several occasions. They believed that flesh and spirit were wholly incompatible and that the entire emphasis of Christianity was upon the spirit and had no bearing upon the body. For them the incarnation was false. Further, they taught that Jesus did not die as He was not truly physical. They also insisted that sins committed in the flesh had no bearing upon a person's spiritual condition. The Gnostics apparently adopted Marcion as their "patron saint." To propagate their views, they also accepted a canon of authoritative books as the basis for their teachings. They used some mainline Christian literature, modifying some of it, reinterpreting other parts, and adding yet new books.

During this time the apologists (defenders of the faith) and the Fathers began to write more extensively, seeking to combat the inroads of such heresies and to proclaim the basic Christian faith. From this time we begin to find references in their writings which quoted from books in our New Testament as sacred, authoritative scripture. It was treated as having the same authority as the Scriptures of the Old Testament. Further, for the first time we find a reference to the "Old" Testament. For there to be an "Old" Testament, there also has to be a "New" Testament.

By the end of this period, it is fairly clear that the churches had accepted the books of the New Testament canon as we now have them. One or two of the books continued to be discussed and debated by the Fathers for some time, but we can conclude with confidence that the New Testament canon was essentially set by A.D. 200. Some segments of the early churches continued this debate on its contents for several hundred years, but mainstream Christianity appears to have had the matter settled here. The basic criteria for their acceptance was that these books came from eyewitnesses or those closely associated with eyewitnesses. Further, these books were also "orthodox" in their presentation of the faith which had been communicated by the first apostles.

For our purposes here, then, we shall use the twenty-seven books of the New Testament canon as the primary sources for our historical study and reconstruction. It is from them that we shall draw the first and primary evidences for our study.

Note

1. For a thorough study of this process, you may read Clayton Harrop's *History of the New Testament in Plain Language* (Waco: Word, 1984).

2
The Nature of Biblical History

At first glance, it appears to the beginning student that history is history, regardless of who writes it or where it is found. History should simply be, so it would seem, a written record of what happened at any given point in time and at any place in the world. However, as we begin to think about the subject, it becomes obvious that the issue is far more involved than this. For example, a person's diary might fit our tentative definition, but it doesn't really appear to be history. Diaries are highly selective, dealing with what happened to or influenced one person and leaving out everything and everyone else. Further, diaries frequently focus on feelings, on the meaning of events rather than on facts. The writer is concerned with what was felt when something happened rather than simply with what happened.

On the other hand, some so-called history has been written to show what political leaders or philosophers believe should have happened rather than what actually happened. The rewritten histories of Europe produced during the early days of Nazi power in Germany or the Russian histories written in the Stalin era are examples of this. Further, histories are always selective. Frequently these judgments are based on national pride or political pressures rather than on fact. For example, the ancient Assyrians almost never recorded a military defeat in their official chronicles. They either ignored such events or rewrote the events in such a way as to appear that Assyria was victorious.

Also, the very nature of history writing forces selectivity upon a writer. Everything which happened at a particular time cannot be written down. Each author records those things which were of interest or apparent significance. Obviously, many things are therefore left out of any particular history which later readers might wish to know or might think to be significant. In addition, the author of a history work does not, and in fact cannot, know everything which went on. Thus some things are omitted which may be the most significant feature of the entire episode.

Finally, the choice of what to include or omit (which may be a far more significant choice) is shaped by the author's purpose and presuppositions.

If this is true of history writing in general, we should expect it to be true in biblical history. As an example of this in the New Testament, both Mark and Luke recorded Jesus' healing of the woman who had the issue of blood (Mark 5:25-34; Luke 8:43-48). They both told the same basic story, but Mark wrote that she "had suffered much under many physicians, and had spent all that she had, and was no better but rather grew worse" (Mark 5:26). Luke, recording the same story, left out that small bit of information. Before we can proceed with a survey of the New Testament era, we need to examine the nature of biblical history in general and New Testament history in particular. In essence, we must ask and try to answer the question: *What is the nature of New Testament history?* This might be more clearly understood if we asked the question this way: What were the New Testament writers seeking to accomplish when they wrote their material?

Biblical History Is Revelation, Sacred Scripture

A major portion of the people of the world accept the New Testament as their sacred Scriptures. As such, we believe it to be a divine-human book. While there is no indication that those who wrote this material knew or believed at the time that they were writing authoritative Scriptures, they clearly believed that they were writing religious truths, taught as much by inference and example as by precept. They expected their hearers to be able to grasp the meaning of the work and words of Jesus, as well as the meaning to be learned from the experiences of the early Christians. For every sentence set forth as a direct general command or admonition in the New Testament, many more are set forth in narratives or specific applications to as specific situations.

On the other hand, and far more important, the Christian churches under the leadership of the Holy Spirit have concluded, at least ever since the formation of the canon, that the New Testament is a divine-human book. This concept should not be surprising, because the basic message of Christianity is the incarnation. The foundation of the Christian proclamation has been that Jesus Christ was God incarnated ("enfleshed") in a human being. He was both God and man. It should not be surprising then to discover that the churches of Jesus believe that the record of that incarnation and its application to human life should claim to be both human and divine.

On one hand, the New Testament is a human book. It was written by people. These people had all the limitations to which humanity is heir. Some parts of the New Testament are written in magnificent Greek while other parts are written in poor, somewhat ungrammatical Greek. Further, some parts are quite philosophical, hinging on precise nuances, while others are written in straightforward language, ignoring the finer refinements of word meanings and sentence structure. Also, different books use different words to describe the same idea, clearly showing the diversity of the authors and their educational backgrounds.

On the other hand, the New Testament is a divine book, inspired by the Spirit of God to communicate His truth to the peoples of the earth. This becomes a matter of faith, based upon each person's perception of and experience with that Book. Its divine purpose of revelation brings a unity to its various parts which would be unexpected outside of such an explanation. Thus the New Testament is accepted by millions of people as an authoritative revelation from God, His guide for life, both now and forever. This assertion should clearly differentiate it from other books and other history writing. It is different from other books, ancient or modern, and therefore must be approached differently and used differently from them. If we treat the history contained in the New Testament exactly as we treat that found in other books from the same era, then we are in essence denying that it is unique. On the other hand, if we ignore that it was written by human beings who were creatures of their own time writing for people who lived in that time, then we shall also have ignored the human dimension of the New Testament. It was written by real people for real people who faced life as it is. Each individual writer had a purpose, even as the God who inspired it had a purpose. It is this combined purpose which we must also consider in dealing with the nature of biblical history.

Biblical History Is Sacred History

One of the terms which became commonly used in the early part of this century to describe biblical history is the German word *Heilsgeschichte*. While not possible to translate accurately into English, it has been variously translated as "holy history," "sacred history," or "sacred story." It is used to describe the idea that the Bible was written to tell the story of God's acts of salvation with His people, Israel, and ultimately with "new" Israel, the church.

This term seeks to call our attention to the fact that the Old Testament is not simply the history of Israel and that the New Testament is not simply the history of Jesus and His church. Rather, both testaments form one sacred story, the story of God's mighty saving acts as He worked out the process of salvation on the stage of human history. The term also calls our attention to the fact that while the Bible is rooted and grounded in history, it is not history as we think of it today. As we study the New Testament, we note that many events of significance were totally left out and others are included with only the briefest mention. Consider, for example, the fact that as we read the Gospels, we would get the impression that Mary and Joseph only had one child, Jesus. Yet we discover later that He had at least four brothers and two sisters (Mark 6:3). All the explanations of them being half-brothers and half-sisters to-the-contrary-not-withstanding, where these people fit into Jesus' family is simply left to our imaginations. As we shall see later, this might be important to our understanding of some factors bearing on His life, but they were unimportant to the ongoing work of redemption.

Further, contemporary historians would probably spend a great deal of time telling the details of an important person's childhood. Obviously, those formative years shape anyone's personality. Yet these important years of Jesus' life are left almost wholly to our imagination.

In addition, to anyone reading the Book of Acts, it would appear that the only real thrust of Christianity was from Jerusalem until it ultimately reached Rome. Further, most of the apostles seem to have had nothing to do with that spread. Were they inactive, ineffective, or what? On the other hand, when the first Christian missionaries reached India, they found a strong Christian movement, called the Mar Thomas Church. This movement claimed to have been founded by the missionary efforts of the apostle Thomas. According to their tradition, he brought the gospel to India in the middle of the first century A.D. Why were his efforts not recorded in Acts? Or for that matter, can we really assume that the other disciples did nothing? Is it not more likely that the New Testament was simply following the one stream of action which God intended that we should have at the moment as a part of sacred Scriptures. Further, it is not that the others' actions were unimportant or insignificant, it is just that they were apparently outside the "history of salvation" which was being recorded. The contemporary historian, dealing with a history of the New Testament era, is concerned with any direction in which Christianity spread and with all who were a part of that spread. The Bible simply was not so concerned. Thus we must conclude that those of us who study the New Testament era must have larger interests and be concerned with other people and influences than the New Testament writers were. On the other hand, we must not discount the New Testament as a source, in fact the major source, of information of the history of the era.

Biblical History Must Be Understood Against the Background of Other Ancient History

The people of biblical times did not live out their lives in a world devoid of other people and nations. Contrary to what we think if we only read the New Testament, Jesus lived and ministered in a relatively small province of the Roman Empire. Although His life is the most important life ever lived, it passed unmentioned in the official records of the empire, even His execution apparently received no mention in the court records of Caesar or correspondence of the Roman governor on the scene to his superiors.

By and large, the same thing is true of the early Christians and the spread of churches throughout the empire. Rome was far more concerned with the steady flow of tax monies from the provinces than with the preachments of a few of the people in one of their rather distant provinces. In fact, it was not until the Christian movement got to the capital of the empire and began to be a source of civil struggle that Rome took any notice of these people called Christians.

However, while Rome did not particularly notice Jesus or His followers during the days of His life or the early days of their movement, these people were most certainly aware of Rome. Jesus was quite aware of the rules by which people could be compelled to carry a soldier's baggage (Matt. 5:41). He and all of His followers were equally aware of the constant presence and pressure of the occupying troops of Rome. He stood before a Roman judge, as did Paul and others at later times. They paid taxes to Rome by means of the hated services of the publicans, considered to be traitors by many people of the land. Further, the major crises of the Roman Empire had an influence upon the administrative policies enforced in the provinces.

In addition to these factors, the actions of the Jews in Jerusalem, Alexandria, and Rome itself had an influence upon Jesus and His later followers. It is of significance for an understanding of the disciples and their Lord that we understand the times in which they lived. This is not only true in regards to the great historical forces at work but is also true of the daily affairs of ordinary life. The men and women of the New Testament were people of their own times. They faced the same issues and pressures which everyone else of their culture and times faced. Thus if we are going to add depth to our understanding of the New Testament and its times, we must understand the times in which they lived. This means that we must come to grips both with the great and small things which affected them.

To do this, we must first of all become familiar with the history of the Roman Empire at the time. We must also add to our store of knowledge the social structures, religious and political pressures, and economic stresses which confronted these people on a daily basis. A thorough student of the New Testament can become familiar with the text of the New Testament. However, to understand the people of the New Testament as real people, facing life as we do, we must see them as they lived their lives in a particular place at a particular time. Certainly Jesus was more than a mere man. Certainly the spread of the gospel was carried out under the leadership of the Holy Spirit, but Jesus and His followers were real people. To see them as such, we must place them in that time. It is a mistake to try to understand first-century people in the light of twentieth-century cultures.

It is this which ultimately serves as a major motivating factor for anyone beginning to study the history of the New Testament. If we are not going to make the effort to understand these people as real people, then we may as well ignore the effort which this study will entail. On the other hand, if you really wish to understand these people as persons similar to yourself and your friends, continue with me in this pilgrimage of knowledge. If we are going to understand the background of the New Testament and its times, then we need to identify those sources where we can go for adding this kind of information to our knowledge. We must also evaluate the relative worth of the various sources which we possess.

3
The Extra-Biblical Sources of New Testament History

The historian who seeks to investigate the extra-biblical sources which are available for the study of the New Testament era is immediately confronted with two seemingly contradictory issues. First, we possess an amazing amount of material which gives us information relating to this era. Analyzing these sources can involve a lifetime of study. On the other hand, however, when we begin to deal with all of this material, we soon discover that we are given far less information relating to the particular subjects and issues than we wish to have. Large gaps are left in our reconstruction of the era, and significant questions are left unanswered. To these questions we can only give educated guesses, or at best, only partially informed answers. Yet even though we might wish for more information, we must work with what we currently possess. The following primary sources are those with which the investigator must deal.

Archaeological Sources

Many of the sites of the biblical world have been excavated. These excavations give us valuable pictures of the nature of daily life in Palestine during the New Testament era, as well as allow us to see remains of the culture of the world and cities into which Christianity spread. These vary from excavations at Jerusalem to those at Capernaum, both cities being ones in which Jesus ministered. In addition, numerous Roman cities have been excavated, giving us not only pictures of daily life in these cities, but allowing us to actually see buildings which were standing when Paul and the other early missionaries lived there. Studying such sites help us more clearly to visualize the nature of the events which are said to have occurred in those places.

Perhaps even more important than these site excavations have been the explorations that have been carried out which allow us to understand the geographical features which affected the ministries of Jesus and the apostles, as well as that of the people of the early churches. We can actually trace the roads over which those early missionaries trod, visualizing the dangers and difficulties which they faced.

Finally, a fairly recent development in the archaeological studies of the New Testament world has been the undersea archaeology in the Mediterranean. Much of the Mediterranean is quite shallow, at least when compared with other oceans and seas. Many ships which sailed the seas in those ancient times were sunk by storms or through other mishaps. With the advent of scuba diving, many of these have been located and their remains carefully studied. Their cargoes have been brought to the surface, giving us yet another dimension in our reconstruction of life in those ancient times. These studies become even more significant for the New Testament historian when we remember just how many times Paul and his companions sailed upon those waters.

Yet archaeological studies at best only give us illustrations of features of life in those times. Such studies seldom give us the hard data which we need to add detail to our understanding of the events recorded in the New Testament or which influenced the New Testament. For this kind of information we need written sources. Fortunately, we have these as well, though not as many or as detailed as we might wish.

Jewish Sources

First and foremost among the Jewish sources to which historians turn in studying the history of the New Testament era are the works of Flavius Josephus. He was born about A.D. 37/38 and was quite thoroughly trained in rabbinic thought. He developed an early reputation as a scholar and a diplomat, gaining respect even in Rome. Belonging to the Pharisees, he sought to remain neutral when the First Jewish War with Rome broke out in A.D. 66. Unable to continue to do this he joined the forces of revolution and became a military leader of the Jewish troops in Galilee. Finally trapped, he surrendered to the Roman forces in A.D. 67. Brought before General Vespasian, he predicted that the Roman would one day become emperor. When that in fact happened two years later, he was freed from captivity and became a companion of the new emperor. Following the war, he settled in Rome where he remained until he died shortly after A.D. 100.

During his years in Rome, Josephus wrote the histories which have become the basis of most extra-biblical studies of the New Testament era. First among these was *The Wars of the Jews,* a seven-volume work covering the history of Palestine from the rise of Antiochus Epiphanes IV in 175 B.C. to the destruction of Jerusalem in A.D. 70. This was primarily a historical work based upon his own experiences and knowledge gained from friends and companions.

Living in Rome, Josephus faced a great deal of prejudice from those who felt that the Jews were a backward and superstitious people. Josephus therefore wrote his second work as a defense of his people. *The Antiquities of the Jews* covered the history of the Jews from their earliest days to the beginning of the First Jewish War. He also wished to establish himself as a man of education, virtue, and leadership in the eyes of the Roman nobility, so he quickly followed this with an autobiography.

In addition to firsthand experience and the Old Testament itself, Josephus also used numerous earlier historians for sources. The works of these have either been wholly lost or remain with us only in small fragments. Among the most notable of these sources are the histories and geographies of Strabo, a Greek; the chronicles of Herod; and those of Vespasian.

While the works of Josephus are the best and most thorough which we have for this era, they must be handled with care. He was viewed with suspicion by the Romans and as a traitor by the Jews. Thus in no way can he be considered to be an unbiased witness. He was consciously self-serving and intentionally defensive. On the other hand, we cannot ignore either his records or the interpretation which he placed upon them.

Two other additional Jewish sources of significance are found in the Old Testament Apocrypha, *1* and *2 Maccabees*. These books cover the period of Jewish history beginning with the Jewish revolt against Antiochus Epiphanes in 167 B.C. First Maccabees appears to be one of the more reliable sources of the entire era; tracing its narrative all the way to about 100 B.C. Unfortunately, this only sets the background for the New Testament era, it does not cover it at all. Second Maccabees deals only with the events in the period from 167 to 161 B.C. It appears to be a far less reliable source for historical research. On the other hand, it does add a few details to our knowledge of that era.

The final group of Jewish sources which add significantly to our knowledge of this era are The Dead Sea Scrolls. These works were the product of a monastic-type settlement at the ancient site of Qumran, located in the rough, rocky terrain on the western side of the Dead Sea. This community has been identified with a fair degree of probability as being the Essenes. Although many of the documents found there are copies of ancient Old Testament manuscripts, numbers of the scrolls reflect the times from the Maccabean era up to the fall of Jerusalem at the end of the Second Jewish War in A.D. 135. While not histories as such, these scrolls give us graphic descriptions and significant information relating to life in Palestine during the New Testament era. Further, there is enough similarity in some instances to lead a number of scholars to suggest that John the Baptist may have either been a part of or at least familiar with that community. The scrolls are clearly a significant firsthand source of contemporary history from the era which we are investigating.

Roman Sources

A number of early Roman historians left works behind which are of value for the student of New Testament history. Livy, who died sometime between Jesus' birth and the beginning of His ministry, wrote a complete history of Rome which helps us understand the larger world in which the New Testament people lived their lives. Shortly before, Cicero wrote a record of the Roman province of Syria, of which Palestine was a part. Suetonius, who lived about a century later, wrote on a number of significant subjects, including chronology. However, his most important work for our purposes was *The Lives of the Caesars*. These dealt with those who ruled from Caesar to Domitian and obviously covered much of the New Testament period.

Of all the Roman writers, however, the one most likely to become familiar to a student of this era is Tacitus. Living from the mid-first through the early part of the second century A.D., he produced two works, his *Annals* and *History*. These dealt with the reigns of the emperors from Tiberius to Domitian. An outspoken critic of the empire and its extravagances, he consistently tended to exaggerate its faults. At the same time, he was quite accurate in identifying the events which were of major importance to the on-going history of Rome. From our standpoint, however, it is his reference to both Jews and Christians which make him of prime significance. His works give us some indication of the importance to the empire of these peoples with whom we are especially concerned.

Greek Sources

Five Greek historians stand out as those who are of primary significance for anyone studying this era. One of the more important of these was Strabo, whose work was used by Josephus. Strabo wrote forty-seven books of history and seventeen books on geography. His historical works have all been lost, except for quotations, but most of his geographies survive. His references to the geography of Palestine make his works of most importance to us, though he does give us some view of the events in Palestine which led to the invasion of Pompey in 63 B.C. Polybius, who died about 120 B.C., and Didorus, who died about a century later, both left historical surveys of the Roman world which help us to understand the intertestamental period. On the other end of our era, Dio Cassius lived in the last half of the second century A.D. He also wrote a major history of Rome, approximately eighty volumes in length of which only eighteen survive. His works obviously cover the entire period in which we are interested. We could only wish that we had all of his writings.

The final Greek historian in whom we are interested is Plutarch. He lived during the last half of the first and early part of the second century A.D. His *Lives* were brief biographies of the leaders who helped shape the Roman Empire and its greatness. He appears to have been a very good historian, and his studies are valuable tools for understanding the forces which shaped the world in which the New Testament figures lived.

Other Written Sources

The remaining primary sources which we can use in gaining historical information fall into three basic categories. (Some might classify these sources differently, but no one disagrees as to the fact that they must be considered.)

First among these are the so-called "Church Fathers." These were Christian writers from the early churches who had personal contact with the apostles and first disciples or who were closely associated with those who did. Basically, they come from the last days of the writing of the New Testament itself (ca. A.D. 70) and continue into the last half of the second century. Although there are not many such writings, several do exist which are of major significance for our study.

Clement was a member of the church of Rome, possibly being responsible for the collection and circulation of Christian manuscripts. His letter, known as *1 Clement*, is remarkably similar to New Testament writings and gives us data for understanding early post-apostolic Christianity. A second letter originally ascribed to him is no longer considered to be by him, almost certainly belonging to a much later time. Another source from the latter part of the first century A.D. is known as the *Didache* or by its English name *The Teaching of the Twelve Apostles*. It purports to be a summary of church discipline, ritual, and organization. It has been variously dated from as early as A.D. 60 to as late as the mid-second century. Though quite brief, it offers a view of early church organization and practice. Remarkably similar to the *Didache* is the so-called *Epistle of Barnabas*. It is unlikely to have been written by the companion of Paul but is a valuable source for studying the operations of the churches around the end of the first century or beginning of the second. Its purpose was to point out that Judaism was not God's final revelation but prepared the way to the life and ministry of Jesus, God's ultimate revelation of Himself.

Also of value in the study of the history of the New Testament era are the writings of Ignatius and Polycarp. Both of these men were early Christian martyrs and both were bishops. Ignatius served in Syrian Antioch, and Polycarp ministered in Smyrna. Both men wrote at about the same time in the early part of the second century, though Polycarp lived into the middle of the century. The writings of both of these men are considered to be quite valuable resources for the study of early Christian history. From the same era also comes *The Shepherd of Hermas*. Hermas wrote over a long period of time; his work gives the impression of being produced over one or more decades. Primarily dealing with doctrinal issues, this work gives numerous hints as to the historical situations faced by the churches during those days. The Christian movement had obviously become quite influential in the communities of his day.

During the second half of the second century A.D., some Christians began to write what have come to be known as apologies. The writers are therefore called the apologists. This term comes from the Greek word *apologia* meaning defense. These people were writing primarily in defense of Christianity and its beliefs and practices. Two of the more significant for our purposes were Justin Martyr and Irenaeus. Justin was primarily a philosopher, while Irenaeus was a theologian, probably the greatest since Paul. Both of these men give us a vivid view of the situation faced by Christians during its most formative years. While neither wrote history as such, both give us significant historical information.

From the mid-second through third century A.D., a large number of writings were passed around among the churches. These writings claimed to be written by the early disciples, giving information to the churches which had been omitted from the canonical writings. While these claims were wholly false and most of the information contained in them is utterly worthless, occasional references are found which appear to give historically valid information. However, when compared with the amount of useless information, few but the most dedicated scholars ever spend much time studying them. These are normally identified as the New Testament *Apocrypha* and *Pseudepigrapha*.

Outside of Luke, the early church does not appear to have produced what would really be called a true historian. However, from the late third century to early fourth century A.D., a man named Eusebius worked in the region of Caesarea. He sought to investigate the sources which were available to him, to evaluate them, and to write a history of the early church, *Historia Ecclesiae*. This is the only historical account of the post-apostolic church which has come down to us. No one can really claim to be acquainted with the early rise of Christianity who is unfamiliar with this source. Once again, however, when we deal with his material, our greatest wish is that he had not left so many gaps in his reconstruction.

As I pointed out at the beginning of this chapter, the student of the history of the New Testament era is faced with the dilemma of more sources than we might expect and not as many as we could wish. However, we must deal with what we have. Thus, in attempting to reconstruct the history of the New Testament era, we will begin with the biblical narratives and try to fill them out with materials from these other ancient sources.

4
How Ancient Dates Are Fixed

"**I** would enjoy studying history if it weren't for having to learn so many dates." More than one student has voiced such an opinion, and I expect far more have had such a feeling without having expressed it openly. Unfortunately, history cannot be studied apart from dates. It cannot even be understood apart from dates. Unless we have some frame of reference by which to relate separate events to one another and other events, we cannot even begin to grasp the factors which made people and nations act as they did. Were it not for dates, we would have no way of separating the lives of Jesus, George Washington, and Abraham. Further, it is the relationship between dates which allows us to consider and perhaps understand the relationship between events in Rome and their effect upon Jesus and His disciples in Palestine. Were it not for dates, the study of history would descend to nothing but a recitation of unrelated anecdotes from the lives of people.

Thus, to study history requires that we study the dates. Further, to study the dates requires that we know something about how the dates for ancient times are established. Once we have made an attempt to survey this complex subject, we shall at least be in a better condition to deal with the chronological material which we have from the New Testament era.

The Nature of the Problem

Luke begins his narrative of the ministry of John the Baptist by writing:

In the fifteenth year of the reign of Tiberius Caesar, Pontius Pilate being governor of Judea, and Herod being tetrarch of Galilee, and

> his brother Philip tetrarch of the region of Ituraea and Trachonitis, and Lysanias tetrarch of Abilene, in the high priesthood of Annas and Caiaphas, the word of God came to John the son of Zechariah in the wilderness (Luke 3:1-2).

Luke was making a bold assertion that the ministry of John was a historical event. It happened. More important for our consideration at the moment, Luke was seeking to nail down in history the actual time when John began his ministry. For modern historians, it would have been easier if Luke had said that John began his ministry in A.D. 26, or A.D. 30. Rather, he sought to establish the historical time in which John preached by referring to seven other people of historical significance who were living and working at that time.

Such historical cross-referencing was satisfactory for those who lived in that time and knew those people. It creates difficulties for those of us who live in this time and do not know precisely when those ancient people lived and worked. To date John we must know something about those other people. This is precisely our problem.

If we were seeking to assign a date to Herod, we would have to know something about the other people to which contemporary writers related his reign. If we wished to date Tiberius, the same thing applies. Ancient writers dated their heroes and heroines by such methods of cross referencing.

This leaves the modern historian with all sorts of information about these ancient worthies. At the same time, it leaves us with a difficult task when it comes to relating them with precision to those whose names are not directly tied in with those ancient people in their records. Further, it leaves us with an even more difficult task when it comes to grasping the great sweeps of history, the mighty empires and lesser nations which shaped the lives of those who shared a part in spreading the gospel, beginning at Jerusalem and continuing to the far reaches of the world.

We need dates for these people and nations if we are going to place them in proper perspective with the rest of history. But, we study the ancient writings in vain for such dates. No one in those times ever wrote that way. There simply was no universal, or even nearly universal, system of dating. The question, then, is how are we going to establish some accurate system of chronology for dealing with such issues?

Astronomical Data, Official Records, and Cross Correlations

There is no such thing as an approximately accurate chronology. Either something happened on a specific date or it didn't. On the other hand, sometimes as we seek to establish when certain ancient events occurred, we simply cannot establish with certainty when they occurred. We can only narrow the limits of the time span within which the particular event occurred. This is accomplished through the study of comparative or correlated chronology.

For example, we have rather full records of the history of most of the major empires of the ancient Near East. We have Assyrian records which span almost a thousand years, Egyptian records which span more than three millennia, and Babylonian and Persian records which span several centuries. To these older empires we can also add the Roman histories covering more than a millennium and Greek histories spanning several centuries. Each of these empires at one time or another had contact with others of these empires. Thus the diligent student can study these records, noting where interinvolvements occurred, and begin to establish a relative history of the ancient world. Doing this does not give us actual dates to which to relate anything. We are still left with uncertainties and approximations.

However, there is one kind of event which can be dated with precision. These are astronomical events. Thus we must search ancient records for the mention of such events. For example, we find the Assyrian records referring to an eclipse of the sun. Modern astronomers can calculate exactly when and where such celestial events occurred and could have been seen. The only possible date for such an eclipse was 763 B.C. This gives us a precise date on which we can begin to establish a concrete chronology for Assyria. Further, working from this, at those places where Assyria came in contact with other nations we can then establish specific dates for the neighboring kingdoms.

Now it must be admitted that, because of gaps in the records and our failure at times to understand such records properly, we can get farther and farther off in our calculations as we get farther from the date with which we began. There are other celestial events that can aid in dating. The Egyptians, for example, knew of a particular celestial cycle in which a star, *Sothis,* took 1,461 years to reappear at the same precise spot on their horizon. We can calculate exactly when this would have occurred and the only time when it could have happened which fits their records was in the second century A.D. This gives us another precise date to tie down a nation's chronology and allows us to begin to cross-check our earlier calculations. Other such events occurred which give us other opportunities for correcting or adjusting our calculations. With the passing years, the discovery of more ancient records, the study and restudy of those which we already have, we come ever closer to the establishment of a precise chronology for the part of the world in which we are interested and the era with which we are concerned.

Deductions from Internal Evidence

For the historian of the New Testament era, however, establishing the dates of kingdoms and empires, while important, is not sufficient. We must also seek to establish, as far as possible, the dates for New Testament events. Some events in the New Testament are related quite specifically to dates which can be established by any good historian of the Roman empire. Yet most dates cannot be so identified. What do we do then?

It is at this point that we begin the task of what I choose to call "biblical detective work." We seek to learn all we can about specific events and the words which describe them and relate these to what we know of the history of the period. Such deductions lead us to probabilities but not to certainties. To make these deductions requires as detailed a knowledge of the times and customs as it is possible to get. At the same time, the student must always be ready to revise conclusions as new evidence is discovered and related.

An example of this kind of process may be seen by noting John the Baptist's baptism of Jesus as it is recorded in John's Gospel. For our purposes, three features stand out. (1) It appears that large throngs are gathered to hear the preaching of John the Baptist. (This is further underscored by the records of the first three Gospels.) These throngs may simply have been attracted by John's preaching. It may also be that this was at a time when large throngs were on the roads, making a pilgrimage to Jerusalem for one of the great festivals of Judaism. (2) During the specific time dealt with, John identified Jesus as the "Lamb of God" (John 1:29).

(3) Further, following Jesus' baptism, Andrew goes to tell his brother Simon that they had found the Messiah (John 1:41).

Among the great festivals of Israel's faith, Passover stands out as one which attracted large crowds from all over the land to Jerusalem. This could explain Galileans being in Judea and on the road to Jerusalem. Further, at the Passover, the minds of the worshiping celebrants would clearly be on the Passover lamb, the one provided by God to spare His people the visit of death at the time of the exodus (Ex. 12:1-30). Finally, a tradition was current among the Jews of that era which held that the Messiah would come to Israel during the celebration of a Passover festival.

Now it is obvious that these three features do not prove that Jesus was baptized at a Passover time. But, it does appear to make it probable that this does provide the best historical setting for the beginning of Jesus' ministry. Now, tying the beginning of John's ministry to the fifteenth year of Tiberius Caesar may give us the year and approximate date for the beginning of Jesus' ministry (Luke 3:1-3).

As we proceed through this study, we shall be forced time and again to make such deductions as we attempt to reconstruct the chronology of Jesus, Paul, and the early church. These conclusions will generally be more or less tentative. The more they support one another and relate properly to one another, the more confidence we will be able to have in our conclusions.

Putting It All Together

The ultimate end of any historical investigation is eventually arriving at an accurate reconstruction of the particular era under investigation. This is what I am trying to accomplish in dealing with the New Testament era. I am seeking to reconstruct, insofar as is presently possible, the historical certainties surrounding the life and ministry of Jesus of Nazareth, as well as that of the disciples and early churches.

However, as any student of the era knows, once we have arrived at the absolute certainties, insofar as actual chronological data are concerned, we are still left with large gaps in the background of the story. It is at this point that we begin to add the results of our biblical and historical detective work: the probabilities and possibilities. For your benefit as you study this book, I will try to make it clear at every point what are the certainties, probabilities, and possibilities.

It is important for you to be constantly aware that the mere fact that we are dealing with dates which are uncertain does not in any way invalidate our faith. For Christianity is precisely that, it is a faith. Whether or not we can arrive at the date of the crucifixion of Jesus does not negate the fact that He did die on the cross. More important, the fact that He died on the cross, while of historical significance, is not nearly as significant as the fact that He died to save sinners. That is a matter of faith.

Consider this as an illustration. The Bible says: "Christ died" (Rom. 5:8). That is stated as a fact. It can be historically investigated. A date can be given to it. For the purpose of the New Testament, the most important thing is that "while we were yet sinners Christ died for us" (Rom. 5:8). That is a faith statement. The fact that *He died* can be investigated. The fact that *He died for us* can only be accepted or denied.

Thus what we are about is an attempt to see the history behind the New Testament narratives. In so doing we will add depth to our understanding of what God was about. However, it will not, or at least it should not, affect our faith. My faith in Jesus is the same whether or not I can ever determine precisely when Jesus died. I may be better able to understand what motivated Pilate, Caiaphas, the Sanhedrin, and the crowd who cried for blood as a result of my historical investigation. In so doing, I may be better able to understand how people relate to Jesus and His movement in the world today. I may also be, and certainly should be, better able to understand the New Testament and the people who were the first Christians. However, this study will not necessarily make me a better Christian, just a more knowledgeable one.

The Problem with Calendars

One last issue needs to be considered before we conclude our survey of the process by which ancient dates are established by modern scholars. This is the calendar itself. We have not always had the present calendar. Throughout human history, years have varied in length as well as the date when they have begun. The same is true of weeks and days. We wish to understand ancient times in reference to our present dating schemes. However, in order to appreciate the difficulty of this, we at least need to know something of the way in which we have arrived at our present calendar and of the difficulties that the process gives to any historian who wishes to reach back into history and assign a specific date to any ancient event.

The present calendar we are using was basically created by Julius Caesar in 46 B.C. However, it was significantly influenced by an older calendar of the Egyptians. This calendar was further adjusted by Pope Gregory XIII in A.D. 1582. Over the centuries, the year has varied from 354 to 445 days in length. It was originally based on lunar months, the time it takes the moon to move one full cycle from one new moon to the next. A lunar month is twenty-nine days, twelve hours, forty-four minutes, and three seconds and isn't readily divided into 365 days, the approximate length of a year. This problem led to a switch to a twelve-month year, but this was no more easily divided into 365 days. Because of the inherent problems in either of these systems, a variety of methods have been devised to try to keep the seasons of the year in proper synchronization. These have included leap months, the short and long Februaries (twenty-eight and twenty-nine days) and other more involved solutions. For example, the Roman years contained 355, 377, 378, 382, or 383 days.

As has so often been the case, however, religion and politics got at cross purposes. When Pope Gregory XIII tried to correct the calendar, a number of non-Catholic countries resisted, particularly England and her colonies. It wasn't until 1752 that these groups made an adjustment to get the seasons back where they ought to be. In that year, England and the American colonies officially changed October 5 to October 15, thus making a 354-day year, the shortest on record. However, the present system should work for about 3,300 years, when an extra day will again have to be inserted into the calendar.

However, establishing a calendar only gives us the length of a year, it does not give us the dates for the years. In the sixth century A.D., a Syrian monk named Dionysius Exiguus calculated the date of Jesus' birth and named that year *anno Domini* 1 (the year of our Lord 1). Years before that were labeled B.C. (before Christ) or B.C.E. (before the Common Era). It would appear that from that point on that everything should have been all right. Unfortunately, that is not so. As we shall note in more detail later, Herod died in 4 B.C. If any date in ancient history is certain that one is.

However, it was he who sought to kill the children of Bethlehem *after Jesus was born* (Matt. 2:16). This is why most scholars now state that Jesus was born in 4 B.C. or earlier. By the time people recognized that an error had been made, we had been using the present calendar too long as a basis for writing history to make any further change. It would have required rewriting all of the world's histories and that was simply impossible.

Thus we now have a calendar which is reasonably accurate. However, in translating any ancient date to a modern one, we are involved with a major and complex discipline. It is one for technicians. Those of us who study ancient history can and must trust those who have become expert in dealing with ancient dates. They give us the bench marks, the modern equivalent of ancient dates. From those, we can then move to the specific task of adjusting those ancient dates with which we are interested into the chronological terminology with which we are familiar.

Part 2
At Sundry Times

Hstory, as we have noted, does not take place in neat little slots, like post office boxes. Unfortunately, for students, the various eras of history never have neat borders, but overlap with those eras which precede and follow them. The parallel eras in neighboring nations overlap with each other, but normally do not end or begin at the same time.

A little thought will help the student to be aware of the truth of this observation. This is clearly true of any period and place under study. It is especially true of the New Testament era. To understand what national and international influences shaped the world and bore upon the life and mission of Jesus and His early disciples, we need to become somewhat familiar with the major influences which bore upon the times.

Jesus simply did not live in a vacuum. Certainly, I and millions of others believe that He was the Son of God, sent to be the Savior of the world. He was also a man, born into a poor Jewish family in Palestine during the height of the Roman Empire. Born in that era, at that time, and in that place, there were numerous factors of historical, religious, and sociological significance which helped influence, if not directly shape both His life and ministry as well as that of His followers. If we are going to understand the New Testament era, we must become aware of the nature of those influences and events.

Obviously, as we study each smaller unit of time which makes up this era, we shall consider those events and influences which helped shape that time. However, the beginning of the era did not just break into history *de novo*. The world into which Jesus was born had also been shaped by those people and events which had gone before. We must seek to understand at least the major features of that world and those things which shaped this era even before it began.

God had already been at work in the world. He who sent Jesus Christ into the world had been shaping that world for centuries. He had been working through His people, Israel, in producing a community of faith. That community of faith had received His revelation which we know as the Old Testament. In addition, through the crises of the preceding few centuries, that community had become a religious community rather than a kingdom. That community was known in Jesus' day and has come to us as Judaism. Both the Old Testament and Judaism significantly shaped both Jesus and His church.

Further, three major political forces had also been shaping the world into which Jesus was born. In 333 B.C., the Greeks under Alexander the Great overthrew the ancient Medo-Persian empire. The Greek empire which was soon formed became a major influence in the world into which Jesus was born. Further, on a far distant peninsula, another empire was soon taking its shape: Rome. This, too, had an enormous shaping power over the world in which Jesus and His disciples lived and worked. Finally, as a direct result of the excesses of the Greeks, a Jewish state raised its head for a time shortly before the birth of Jesus. This state gave rise to the political-religious parties which sought to influence and control the minds, hearts, and allegiances of the Jews in the world through which Jesus and His disciples moved. All of this was clearly under the sovereign power of God. These all directly or indirectly shaped the New Testament era, the life and ministry of Jesus and His disciples, and the writing of the New Testament itself. In the chapters which make up part 2 of our study, we are seeking to outline the major influences that each of these nations or movements had in shaping the world into which Jesus was born. It was an exciting world, used to tumult and uncertainty. It was also a world desperately seeking for something to give life stability and meaning. It was a world which was basically hopeless, but which was looking for something in which to hope and something worth hoping for.

5
The Old Testament Root

Anyone who knows anything about the Bible at all is aware that it is made up of two major parts—the Old Testament and New Testament. Even without reading either, one might suspect that the second is based upon the first. When you read the New Testament, it becomes quite obvious that what you suspected is true. Quotations from the Old Testament abound in the New Testament. Further, and even more significant, many concepts of the Old Testament underlie the teachings of the New Testament. For example, the Epistle to the Hebrews appears to be a Christian commentary or exposition of the Book of Leviticus. Also, many of Jesus' teachings in the Sermon on the Mount are based upon and are enlargements of teachings of the Old Testament (Matt. 5:17-48).

We can be quite sure, therefore, that if we are going to understand the history of the New Testament era, we must become aware of the influence which the Old Testament had upon Jesus and His followers. The Old Testament root of the New Testament background is one of the more important, if not the most important with which we need to become familiar. It shaped much of the thought and influenced a great deal of the activities of those who were the participants in the beginnings of Christianity. We cannot survey all of the teachings of the Old Testament which may have influenced the New Testament. On the other hand, several features of the Old Testament faith stand out as being of major significance.[1]

The Covenant

The names of the two divisions of the Bible reflect the fact that the concept of covenant is of major significance. *Testament* is actually a synonym for *covenant*. Old "Testament" is simply another way of saying Old "Covenant." However, the concept goes deeper than the titles of these two sections of the Bible.

First, a number of Old Testament scholars believe that the covenant concept is actually the central feature of the Old Testament itself. To them, there is no way of understanding either the ongoing history of Israel or the faith reflected and propagated in the book which ancient Israel produced without seeing it all as the outgrowth of the covenant relation with their God. Even scholars who do not believe that the covenant is the absolute center of the faith of Israel (and I am one of them) do believe that it is quite important for understanding that faith. Yet, whether or not it is central or merely important to Israel's faith is unimportant if we do not understand what it means. *Covenant* is a term which is not commonly used by nontechnical biblical scholars.

The covenant concept which is used to describe the relationship which exists between God and Israel has at least a part of its basis in the old "suzerainty" treaties or covenants of the ancient Near East. These treaties were entered into by suzerains or "great kings" with those who were their vassals. Such agreements were based upon the historical relations between the two kings and their peoples, promising the benefits which the suzerain would bestow upon the vassal. Equally as important, the covenant also set forth the obligations laid upon the vassal. These features clearly show up in the Old Testament. God's covenant with Israel was based upon His historic acts on their behalf, the most important of which was His deliverance of them from the slavery in Egypt through the exodus experience. This was consummated in the covenant sealing at Sinai, where the stipulations were laid upon Israel in the Ten Commandments (Ex. 20:2-17).

This covenant was reconfirmed on numerous historic occasions with great religious celebrations (Josh. 8:30-35; 24:1-27; 2 Kings 18:3-6; 23:1-25). Further, the prophets also regularly called the Hebrew people back to their covenant commitment to the Lord (Isa. 1:2-20; Jer. 11:1-7; Hos. 2:16-20; Mic. 6:1-4). Ultimately, the failure of Israel to keep their covenant commitment to the Lord prompted a promise that one day God would make a new covenant with His people (Jer. 31:31-34).

But what actually was Israel's understanding of *covenant?* No simple answer can be offered because the concept was quite complex and involved. First, it is obvious that the covenant involved a relationship between God and Israel, a relationship which had been established by God, not by Israel. In addition, the covenant also laid obligations upon Israel. While God Himself had already taken up the obligation of redeeming Israel from their slavery, His obligation was voluntary and not compulsory. Israel on the other hand could choose either to accept or reject the covenant which God offered. However, once they had accepted its terms and entered into it, they could not leave it without being treacherous and deceitful.

The covenant was also frequently understood in terms of marriage. God was viewed as the husband and Israel was seen as God's bride. In addition, the covenant was understood in terms of the parent-child relationship. God was the Father, and Israel was His firstborn. The family relationship was clearly understood as being established or at least reflected by the covenant relation. The covenant was also understood as establishing responsibility upon the two partners. Each bore certain responsibilities to the other in making the covenant effective. Once again, God had taken the responsibility of caring for Israel upon Himself before the covenant. On the other hand, Israel accepted her responsibility as a part of entering into the covenant. Finally, it is important to note that the covenant was entered into by Israel as a community. It was national in scope, rather than individual. The entire nation entered into it and accepted its obligations. If, and as it turned out when, Israel repudiated the covenant by her rebellious, idolatrous actions, it was considered to be an utterly despicable act of treachery. At such times the entire nation suffered the consequences. This brings us to the consideration of the Old Testament's understanding of the community, the congregation of Israel.

The Community

While the Old Testament does speak to individuals, one of its more significant features is its sense of community. This is sometimes referred to by scholars as "corporate responsibility." Thus when one Israelite violated the covenant by disobeying God, the entire nation suffered. For example, when Achan disobeyed the command of God by stealing some of the goods from Jericho, it was the whole nation which suffered defeat at Ai. Further, when Joshua inquired of God for the reason for that defeat, he was told that it was due to the sin of Israel (Josh. 7:11).

In fact, although this seems strange to modern students, this concept became so strong in Israel that they frequently used it as an explanation for the judgments which befell them. At such times they blamed their fathers for the guilt which brought judgment upon the nation. To counteract the one-sidedness of this concept, both Jeremiah and Ezekiel proclaimed that individuals were also responsible for the consequences of their own sinful acts (Jer. 31:29-30; Ezek. 18:1-4). However, we should also note that these prophets pointed out that the sense of corporate responsibility was still a strong feature of Israel's faith.

The Faith

In addition to the covenant and community, Israel's faith had two distinct features. The first and primary one of these was the nature of God. The second was closely related to this and focused upon Israel's own sense of election, of being the "chosen people" of God.

In contrast to the modern world, particularly the Western cultures, Israel existed in a world where people were very religious and gods abounded. Israel's distinctive view of God was in their awareness of His sovereignty and in His personal nature. Israel was first of all aware that God was best understood in personal terms. He related to them on the personal level. Although they were forbidden to make an image of God, when He chose to reveal His own image, it was in persons who were related to one another in a relationship of love. "So God created man in his own image, in the image of God he created him; male and female he created them" (Gen. 1:27).

Further, in describing God, Israel perceived Him as holy (Isa. 6:3). In fact, one of the more common titles for God was "the holy one of Israel." Holiness was that which differentiated God from humanity. While people were perceived to be in God's image, there was never any doubt that He was wholly other than people.

Israel also perceived God as being revealed in His actions. He acted in history and the events of their national existence. Primary among these acts were His acts of choice. He obviously chose them first in Abraham. As his descendants, the whole nation was a part of that choice (Gen. 12:1-3). However, God's supreme act of election was seen in the exodus event when God brought them forth from the land of Egypt (Ex. 3:8). It was this act of redemptive choice to which they always looked back as the supreme example of God's redemption (Ps. 78:42-53).

Further, it was in God's acts of redemption that both Israel and Egypt experienced God as sovereign over the world of nature and humanity. These were intended as visible demonstrations of God's sovereign power (Ex. 7:5,17). The prophets also perceived and proclaimed this. Among the other nations of the ancient Near East, a defeat was understood as a defeat for their gods. In Israel, to the contrary, God used the pagan nations as the instruments of His judgment upon His own people.

God was also understood in the Old Testament as righteous. The gods of the pagan nations were understood by their followers as being capricious, undependable. In Israel, however, God was seen as being consistent and consistently righteous. He set His standards for the behavior of His people, and they were the same regardless of the circumstances. God was good and He expected His people to be good in return.

An old cliché still remains in the minds of many Christians about the Old Testament concept of God. It says that the Old Testament is a book of law, while the New Testament is the book of love. Like most such sayings, this is passed on from one person to another without anyone really seeking to investigate its truth. It simply is not so. Even in the midst of the great sermon on the covenant, the people of Israel were told of God's love for them (Deut. 4:37). Further, through the heartbreak of an unfaithful wife, Hosea became aware of the amazing love of God for Israel. He described this both in terms of the betrothal of Israel to God and a brokenhearted Father seeking His son (Hos. 2:19-20; 11:1,8-9).

Growing out of Israel's understanding of God's sovereign love, as well as His holiness and righteousness, was the Old Testament understanding of Israel as God's chosen people. It was this idea which became quite characteristic of their own self-awareness as the people of God. Unfortunately, Israel's awareness of God's sovereign grace as experienced in His choice led to a sense of self-confidence which it was never intended to have. Because of their sense of being chosen, they began to presume upon God's favor.

Amos addressed the issue of Israel's presumption in the midst of the eighth century B.C. They were looking forward to the "day of the Lord," expecting it to be a day of judgment upon God's enemies. What they failed to perceive was that they themselves had become the enemies of God (Amos 5:18-24). Because they had been chosen by God, they assumed that those who were their enemies were God's enemies as well. What they failed to perceive was that being chosen did not excuse them from faithfulness but laid an even greater responsibility upon them.

Further, as the chosen people of God, Israel also wrongly assumed that all which they had to do was properly observed as the ritual. Proper worship was, and is, important. But, it will not cover unrighteousness. This brings us to the next branch of the Old Testament root which led into the New Testament era, Israel's sin and rebellion.

The Failure

Linguists have long been aware that various peoples develop a large vocabulary to describe terms with which they are most familiar. On the other hand, things or ideas with which they have little experience never develop such a rich vocabulary. The Arabs, for example, have more than twenty words describing sand, something with which they have abundant experience. Snow, on the other hand, something with which they are far less familiar is described with only a few words. The Eskimo people however are quite the reverse. Their language has a very full vocabulary for snow and only a limited number of words for describing sand.

The point behind this seeming digression is that the Old Testament has an extremely rich and varied vocabulary for sin. Ultimately, sin was considered to be the mark of human failure. Springing from pride, it led to disobedience and rebellion against God.

Sin is first described in the experience of Adam and Eve in the Garden of Eden. There they listened to the serpent's lie and thought that they should be equal, or at least similar, in knowledge to God. This clearly sprang from a basic pride, a self-confidence in their own ability to know what was best for them. It also sprang from the fact that they were free to make choices. They were not forced into obedience but were left by God free to obey or disobey. At the same time, our primeval parents were also faced with the necessity of accepting or enduring the consequence of their actions, the first of which was guilt (Gen. 3:1-10).

The second major description of sin in the Old Testament is also set forth in terms of disobedience and human pride. This is the experience of the tower of Babel (Gen. 11:1-5). At that point, humanity had been commanded to "fill up the earth" (Gen. 9:1). In direct disobedience, they sought to "make a name" for themselves. They also sought to gather together in one place rather than scattering over the earth as they had been commanded (Gen. 11:4). Throughout the rest of the Old Testament, these same two roots for sin keep cropping up again and again. It is worth noting that in the aftermath of this story; the Lord paid a compliment to His human creatures when He said that so great was their ingenuity that they would be able to accomplish anything to which they set their mind (Gen. 11:6).

Based upon their own experience of pride and disobedience, the Israelites developed their understanding of sin. The words and phrases which describe the Old Testament sin experience fall into five different categories. (Although here I am only going to summarize them, these ideas can be investigated further in any good theology of the Old Testament or the Old Testament text itself by using one of the major biblical concordances.) Each of these descriptive categories was first drawn from its normal daily experiences. The image was then applied to what they sensed about sin.

First and foremost, *sin* is "missing the mark." This word was originally drawn from the military or hunting vocabulary of ancient Israel. It described an archer whose arrow missed the target. It also described a slinger whose stone failed to hit the object at which it was thrown. Words used to describe this idea of sin do not in and of themselves carry any moral connotation. Rather, they are simply descriptive of the fact that the sinner failed to do what God had intended. In some way, such a sinner had fallen short. This may have happened by accident. It may also have happened through ignorance. It may even have happened intentionally. Decisions on the basis or nature of the responsibility for such acts can only be made as we study the context. This description of sin is the most common one found in the Old Testament.

A second basic Old Testament understanding of sin can best be described as rebellion. This concept is also found in some translations as *transgression,* a term which is relatively unfamiliar to most contemporary students. The idea which was originally behind this was twofold. First, it described a person or nation who willfully crossed over the boundaries which had been established by someone else, such as crossing over property without the owner's consent. It was also used in a legal sense of consciously disobeying the laws set forth by a ruler or master. Its relationship to the Old Testament understanding of sin can be clearly seen. In this sense it describes a conscious act on the part of a sinner to disobey the command of God.

With this concept we have clearly moved into a moral understanding of sin. In this case the sinner has decided that he or she knows what is best. Either that or the decision has simply been made to proceed along a particular course of action regardless of God's command and the possible consequences. Here is a child, knowing the parent's command not to cross the street, but doing so anyway. At the very least there is the risk of parental displeasure and punishment. At the worst, the child runs the risk, perhaps without even being aware of it, of being run over by a speeding car. When this term is used, the sinner knows that the will of God is being violated. Without knowing or being aware of all of the possible consequences but clearly knowing that such an act runs the risk of God's displeasure and judgment, the sinner proceeds to act. Intentionality is clearly present in such an act. The sinner is bluntly saying, "I'm going to do it my way."

The third concept of sin in the Old Testament is best understood as stubbornness. The people of Israel were consistently described as being stubborn and stiff-necked. Having experienced both God's mercy and His sovereign power, they refused to accept His correction but set their hearts upon following the way of their own devices. Not only had they rebelled, they refused to turn back to Him when they were invited. The idea is also set forth in terms of being hard of heart. This is a step beyond rebellion. It is at this point that rebellion has become a habit, a way of life. The concept is also fully moral and describes a moral bankruptcy on the part of God's people.

A fourth concept of sin in the Old Testament is best described as perversion. At times, it appears to be a further step beyond stubborn rebellion. In these terms, the sinner has so set the pattern for life that from this point on one's way is permanently set. At the same time, in some contexts, this sense of being perverted also appears to be the result of outside factors. Thus a person may find himself almost forced into the path of evil. This idea had its pictorial root in an arrow which is twisted or bent and simply cannot fly straight when it is shot. In such terms, the sinner is bent toward evil. This partially comes from being the children of rebellious Adam. It may also come from other factors. The end of such a characteristic however is the fact that the person is certainly going to sin. At the moment of choice you may be free, but because of your nature you are going to choose to do wrong.

The fifth major concept used to portray sin in the Old Testament is that of guilt. In this sense, the sinner knows that he or she stands guilty before God. Rather than describing the act of or the reason for sin, this idea points to the consequence of sin. We must be careful not to perceive this as focusing upon the judgment which was going to follow sin. Instead, it directs our attention to the fact that when the human conscience is awakened, we honestly know that we are guilty. We are simply without excuse. This is not descriptive of Adam and Eve in the garden, blaming someone else for their sin (Gen. 3:12-13). Rather, this idea is more easily seen in David standing before the prophet Nathan. There he cried out his awareness of guilt, saying bluntly and without excuse, "'I have sinned against the Lord'" (2 Sam. 12:13).

The Hope

The final dimension of the Old Testament which helped prepare the way for the New Testament era was Israel's hope. Israel's awareness of sin might appear to have left her in an utterly hopeless condition. God, however, had given to her a distinct hope which was founded upon His love. This was first seen in the story of the garden. Even when God drove Adam and Eve from the garden in punishment, He protected the way back as a mark of His mercy. He did not wish them to "live forever" in their alienated state (Gen. 3:22,24). This implied a hope even though it did not offer one directly.

Their specific hope had two major dimensions, both based upon God's acts of power and love. Israel had experienced God's deliverance from Egypt in the exodus. During the exile, they looked forward to an ultimate deliverance from their exile in the time of the Babylonian captivity. From these foundations they realized that they had a realistic hope that He would ultimately deliver them from their enslavement or captivity to sin. This hope was based upon the actions of God's Messiah—His Suffering Servant (Isa. 9:2-6; 53:5-11). This hope was viewed at first in national terms, but it also came to be understood in personal terms. Each one could individually experience God's acts of redemption for themselves (Jer. 31:33-34; Job 19:25-26). At the same time, Israel also looked forward to the cataclysmic institution of God's kingdom at the end of the age. On a more personal level, God's prophets were beginning to perceive that there would be some form of resurrection (Isa. 26:19; Dan. 12:2).

Perhaps the most important part of the Old Testament hope which developed before the New Testament era was their dependence upon God's love and mercy. Even as they lived in the present, they looked forward to whatever future He would provide.

In each of these parts of the Old Testament faith which came before the New Testament era, God was setting the stage for His new thing. At times this faith was cloudy; at times it was more clear. However, through every instance, He was setting the stage for the development of the Christian church. Jesus and His disciples walked upon the stage of history, one of whose major supports was the faith of the Old Testament.

Note

1. Those who wish to make a more detailed study of the Old Testament influence upon the New Testament will find help in Robert Cate, *Old Testament Roots for New Testament Faith* (Nashville: Broadman Press, 1983).

6
The Greek Root

Most people are aware that the Old Testament is written primarily in Hebrew with a few passages in Aramaic, a close descendant of Hebrew. The New Testament, however, is written in Greek. This shift in language would be striking enough when taken by itself. It is all the more striking when we realize that most of the disciples who wrote the various New Testament books were Hebrews. We must immediately ask the question "why?" Why are the two halves of the Bible in different languages? Why did loyal and faithful Jews write books about a new development in their Jewish faith (for this is what many people thought Christianity was at first) in the Greek language?

These questions bring us to the next issue in our study. As we shall discover, the world in which Jesus and His disciples lived was significantly shaped by the ancient empire of Greece. We need to discover exactly what influence that kingdom had upon the world of the New Testament and thus upon the New Testament itself. The Greek root of the New Testament era is one of the more important roots which we shall consider.

The History

The Rise of Greece (333-301 B.C.)

From the time when the Medo-Persians overthrew Babylon (539 B.C.), the Persians ruled the ancient Near East with very little threat or opposition. During this period, the Hebrew people in Palestine were governed by their Persian overlords with a relatively small amount of interference. Further, the Persian province of Judah generally enjoyed one of the more peaceful eras which the region ever experienced.

However, about the middle of the fourth century B.C., that situation began to change. Up until then, the Macedonian peninsula had been the site of several city states which had competed with one another. However, the rise of Philip of Macedon changed all that. He was able to unite the various city states of that region into one political power.

Upon the death of Philip, he was succeeded by his son Alexander, later to become known as "the Great." It was he who changed the fate of Palestine, reshaped the map of the ancient Near East, and helped prepare the world for the coming of Christ. During Alexander's youth, he studied with Aristotle. From that experience, he became convinced that Greek culture and language was the greatest thing in the world. He considered it his special purpose to carry that culture and language into the rest of the world. Alexander did not, however, seek to convince the world by logic that his native culture was better than theirs. Rather he sought to force the world to accept this gift of culture. Thus he purposefully set out to conquer the world in order to make the world Greek. He intended to force a cultural revolution rather than simply trying to establish a world empire. To the Greek mind, everyone was either Greek or barbarian. Paul reflected this idea of opposites when he contrasted Greeks with barbarians (Rom. 1:14). He may even have been implying that Greeks were wise, and anyone else was foolish. At least, this was certainly what the Greeks believed.

Upon the death of his father, Alexander took control of the Macedonian army, quickly won or forced allegiance from those who sought to reestablish the old city-state system of Greece, and turned his eyes eastward toward the "barbarians" of the Persian empire. To any unbiased analyst of the times, such a move would have been unthinkable because it appeared impossible. At the Battle of Issus in 333 B.C., however, the Persian armies were defeated, and the ancient Near East lay open and undefended before the Macedonian youth and his armies.

To the far east, Alexander could see (or at least sense) the regions of Syria, Persia, Media, and even India. To the south his mind's eyes rested upon Egypt. At this point, as far as the Jews were concerned, it was geography which forced them to play a part in this great drama. Palestine in general and its coastal plain in particular formed a land bridge over which any army had to cross in order to reach Egypt, at least with any significant forces. Alexander began moving through Syria but rather than leave an exposed flank, turned his troops southward through Palestine. The island fortress of Tyre held out for a few months but was finally overcome. Gaza resisted the Greek advance for a much shorter period, and finally Egypt lay open before them. Not even remaining with those troops to finish the campaign, Alexander turned the main body of his troops north and eastward, first returning through Palestine. The Jews submitted to the Greeks and pledged their allegiance. Because of this, they were basically allowed to remain free to govern themselves and especially to practice their religion, a matter of utmost importance to them.

During Alexander's brief turn southward, the Persians had time to regroup, and they faced the advancing Greeks for a second major battle at Gaugamela in 331 B.C. There the Greeks were again victorious, and the back of any significant Persian resistance was broken. Alexander and his armies continued their march to the east. He died at the age of thirty-three in 323 B.C. in the Indus Valley. Truly he had earned the name "the Great."

Since Alexander had set forth on his brilliant march of conquest with the goal of spreading Greek culture, we should note that he did precisely that. When cities were conquered, they were immediately settled with a garrison of Greeks, usually retired soldiers. New cities, such as Alexandria in Egypt, were basically Greek in design and were heavily populated with Greek citizens. The Greek language became the official language of all the eastern Mediterranean world. Gymnasiums, centers of public baths, and all sorts of athletic contests were established wherever the Greek armies moved. Theaters were built and Greek dramas were performed. Greek temples were erected and Greek gods were worshiped in all major cities within the empire. Since the official name for the Macedonian peninsula was Hellas, the process of inculturating the world was called Hellenization.

This Hellenization became a major source of trouble for the Hebrews. Obviously, they resisted the worship of the pagan gods. At the same time, some among them welcomed the new culture, while others resisted it as pagan and immoral, particularly since the athletic events in the gymnasiums were performed nude. Much of the Greek drama was highly licentious, further offending the Hebrews' morality.

The unexpected early death of Alexander brought chaos to his empire. During this period, the Diadochi ("successors") struggled for supremacy over the empire. For a while, this conflict was behind the scenes in a pretense of ruling for Alexander's infant son. It finally broke out into the open. The Jews of Palestine were particularly caught in the middle of the struggle between Ptolemy I in Egypt and Seleucus I in Syria. However, at the Battle of Ipsus (302 B.C.) the issue was settled for the time being with a total victory for the Egyptians. This gave Ptolemy I absolute and undisputed control over Palestine.

The Ptolemaic Era (301-198 B.C.)

The century during which the Ptolemies ruled over Palestine was characterized by two major features. First of all, it was a time of several very intense conflicts interspersed among longer periods of peace. During this time there were five major wars between Egypt and Syria (274-272, 260-252, 246-241, 221-217, 201-198 B.C.). Second, the Hebrews were allowed somewhat the same degree of freedom to determine their own destiny insofar as their internal affairs were concerned.

We must note, however, that every time an army marched in either direction between Syria and Egypt, the Hebrews were immediately involved in international affairs. Choices of giving or withholding aid had to be made with care because the future of the nation depended upon siding with the victor in each instance. These decisions had to be made by the high priest in Jerusalem because he was the leader of the nation during this time. Of course, he had the advice of the scribes and Sanhedrin. During this era, the three major sources of power and influence among the Hebrews were these two groups, plus the priesthood itself. Neither group was exclusive or independent of the others, and numerous people were part of more than one of these groups.

The Seleucid Era (198-167 B.C.)

The tide of control over Palestine turned in favor of the Seleucids in the Fifth Syrian War (201-198 B.C.). The Jewish leadership realized that this was occurring and took advantage of this change in fortunes by switching their allegiance, fighting on the side of the Syrians in this conflict. Because of this, when the Syrian forces won, the Hebrews were again able to maintain their relative independence. In fact, the Hebrew's position was so strong that Syrian funds were used to repair damage done to Jerusalem during this conflict. Further, the officials in Jerusalem were exempted from taxation. However, due to problems on the western side of Syria these conditions did not last long.

First, the Seleucids entered upon a thoroughgoing process of Hellenization, a process which had not been pushed during the period of Ptolemaic rule. This antagonized the Jewish leaders who were loyal to the Torah. As such, they were unwilling to compromise in any way with the Syrian rulers.

Further, Antiochus III (223-187 B.C.), having expanded his kingdom to the south, sought to expand to the west, attempting to gain control of Greece by conquering its old city states. This, however, was a threat to the rising empire of Rome. They quickly invaded, forcing the Syrian troops into retreat until Antiochus was defeated by Rome. That peace was sealed by the treaty of Apemea (188 B.C.). As a part of the so-called Peace of Apemea, the Syrians were forced to make massive payments of tribute to Rome. These payments utterly depleted the national treasury, and Antiochus III and his successors had to raise the money through massive taxation. A part of this was accomplished by seizing the treasuries of the temples in territory under his control. This affected the Hebrew temple and worship in Jerusalem.

As a part of this process, the rulers of Syria began to appoint the high priest, an affront to the Jews. However, among the priesthood numerous rival claimants sold their souls by bartering with the Syrian kings for that appointment. What was usually offered by these priests was massive tribute and aid in the ongoing process of Hellenization. All of this created serious unrest among the loyal and orthodox members of the Jewish community. We need to note that most of the people seem to have been unaware of these issues. Life was difficult, and the mere struggle to survive took most of the common people's attention. Taxation was a concern. The concerns of political power were basically unimportant to them if it did not affect them immediately and directly.

With the accession of Antiochus IV Epiphanes to the throne of Syria, a new crisis arose which had far-reaching consequences for the Hebrews. Antiochus sought to carry out the long term goal of his ancestors—the conquest of Egypt. When he believed his forces were of sufficient strength, he marched against his ancient enemy. However, Antiochus was forced to abort this campaign by the intervention of Rome, with whom the Egyptians had made a treaty.

The Jews in Jerusalem heard a rumor that Antiochus had been killed in a battle and rebelled against Menelaus, the high priest who had been installed by Antiochus. However, when Antiochus arrived at the unfruitful end of his Egyptian campaign, he was incensed at the Jewish actions. He reinstated Menelaus and plundered the temple treasury. In a second attack upon the Hebrew nation, he decided to finish his process of Hellenization by force. The walls of Jerusalem were torn down, and a Syrian fortress was built on the Temple Mount (the Acra). Furthermore, the Hebrews were forbidden on penalty of death to celebrate the Sabbath or circumcise their children. These latter two things were the basic symbols of the people's Jewishness. The actions by Antiochus aroused the wrath of large portions of the Jewish people.

Furthermore, an altar to Zeus was erected on the site of the temple altar, and swine flesh was offered there in 167 B.C. This final act was seen by the Hebrews as the abomination of desolations predicted by Daniel (Dan. 11:31; 12:11). Antiochus had fanned the feelings of the Hebrew populace to a white heat. Rebellion was boiling just beneath the surface, lacking only the right spark to blow the lid off the entire situation.

The Hellenizing Tendencies

We have already noted that the major purpose of Alexander's conquests was the spreading of Greek culture and civilization. This was carried on with an even greater intensity but with less understanding by the Seleucids from their base in Syria. Alexander established new cities and settled Greeks in old ones. However, he does not appear to have been as militant in forcing the defeated to take on Greek culture. The Seleucids, particularly after the peace of Apemea, were far more aggressive. Further, they also appear either to have been ignorant of the cultural and religious sensitivities of conquered peoples or to have intentionally sought to force them into submission and acquiescence.

Insofar as the people of Jerusalem and Judea were concerned, several of the major Hellenizing tendencies were particularly distressing. First among these, at least to the more orthodox of the Hebrews was the actual buying and selling of the office of high priest. This had been hereditary and was thus understood as the gift of God. However, although it would have been bad enough for the Jewish people to have simply seen the office become so politicized and commercialized, it was even worse to see the office under the power of a pagan. In fairness to the Greeks, we should note that this became a part of the Hellenizing process only when their financial situation became desperate. It had not been a part of the process from the beginning.

The settling of Greeks in ancient cities and the establishment of new Greek cities may have disturbed the Hebrews. However, what really became difficult for them was the garrisoning of soldiers on the Acra in Jerusalem. This put pagan soldiers on the sacred mountain, a major affront to Hebrew sensibilities. It would have been bad enough to have any foreigners there. To have troops from an occupying power on that sacred site was especially despicable.

The third major problem for the Jewish people which was raised by the process of Hellenization was brought about by the gymnasiums. These places of baths and athletic contests were particularly difficult for the Hebrews to accept due to the fact that these activities were done in the nude. This was considered to be immoral by the orthodox Jews. These activities became a source of difficulty even for those Hebrews who sought to participate because to the Greek mind circumcision was wrong. Greeks disapproved of any alteration of the natural body. Numerous Jewish young men who sought to participate had operations to try to reverse the effect of circumcision. This created other problems because to the orthodox Jews such operations were a denial of their Jewishness. Thus the end result of the activities of the gymnasiums was not merely the hatred of the Greeks by the Jews, it also created a major division among the Jews.

The fourth major area of Hellenistic activities on the part of the conquering Greeks was the introduction of their language. Such a practice was beneficial to the world in that it allowed easy communication across national and ethnic barriers. On the other hand, to the Hebrews the substitution of Greek as the language of government was another affront. We shall return to this issue later.

From the Hebrew standpoint, the final negative step in the process of Hellenization of the Jewish cities was the building of theaters in most major cities. As we noted before, many of the Greek dramas were quite licentious. To the conservative Hebrews, such activities were immoral. On the other hand, Jewish leaders who sought for power under the Greeks attended these plays and thus were alienated from their fellow citizens. Further, to the very orthodox among the Jews, the actors in a drama were thought to be making images and thus such activities were thought to be a violation of the Commandments.

Not all of the steps in the Hellenizing process were negative for the Hebrews. The Greek system of logic (question and answer in seeking for the truth) was adopted by the scribes and rabbis as means of searching for deeper understanding of their faith and its teachings. It shows up in later rabbinic writings of the Hebrews. This method also shows up occasionally in the New Testament.

A further beneficial consequence of Hellenization for the Hebrews was Greek medicine. The Hebrews already had, by ancient standards, a fairly well-developed healing ministry. However, Greek medicine was apparently much further developed. In fact, the Greek influence on medicine is felt today as contemporary American physicians take the medical oath of an ancient Greek physician, Hippocrates.

The Greek conquerors sought to make the world Greek in thought and action. That may have been all right for most of the world. It was all right for some of the Hebrews, particularly those of the wealthy and powerful families who dwelt in Jerusalem. However, for the more religious Hebrews, the process of Hellenization would bring an ultimate confrontation with their faith.

The Purifying Tendencies

The rise of Hellenization among the Hebrews brought about a reaction which was only to be expected. Throughout history, whenever any conqueror has taken over a nation, two immediate results occur. First, some of the conquered people begin to collaborate with the conqueror. This is usually done for power, wealth, or both. Many such people were certainly found among the Hebrews, including those who eventually served as high priests. On the other hand, in reaction to the collaborators and to the very fact of conquest, some form of a resistance movement grows. The strength of the resistance movement is usually in direct proportion to the harshness with which the conqueror governs. This was again true among the Hebrews. There were those who resisted the Hellenization policy from the earliest days. As the ruling authorities became more harsh under the Seleucids, the strength of the resistance grew.

This resistance flashed out in open revolt at the rumor of the death of Antiochus IV Epiphanes (168 B.C.). Interestingly, the revolt was aimed at the Jewish collaborators more than at the conquerors themselves. Jason, a high priest who had been deposed by Antiochus, gathered an army of the disaffected around him and drove the reigning high priest from Jerusalem.

Antiochus came to Jerusalem, put Menelaus back on the priestly throne, and began a systematic attempt to stamp out the Jewish religious observances. Such actions drove the resistance back underground. However, the harsh and oppressive policy greatly intensified the hostility of those who hated Hellenism. It also caused more people to flock to the support of the resistance. For the moment the resistance was waiting for the spark which would create the explosion.

The Language

Perhaps the most significant part of the Greek root from which the New Testament era was an outgrowth was the Greek language itself. By the time Alexander's conquests were concluded, Greek was spoken in every major nation between Macedonia and the Indus Valley. This made it possible for people of very diverse cultures and different nations to communicate with one another with ease. Greek became the language of commerce and international diplomacy.

For the people of the New Testament era, this gift of the Greek language had two major consequences. The first of these has to do with the Old Testament Scriptures. In the centuries following the conquest of Jerusalem, Jewish refugees were scattered over the Mediterranean. Most of the major cities soon had Jewish communities. As the years passed, these Jewish communities began to speak the language of the nations where they lived. The ultimate consequence of this was that it became more and more difficult for the various groups of Judaism to communicate with one another or understand their sacred Scriptures.

To counteract this problem, the Jews translated their Scriptures into Greek. According to an ancient but wholly unreliable tradition, this was done by seventy men in seventy days. Though the tradition is unreliable, it gave the Greek translation its name. It is called the Septuagint, which means seventy. This is usually abbreviated LXX. Because of its international character, this gave the early Christian preachers and missionaries a Scripture which was understandable in the various nations to which they went with the gospel.

In addition, the spread of Greek as a universally understood language made it possible for the early Christians to be understood wherever they went. The spread of Christianity was resisted at first by the Hebrews. But, that very universality did make it possible for the gospel to be proclaimed to the ends of the earth. Alexander's conquest was a major step in preparing the world for the proclamation of God's good news of redemption.

7
The Maccabean Root

Great trees stand tall and strong because they are supported and nurtured by many roots. The same thing is true of various historical eras. Each one builds upon and is shaped by those which have preceded it. This is certainly true of the New Testament era. We have already examined two of the historical roots which fed into it: the Old Testament and the Greek empire. For the Hebrew people of Judea, the Greek period ended with the oppressive and devastating policies of Antiochus Epiphanes. As a result of those policies, the tension in Jerusalem and Judea was almost palpable. For the first time, the people of the land were aroused. Other crises had appeared, but they were significant only for the political and religious leaders, Insofar as most of the people were concerned, life had not changed. The present issue, however, touched them all at the point of the practices of their faith. Being forbidden to practice circumcision or keep the Sabbath involved everyone. All that was lacking was the proper spark, and the whole land would explode into rebellion. That spark was not long in coming.

The Revolt and Purification

The flash point among the Jewish people was reached when Antiochus sought to enforce his renewed emphasis on Hellenization throughout the Judean countryside as well as in the capital. The people outside of Jerusalem had held on to their faith with loyal tenacity. In what he perceived as the last step in turning the Hebrew nation into a Greek state, Antiochus IV sent his troops and commissioners throughout the land with orders to enforce his Hellenization of the worship practices of the Jewish people.

When they came to the town of Modein in 167 B.C., the Syrians sought to force an aged priest named Mattathias to sacrifice swine flesh. Upon his refusal, another Jew of the community volunteered to perform this act of sacrilege. Mattathias was so enraged that he leapt forward, killing both the Jew who was so willing to collaborate and the Seleucid officer who had ordered him to do so. With that act, the die was cast and the nation burst into open rebellion. Mattathias and his sons immediately fled into the Judean wilderness, where they were quickly joined by growing numbers of the patriotic and the disaffected. To this group also came the religious rebels or "pious ones," better known as the *Hasidim*. This latter group was concerned with religious issues only, having no desire to get involved with political issues except where their religion was affected.

The makeup of this band of rebels had within it the seeds of future problems. The *Hasidim* only sought the purification of their religion. The rest of the band sought varying degrees of political independence from the hated Antiochus IV, his Hellenizing policies, his occupying troops, and the oppressive Syrian taxation.

After the death of Mattathias, the leadership of the rebel forces fell upon his son Judas. His quick actions, sudden and surprising attacks, and solid blows against the Syrian forces soon led the people to nickname him "the hammer." The Aramaic term for this, *makkaba*, caused Judas to be called by its Greek transliteration, Maccabee. From this, the entire movement came to be known as Maccabean.

At the beginning of the revolt, the Maccabean forces made numerous guerrilla attacks on both Syrian forces and Jewish collaborators throughout the countryside. Antiochus, who was engaged in a major conflict with the Parthians far to the east, sent his general, Lysias, with orders to deal quickly with these upstart rebels. Unfortunately for the Syrians, not only were they unable to destroy the Maccabees, they themselves suffered several major defeats. As a consequence, Judas and his forces soon marched into the city of Jerusalem and took over the temple. Under his leadership, the holy place was cleansed and rededicated with a major celebration on the twenty-fifth of Kislev (late December) in 165 B.C. This great celebration, an eight-day festival of exuberant joy, has come down to modern times in Jewish religious observances as Hanukkah, the Feast of Lights (John 10:22). It is still one of their most joyful celebrations.

However, although the temple had been reconsecrated, the Syrian troops continued to occupy the Acra in Jerusalem. Along with a few other minor skirmishes, Judas directed his major attention to the task of forcing the Syrians from that position by besieging their fortress.

In the meantime, Antiochus had died in the east, throwing the entire Syrian kingdom into conflict because his minor son was unable to rule in his own right. General Lysias, however, served as regent. Lysias and his army marched on Jerusalem, defeating the Jewish forces in the field and then besieging Judas and his troops inside the city of Jerusalem.

At this point, international affairs took a hand on the side of the Jews. A rival sought to take over the throne of Syria in the absence of Lysias. This crisis left Lysias two choices. His first option was to continue the attack on Jerusalem, almost certainly winning the battle but losing control of the situation in Syria. A second option for Lysias was to abandon Jerusalem, allowing the Jews to be victorious by default, but regaining control of the situation in Syria. Lysias chose a middle path. He entered into a treaty with Judas, granting the Jews absolute religious freedom in return for the Jews' recognition of the political suzerainty of Syria. This treaty gave both Judas and Lysias the freedom to operate with relative independence in their own circles.

The Rise of Nationalism

As far as the Hebrews were concerned, the result of all of this conflict was that the hated Menelaus had been deposed from the high priesthood while they had regained the right to practice their faith with freedom. The initial goals of the revolt had thus been achieved.

Even though a new Syrian king, Demetrius I (162-150 B.C.), had appointed a new high priest in Jerusalem who was sympathetic to the process of Syrian Hellenization, the *Hasidim* withdrew their support of Judas and his revised goals. These pious ones were willing to accept Alcimus, Demetrius' appointee, as high priest since he was of the line of Aaron and thus qualified to serve. They had sensed that Judas and the more politically motivated of his followers had changed their perception of the purpose of the revolt. No longer was religious freedom enough for the Maccabees. They now were looking for political independence as well. While Judas and his more loyal supporters perceived this as the only way they could ensure their independence, the *Hasidim* viewed it as a betrayal of their original purposes.

With the departure of the *Hasidim* from among his supporters, Judas' forces appeared to be significantly weakened. However, he so believed in his divine destiny that he and those troops who remained with him were undaunted as they sought to continue the revolt without the aid of the *Hasidim*. In a sense, his sense of destiny appeared to have been confirmed when he negotiated a treaty with Rome confirming his claim to the leadership of Judea. Although Rome was in no position at that time to offer real support, the fact that such a treaty had been signed was significant to Judas as well as to Syria. It showed that he was a force to be reckoned with on the international scene. However, it also further confirmed the belief of the *Hasidim* that his goals had changed.

Judas then decided that even though he had negotiated a treaty with the Syrians, he could not depend upon that for the future religious freedom of his people. To the contrary, as far as Judas was concerned, the only way he could ensure the continuation of their present freedom was by attaining political independence as well. To this end, Judas attacked the troops which the Syrians had placed at Alcimus' disposal, seeking to depose the high priest. That was not merely a challenge to the high priest and his supporters, it was a challenge to the Syrian ruler, Demetrius I, as well.

As a result of this confrontation between Judas, Alcimus, and the Syrian forces, the Maccabeans and their enemies were involved in a number of military engagements. These varied from pitched battles to guerrilla-type engagements. Perhaps the most important immediate result of these battles was the death of Judas himself in 161 B.C. It might be supposed that his death would have brought the entire revolt to an end. However, the opposite turned out to be the case.

Jonathan, the brother of Judas, succeeded to the leadership of the Maccabean forces. The renewed fighting, coupled with Judas' death, resulted in a number of defeats and intense persecution of the rebellious Jews by the Syrian forces. The Maccabean forces were in retreat and disarray, but only for a while. In the wilderness of Judea they regrouped and began to take the offensive against the Syrians and the supporters of Alcimus.

Jonathan seems to have had more political skills than Judas, although he may not have been his equal in generalship. However, his political acumen more than offset any other weaknesses. Throughout this period, rival leaders and factions struggled over the Syrian throne. Jonathan was able to take advantage of this internecine warfare, supporting first one claimant to the throne and then another. Each time he changed sides, he was able to gain new concessions, while seeing the opposing forces steadily weakening due to their ongoing conflicts and the continued drain on the Syrian resources. All of this added further strength to his own position.

Three major developments came out of this period of conflict and negotiations. First, Alcimus the high priest died about 159 B.C. This left the high priesthood vacant. The ongoing conflict over the throne of Syria took so much attention that the Syrians did not bother to appoint a successor. In fact, until 152, there was no official high priest in Jerusalem. (This period has been called by historians the "Intersacerdotum," meaning the time between the priests.)

The second major development was the enlargement of the territory over which Jonathan ruled. Because of the steady concessions granted by the claimants to the Syrian throne, Jonathan was even granted authority over the southern part of Samaria, as well as increasing the boundaries of his possessions which surrounded Jerusalem.

However, the third development of the era ultimately became the most significant. During the ongoing conflict for the throne of Syria there was no high priest in Jerusalem. Playing his political skills to the utmost, Jonathan eventually got himself appointed to that position about 152 B.C. With that appointment, the entire revolution took on a new dimension. It had begun partially because the Jews resisted a foreign ruler appointing high priests. It had now so changed that its own leader accepted such an appointment. It had begun because the religious sensibilities of the Jews had been affronted by the high-handed actions of Syrian rulers. It had now come to the place that the Maccabeans not only accepted but welcomed as the high priest one whose hands were stained with blood, one who, though of Aaronic descent, was not of the Zadokite priesthood of Jerusalem. Personal ambition and lust for power had altered the course of the revolt. The historian cannot help but wonder what the aged Mattathias would have thought of his son. The rebellion which had its roots in the idealism of religious purists had been sacrificed on the altar of so-called political realism.

These changes were viewed with horror, fear, and suspicion by the *Hasidim*. The revolt which begun with a united Jewish front against the forces of Hellenism had now created a division among the people of the land. Jonathan now had it all: relative independence coupled with political and religious authority. The price for the people of Judea was going to be quite high. These hidden costs were going to be discovered later.

The Kingdom of Priests

As a part of the ongoing crises in the kingdom of Syria, Jonathan continued to try to play the various claimants to the throne against one another and to his advantage. This time his skill failed him. Further, he had never been as great a general as he had been a politician. As a visitor (captive?) of the Syrians, he was murdered in 142 B.C.

Once again, the Maccabees were without a leader. Another of the brothers of Judas—Simon—succeeded to the leadership of the revolt. Instead of following the policy of Jonathan in expanding his territorial borders, Simon turned his attention to the Syrian garrison which was still within the city of Jerusalem. He realized that any attempt at independence was untenable as long as foreign troops were garrisoned within the holy city. The Maccabean leader also believed, probably correctly, that driving those troops from Jerusalem would win the renewed support of the *Hasidim.*

Simon's assault on the Acra met with success, and for the first time since the days of Antiochus Epiphanes, Syrian forces were no longer garrisoned in Judean territory. The Hebrew people and particularly the *Hasidim* were overjoyed. If Simon had been content at that point, he might have once again united the Jewish people behind him. However, his own ambition, like that of his brother before him, became his downfall.

Simon took advantage of his victory and the continuing conflict in Syria over the throne and negotiated a treaty with the Syrians which was extremely beneficial. Unfortunately for the Jews, it was more beneficial for him personally than it was for his people, although they did gain major concessions as well. For the nation, their independence was confirmed by the elimination of all Syrian taxation. Such a benefit was received with great joy. However, the major beneficiaries of this particular concession were the wealthy, who were primarily the merchants and priestly families.

However, the major benefits fell to Simon. First, he was installed as high priest, even as his brother had been. While making him the leader of the Jewish people, that once again alienated the *Hasidim*. Next, Simon was recognized as the military leader of the Jews, a position which was made official through his appointment by the Syrian ruler. The most important concession to Simon, however, was that he was granted the hereditary rulership over the Jews. For all practical purposes, he had been made king of the Jews.

Simon's accession to the throne established the Hasmonean dynasty. (The name came from an ancestor by the name of Hashmon.) To confirm the real authority behind that appointment, the Jews were allowed by the Syrians to mint their own coins. Such a right was recognized by ancient nations as being the outward, visible sign of an independent kingdom. Subject kingdoms were not allowed that freedom. Again, in a decision which was to have even more far-reaching influence, the Romans recognized Simon's kingship. For the first time in its history, the Hebrew nation had actually become a kingdom of priests.

To the Maccabeans and their supporters, the reign of Simon was viewed with almost the same ecstatic joy with which they would have greeted the messianic kingdom. He does appear to have been a relatively wise ruler (1 Macc. 14:8-15). For the first time since the revolt had begun, peace settled over the territory of Judea. Further, Simon appears to have been a loyal follower of the Torah. Coupled with his religious orthodoxy and political wisdom was a genuine compassion for the people of the land. His reign brought, at least for a time, a period of real peace and goodwill among most of the people of his land.

But once again, the *Hasidim* were not so easily swayed. They viewed the reign of Simon with great distaste. Although he was of the house of Aaron, he was not of the Zadokite line, the ones from whom the high priests were to be selected. Further, he was not of the house of David from whom the Hebrew kings were to be descended. Both of these factors were major affronts to Hebrew tradition. Some open hostility was voiced, and a deep undercurrent of resentment was present among these pious ones. Further, some of the pious ones were so disturbed by these developments that they simply left the land, moving to the shores of the Dead Sea and establishing a community there which has become known to us as the Qumran community.

Human Failure

With the rising hostility toward Simon, the stage was set for the ultimate collapse of the Maccabean revolt. Slowly, but inexorably, it continued to grind toward its final dissolution. Simon was murdered about 135/34 B.C. in an abortive attempt at rebellion. That failed and he was succeeded in the priesthood and on the throne by his son, John Hyrcanus (135/34-104 B.C.). At that point, the Syrians sought to regain some control over Judean affairs. They failed, however, allowing Hyrcanus not only the opportunity to consolidate his authority but to expand his territory. He conquered both Samaria to the north and Idumea to the east and south. During his reign, there was a decisive break with the Pharisees. They had sought to get him to resign his high priesthood, raising some question as to whether or not he might have been illegitimately conceived by his mother.

Following the death of John Hyrcanus, his son Aristobulus seized the throne, throwing his mother and three of his brothers into prison in order to do so. For a brief time Aristobulus shared the power with one brother, Antigonus. However, he eventually had Antigonus murdered, thus ruling alone. The earlier members of the Hasmonean dynasty had ruled as kings, but Aristobulus was the first one to claim the title of king. He continued the military successes of his father, expanding his territory into Galilee. He died in 103 B.C., after a reign of slightly more than one year.

Salome Alexandra, the widow of Hyrcanus, freed her imprisoned brothers-in-law, marrying the eldest and delivering the throne to him. Upon his accession, he adopted the Hellenized name of Alexander Jannaeus. He continued the expansion of the kingdom, conquering territory along the coastal plain to the west and into the region of the Nabataeans to the east. However, at home Alexander was able to maintain his power only by means of the harshest cruelty. An open break with the Pharisees led to a civil war. That was crushed when Alexander had eight hundred of the Pharisees crucified while he, his wives, and supporters watched from a banquet table. He even had the wives and children of the Pharisees slaughtered before their crosses, making the dying victims witness that scene of horror. For Alexander and his followers, the entire episode was simply a form of after-dinner entertainment. His brutality brought an end to the rebellion and initiated a time of peace during his final days, but the opposition of the people of the land was only buried beneath the surface.

Once again, Salome Alexandra was a widow. This time she ruled in her own right (76-67 B.C.). As a woman, however, she could not fill the office of the high priest, so she installed her son, Hyrcanus II, in that position. Further, following the deathbed advice of her late husband, she sought a reconciliation with the Pharisees. This was accomplished by appointing some of them to the Sanhedrin, positions which had essentially been held only by the Sadducees up to that point. This alienated the Sadduccees, who formed an alliance with another son, Aristobulus II. However, Salome managed to maintain peace at home and abroad. Thus her reign is looked upon as a time of relative quiet. That did not last beyond her death.

With his mother off the scene, Aristobulus II fought for the kingship with Hyrcanus II. Aristobulus quickly showed himself to be the superior, and the forces of Hyrcanus abandoned him in favor of his brother, who became both king and high priest (67-63 B.C.). The conflict did not end so easily, however. Hyrcanus was soon joined by Antipater of Idumea and Aretas of the Nabataeans. Their united forces marched on Jerusalem, laying siege to the army of Aristobulus. At this point, Rome appeared on the scene as the troops of Pompey marched into Palestine through Syria. Both sides appealed to him for help. With such an invitation, Pompey invaded Jerusalem in 63 B.C. and the Hasmonean kingdom came to an end.

The influences of that era upon the Hebrews are still present in Judaism today. Further, since it was such an influential time, it obviously added a dimension to the world of Palestine, and this in turn influenced the rise and spread of Christianity.

8
The Roman Root

Anyone familiar with the New Testament is aware, at least to some extent, of the Roman influences on the life and ministry of Jesus and on the subsequent spread of Christianity throughout the Mediterranean world. Luke anchored his Gospel solidly into the Roman world with his introductory words to the birth narrative of Jesus. "In those day a decree went out from Caesar Augustus," he asserted, relating Jesus to the ruling authority of the Roman empire (Luke 2:1). Further, Roman soldiers figured on more than one occasion in the gospel stories, and a Roman governor issued the final judgment of crucifixion against Jesus (Matt. 27:2,26).

In addition, the same sort of thing is found in reading the Book of Acts. Roman soldiers and officials are found on many pages, and Paul's Roman citizenship protected him at Philippi (Acts 16:35 39). Under Roman law Paul was able to appeal to Caesar for justice. This eventually made it possible for him to reach Rome and proclaim the gospel, although he went there as a prisoner (Acts 25:10-11).

Furthermore, a survey of the Epistles reveals numerous phrases and references which can only be understood against the background of Roman authority, laws, and practices. Whatever else may be said about their environment, the early Christians lived and died in a Roman world. Therefore, in order to understand their history, we must first of all be aware of and try to understand the Roman root of that history.

Expansion of the Empire

For more than a century, life on the eastern edge of the Mediterranean had been lived under the growing shadow of Rome. For the

Hebrews, that shadow had turned into a brutal reality when Pompey marched into Jerusalem in 63 B.C. From that time onward, the Jewish people experienced not only the presence of Rome but the iron fist of Roman oppression. They learned that Rome knew what the ultimate purpose of foreign conquest was all about: gold! More clearly than any nation before her and probably with more clarity than those empires who followed, Rome realized that the chief business of a world conqueror is the collection of taxes. Her imperial rulers also recognized quite clearly that peace in a conquered territory is necessary for the steady flow of tribute and taxes into the general coffers of the conqueror. Thus Rome's overall policy was directed to the accomplishment of this purpose. The Hebrews were to learn this from bitter experience. They had invited Rome in. They would not be able to "invite" Rome out.

For all of her history after the Babylonian capture of Jerusalem (587 B.C.), with the brief exception of the Maccabean era, the Hebrews had lived under foreign domination. Rome was just one more in a long string of foreign rulers. This was nothing new. However, Roman domination brought two major changes to the fortunes of Judea.

With the advent of Rome on the Palestinian scene, the official seat of foreign authority was now far to the west. Further, when Rome invaded Judea, the Parthians moved into Mesopotamia from the east. This meant that Judea was no longer somewhere near the center of an empire, as she had been with Persia and Greece. From the perspective of Rome, Judea was on the frontier. The Jewish nation was simply a frontier outpost, not a significant central feature of the imperial strategy.

In a parallel development, Rome also had a fairly significant navy. This meant that for her to move troops into Egypt, she did not necessarily have to move them through the land bridge of Judea. This further reduced the strategic significance of Judea for the rulers of Rome.

Each of these changes in the Jewish relationship to the policies of her rulers was to have a significant effect upon both the Jewish nation and the rise of Christianity. The Roman rulers were not overly concerned to send the most able governors to that insignificant part of their empire. This was to have major consequences for the people who lived in that region.

Political Realities

Following Pompey's conquest of Jerusalem in 63 B.C., Judea was made a part of the Roman province of Syria. That meant that the Jewish nation was officially annexed to the empire of Rome. From that time on through the New Testament era, the fortunes of Judea were intimately intertwined with those of Rome. In a fortunate development for the Jewish people, during the early days of this period, Judea was led by a man who was unusually qualified to make the best of that situation. He was able to utilize the political fortunes of Rome to best advantage of the Hebrews.

Antipater and Hyrcanus II (63-ca. 43 B.C.)

Antipater of Idumea had joined forces with Hyrcanus II in an attempt to place the latter upon the throne of Judea and reinstate him as high priest. Hyrcanus was the one with the legitimate claim, but Antipater was the strong one in that coalition. He was a masterful politician, one who at the first was content to wield the real power while allowing someone else to be the figurehead.

Recognizing the awesome power of Rome, Antipater adopted as his basic policy the maintenance of good relations with Rome. He sought to accomplish this by wholeheartedly supporting whoever was in power at any given moment. He also made sure that both the Romans and Jews were regularly made aware of his good works.

Antipater's first achievement after the Roman annexation of Judea was to seek and receive Hyrcanus' appointment to the office of high priest. This might have been considered a major concession to Hyrcanus; however, no one in authority had any doubt that Antipater was in control in Jerusalem.

Although Hyrcanus' appointment gave him no real power, significant concessions were made to the Jewish state because of Antipater's influence. Even though the Jews were forced to give up all of the non-Jewish territory which the Hasmoneans had conquered, Judaism was recognized as a legal religion. This allowed the spread of synagogues throughout the Diaspora without governmental opposition. In addition, Jews were exempted from military service, Roman troops were withdrawn from Judea, and religious freedom in Jerusalem was reconfirmed. In order to allow the Jews a better opportunity for international trade, they were also given a seaport, Joppa. Finally, they were also given permission to rebuild the walls of Jerusalem.

For about thirty-five years following the victory of Pompey in Jerusalem, affairs in Rome were quite turbulent. Rome itself was going through a political transformation. The first triumvirate was established in 60 B.C., made up of Julius Caesar, Pompey, and Crassus. Crassus ruled over Syria and thus over Judea. Crassus was killed in a battle with the Parthians in 51 B.C. Caesar and Pompey soon clashed and Caesar defeated Pompey in 48 B.C. Pompey promptly fled to Egypt where he was assassinated upon his arrival. Caesar, left in sole authority, was made virtual dictator in 45 B.C. Fearing the consequences of that, a conspiracy led by Brutus assassinated Caesar on March 15, 44 B.C.

A new triumvirate of Antony, Lepidus, and Octavian was formed in 43 B.C. They quickly dealt with the conspirators. In the division of responsibility which followed, Antony was given authority over Syria, which still included Judea. However, once again the leaders of Rome shortly fell out among themselves. That series of conflicts left Octavian as sole ruler of Rome. He took the title of Augustus, ruling from 27 B.C. to A.D. 14.

These turbulent years gave Antipater abundant opportunities to demonstrate his political skills. However, they were also dangerous years for him because a false step could have deposed him from power or cost him his life at any time. Julius Caesar brought Antipater's power into the open when he appointed him to be procurator. During the years of turbulence, there was never any question of Antipater's loyalty to Rome, which allowed him to continue to function regardless of which faction controlled the empire.

Following the murder of Caesar, Antipater took the opportunity of appointing two of his sons to power (ca. 44 B.C.). Phasael, the eldest, was named governor of Judea; and Herod, the second son, was named governor of Galilee. These high-handed acts aroused the hatred of the Jews. Antipater was poisoned in 43 B.C. His sons now ruled on their own, under Rome of course.

Phasael and Herod (ca. 44-40 B.C.)

Although Phasael's appointment in Judea created no real problem, Herod's in Galilee most certainly did. Galilee was a center of

Hebrew nationalism (a fact which later created problems in Jesus' ministry). Herod executed one particular insurrectionist and all of his followers. For this Herod was praised by the Romans and was called to face a trial in front of the Sanhedrin in Jerusalem. Arriving like a royal potentate, Herod obviously sought to intimidate the Jewish court. Instead, he further alienated them. He was almost convicted, avoiding this only by the expediency of having Hyrcanus disband the court just before their decision. In anger, Herod planned to attack Jerusalem but was talked out of it by Phasael who sought to avoid Jewish civil war. Herod, however, was rewarded by the Romans by having additional territory to the north added to the region which he ruled.

Following the assassination of Caesar and the ultimate defeat of Brutus, a delegation of the Jews appealed to Mark Antony to replace Herod and Phasael. Rather than granting this, Antony made them both tetrarchs. Their elevation did not last long. While Antony became involved with Cleopatra, the Parthians invaded Palestine from the east, placing Antigonus (a son of Aristobulus II) on the throne of Judea. Phasael committed suicide and Hyrcanus was mutilated, thus disqualifying him as high priest. Meanwhile, Herod fled to Rome, biding his time and leaving Antigonus in effective control of Judea.

Antigonus (40-37 B.C.)

With the high priesthood vacant, the Parthians installed Antigonus in that office, making him both king and high priest. All observers were quite aware that though he bore those elevated titles, Antigonus was nothing more than the puppet of the Parthians. Rome could not ignore this situation because it threatened their control of the entire eastern end of the Mediterranean.

Herod gathered some Roman troops together and with their aid invaded Palestine in 39 B.C. Overrunning both Joppa on the western coast and Masada in the eastern wilderness, Herod launched an unsuccessful attack on Antigonus in Jerusalem. However, other Roman forces defeated the Parthians to the east in 38 B.C., breaking their line of support to Jerusalem and sealing the fate of Antigonus. With the Parthian support gone, Antigonus could no longer hold out and Herod overran Jerusalem early in 37 B.C., slaughtering the defenders and carrying Antigonus captive to Antioch, where he was beheaded.

Herod as King (37-4 B.C.)

When Herod had fled to Rome at the time of the Parthian invasion, he had met Octavian, who was impressed with the Idumean's ability and his heritage of loyalty to Rome. Upon the recommendation of both Antony and Octavian, Herod was elected King of Judea by the Roman senate in 40 B.C., being granted exceptionally wide powers. Furthermore, Herod pleased both the politicians and the people by offering public sacrifices to Jupiter. This act leaves no doubt as to his real religious convictions, showing that for him religion was little more than a political tool by which one gained or kept power. Though Herod was King of Judea as far as Rome was concerned, Antigonus ruled in Jerusalem as a Parthian vassal. Herod was in fact a king without a country.

This situation was soon though not immediately, remedied. By 37 B.C., Herod was king of Judea by Roman election, beginning a reign which was to last more than thirty years. However, though he reigned over the Jewish state, he was hated by most of the Jewish leaders with a passion that was almost unlimited.

Four basic reasons have been identified for the hatred of the Jews for Herod. (1) Herod had become king by overthrowing the last of the Hasmonean dynasty. Although these Hasmonean rulers had themselves been hated by this time, they were at least Jews. Herod was openly the representative of the Roman oppressors. (2) Herod was an Idumean, making him half-Jew and descendant of the hated Edomites. (3) Herod realized that with little local support, he could sustain his authority only through fear. To this end, upon his accession to the throne he immediately executed many of the leaders who had supported Antigonus. That bred deep hostility among those who survived, even though they kept it under cover. (4) In order to maintain his authority, Herod needed Roman support. That cost money in the form of tribute and taxes. This generally was exacted from the wealthy, eliminating any possible support for him from them.

On the other hand, Herod was never one to long for what might have been. He was a political realist and set out to make the best of conditions as they were. During the conflict, lawlessness had become the rule of the day and outlaws wandered the wilderness of Judea, threatening all who passed through. Jesus' later parable of the man who fell among thieves (Luke 10:30) described events which were regular occurrences in these times. The king set out to restore law and order and was far more successful than King Saul had been with David or than Antiochus Epiphanes had been with the Maccabees. By the time Herod was through, having dealt with these outlaws both swiftly and ruthlessly, the land was safer than it had ever been.

King Herod also sought to win the people's loyalty, if not approval, by negotiating with the Parthians for the release of Hyrcanus II. These negotiations were beyond the authority granted to him by the Roman senate, but such niceties never concerned him. Although Hyrcanus had been mutilated and could no longer serve as high priest, Herod furnished him with lush living quarters and honored him publicly. Herod also sought to establish ties of legitimacy for his reign by marrying the Hasmonean princess Mariamne. This marriage was an astute political move on Herod's part. However, he also seems to have loved his wife with a deep devotion. In addition Herod also sought to win Pharisaic support by honoring two of their leaders and refusing to have images stamped on the coins of Judea. He also refused, for the time being at least, to have any of the usual Roman images brought into Jerusalem.

As far as Rome was concerned Herod could have acted as high priest. However, he wisely turned to a Babylonian Jew, Hananel, naming him to that office. This choice was a masterpiece because Hananel was a part of none of the Jerusalem parties and thus did not alienate any who would have been left out if a local priest had been so appointed.

However, Herod's mother-in-law persuaded him to depose his initial appointment in favor of her son Aristobulus, the grandson of Hyrcanus II, who thus had a legitimate claim to the office. Aristobulus drowned shortly thereafter in a swimming accident, and Herod reinstated Hananel, who served as high priest until 30 B.C. It was rumored that Herod had actually been involved in the death of Aristobulus. Though no evidence exists, his later actions make such a rumor quite plausible.

This whole crisis over the priesthood created other problems for Herod. He was called to give an account of his actions to Antony. It is also rumored that he bribed Antony. In any case, he was acquitted, returning home more secure with Rome than ever.

In a further effort to win the support of the Jewish people, King

Herod entered into massive building projects all over the land. Some twelve to fifteen major cities were built or rebuilt during his reign. Numerous fortresses along his borders were added to these. He proceeded with other major building projects in Jerusalem. In addition to his palace, the most significant of these was the temple itself. This was actually begun ca. 20 B.C., was in process during the lifetime of Jesus, and was not finished until A.D. 64, almost seven decades after Herod's death.

Sadly for Herod and the Jewish nation, none of this worked. Although he brought glory and honor to the nation, the people still viewed him as an outsider, a foreign interloper. Even using his own wealth to purchase grain for the people during a severe famine did not win their support. Again, being a realist, in the latter years of his reign, Herod gave up any attempt to win friends and influence among his hostile subjects.

When Herod became king of Judea, the international situation insofar as Rome was concerned was in a state of great flux. Herod followed in the steps of his father and remained resolutely loyal to Rome, fully supporting whichever Roman leader was in control of Palestine.

During these early years, conflict arose between Antony and Octavian due to Antony's marriage to Cleopatra. Antony gave Cleopatra a great deal of land which had belonged to the Ptolemies in the third century B.C. Among this was some land near Jericho for which Herod had to pay an exorbitant rental. In 32 B.C., the Nabateans failed to pay Cleopatra the annual tribute on their part of the land. Herod set forth with his troops to force them to pay her. That act may have saved the kingdom for Herod because at that same time Antony and Octavian met in what was to be the final battle between them. If Herod had not been involved with the Nabateans, he would have been fighting alongside of Antony at the Battle of Actium, where Antony was defeated.

Following his victory, Octavian summoned Herod along with a number of other vassals to meet him at Rhodes. Herod acknowledged his absolute loyalty to Antony but claimed a prior allegiance to Rome and promised the same kind of support to Octavian. Octavian accepted him on those terms, restoring to Herod those lands which Antony had given Cleopatra, along with several additional regions.

This new relationship was not only profitable to Herod but was profitable both to Rome and Judea. Augustus, as Octavian came to be known in 27 B.C., gave additional territories to Herod on at least two other occasions, eventually giving him some authority over all of Syria.

Herod was as good as his word, insofar as Augustus was concerned, sending both troops and money to his aid on more than one instance. The Judean king also engaged in a number of building projects aimed at honoring Augustus. Finally, near the end of his reign, Herod did institute in Judea an oath of loyalty to Rome. This created a major problem with the Pharisees and Essenes, but their support for Herod had always been doubtful at best.

Herod's major problems and greatest failures were in the arena of his family life. They began with the drowning of Aristobulus, which alienated his mother-in-law and perhaps began the alienation of his wife, Mariamne. Herod was so jealous of her that at one point he had ordered his uncle, Joseph, to kill her if he died first. Joseph revealed this to Mariamne as evidence of Herod's great love for her, but she was not particularly impressed. It is no surprise that her love for Herod soon cooled significantly. Herod was convinced that Joseph had revealed his secret while having an adulterous relationship with Mariamne, so he had Joseph executed. He also shortly thereafter had Hyrcanus II executed, accusing him of treachery. In 29 B.C., Herod had another suspected lover of his wife executed, along with Mariamne herself. This was followed a year later by the execution of his mother-in-law.

The family situation was more peaceful for a while, but Herod began to suspect his sons of treachery. Two of them, Alexander and Aristobulus, were executed by strangulation in 7 B.C. Discovering some unrest among his troops over this act, Herod then had some three hundred officers executed because of his suspicions that they were about to rebel. This was followed in 4 B.C. by the execution of Antipater, another of Herod's sons. Antipater had been designated as Herod's successor, but was suspected of wanting to hurry the process along. It was at that time that Augustus made his famous pun: "It is better to be Herod's pig (*huis,* which as a Jew he would not eat) than his son (*huios*)."

All of this reveals that Herod was insecure, insanely jealous, and violent. Such a person could easily have ordered the slaughter of the children of Bethlehem (Matt. 2:16).

Throughout his last year, Herod was a dying man. The nature of his disease is unknown and cannot be diagnosed from this distance. It was possibly some form of cancer. The citizens of Judea knew of his approaching death and looked forward to it with eagerness. In his latter days, Herod had placed a Roman eagle over the temple gate. Hearing that he was dead, the Pharisees pulled the hated emblem down. But their rash act was somewhat premature. Herod was not yet dead. In retaliation he had numbers of the Pharisees and two leading rabbis burned at the stake.

Fearing that there would be no mourning, Herod made preparations to have a large number of Jewish leaders executed after his death. In this way he felt that the land would be plunged into mourning when he passed away. When he died in 4 B.C., his funeral was held with great pomp and luxury. At the same time, riots broke out over the land. Archelaus, his son and successor, dealt with them in summary fashion, and some three thousand Jews died in the fighting. As Herod had wished, the land was filled with mourning at his death, but not for him and not in the manner he had planned. With his death, the stage was set for the coming of the New Testament era.

Peace and Prosperity

Two major features of the Roman period helped prepare the way for the ministry of Jesus and the early church. The first of these was the *pax Romana,* the peace of Rome. The early days following the conquest of Jerusalem by the forces of Pompey brought no peace to the empire in general or Judea and Jerusalem in particular. However, by 31 B.C. with the ultimate victory of Octavian, a general peace settled over the region. Borders were open from the provinces at the edge of the empire all the way to Rome itself. As a part of her world rule, Rome built roads; many of which still exist today. These were designed for the rapid and easy movement of troops. They also served as highways for trade. This meant that in the empire, travel and trade were easy and accessible to most people, at least by ancient standards.

However, the peace of Rome under Herod was no gentle peace but was harsh and cruel, especially for those who opposed either Rome or Herod. Most of the common people viewed peace as the absence of war. This period brought that kind of peace, and it extended, with the exception of the rioting around the time of the death of Herod, into the New Testament era and beyond. On the other hand, the seeds of dissent had been sown which were to bear bitter fruit in the Judean future. The deep-felt resistance to Rome was a reaction to Herod's cooperation with them. The Jewish people began to long as never before for the coming of a Messiah who would drive the hated oppressors from the land.

Prosperity, on the other hand, was real during the reign of Herod, at least in most of the cities, including Jerusalem. His extensive building projects put many people to work and brought a significant rise in income for the land. On the other hand, its cost had to be borne by heavy taxation. Archaeological excavations show that the rural areas of Judea and all of Galilee were significantly impoverished. Thus the era appears to have been one where the rich got richer while the poor got poorer. This growing gap between the economic segments of the community bred envy and hostility and created disharmony between the major groups.

Thus the Roman root furnished the New Testament era with a mixed background. Many good features had been inherited but the common people were suffering. Further, they were looking with eager longing for someone or something to deliver them from their misery. It was not long in coming.

9
The Judaistic Root

The final root which fed into the growth of the New Testament era was Judaism. Of all the external influences which shaped the thinking and actions of the first disciples, none was probably as significant as Judaism itself. Yet we must note that Judaism was significantly modified and influenced by each of the other roots which we have considered. That is why we considered them first.

Judaism is the religion of the Jews. It primarily involved the faith of the Hebrew people and the practices of that faith as it related to their lives apart from temple worship and the sacrificial ritual. It apparently had its real beginning during the Babylonian exile, when major portions of the Hebrew people were captives in Babylon or were refugees away from the region of Judah and Jerusalem. For them, the temple was no longer a present reality. Yet they needed and wanted to worship God where they were.

Like most such institutions, religious or otherwise, Judaism did not spring full grown onto the stage of history. Rather it took shape and developed over the years as it sought to meet the religious needs of the Hebrew people wherever they were. The most formative time for the development of Judaism was the period of the interbiblical era up to and including the final destruction of the Hebrew state in A.D. 135. These are precisely the years with which we are concerned in our study.

The Parties

From the standpoint of the New Testament, the most significant development within Judaism was the rise of the various parties or sects. These were all separated from one another by their views on philosophy, theology, economics, and patriotism. Perhaps more than anything else, they were divided by practical politics. They differed from one another primarily on the basis of how the nation ought to be run and how it ought to relate to the international powers which threatened or ruled over them. We need briefly to consider seven of these parties, their roots, their similarities, their differences, and their influences upon the people of the world in which Christianity grew and developed.

The Pharisees

Like most such groups, we have no clear indication of when or where the Pharisees first arose as a distinct party. In at least one place, Josephus places their origin in the time of Jonathan's leadership during the Maccabean revolt (161-142 B.C.). In other references, their origin appears to be a little later. The point is, we do not really know when they arose.

Because of the scathing denunciations of the Pharisees in the New Testament (Matt. 23:13-36), we have generally assumed that they were people of the worse sort. Nothing could be further from the truth. Their primary concern was to do exactly what God wanted of them. To them, this meant keeping the law, the whole law. This made life both meaningful and livable to them. In order to accomplish their goal of observing the law, they went to what some would think were ridiculous extremes. Yet they never intended to make the law a burden. Jesus did not denounce them for keeping the law. To the contrary, He commended them for this. What He did denounce was their lack of compassion.

The Pharisees were certainly the descendants of the *Hasidim,* although that group was never as unified or distinct a group as the Pharisees became. Further, the Pharisees were clearly on the scene by the time of Pompey's invasion, if not almost a century earlier. At least during the time of the Hasmonean era (142-63 B.C.) the open conflict between the Pharisees and the Sadducees took form. This continued to some extent into the period of the New Testament itself.[1]

During the period of the early Roman domination of Palestine (63-4 B.C.) the Pharisees became ever more visible and influential. Herod the Great actively sought their support. However, due to his Idumean ancestry and Roman allegiances, he was never able to obtain it. Although Herod excused them from swearing allegiance to him, he did seek to force them to make such a pledge to Rome and Augustus Caesar. They refused to do this as a violation of the Torah and thus a rejection of God. However, they do seem to have accepted the domination of Rome as an accomplished fact, apparently seen as a divine punishment for His people's disobedience of the law.

The disagreements between the Pharisees and Herod eventually led to his treating them as enemies. This they certainly were. Some of them were actually put to death by Herod, and he planned the death of many more at the time of his own death. During his reign, they wielded a major influence upon the Hebrew people, especially those of Jerusalem. It is estimated that at their greatest, they never numbered more than ten thousand actual adherents. At the time of Herod's death, their numbers had probably been reduced to about six thousand.

The major beliefs of the Pharisees are quite straightforward. First, they were people of the Torah, the law. They believed that God gave the law to make life livable. Just as a game is unplayable without rules, so they believed that life could only be fully experienced when a person was obedient to God. In order to make the law understandable and more easily obeyed, they multiplied its explanations. However, there was never any intention of making it a burden.

The other dimension of the Pharisees' faith which we need to note is their belief in life after death and in resurrection. This was a major new development in the interbiblical era. Prior to this time, few people among the Hebrews held such a belief. This new belief gave them a wholly different outlook on life, as well as upon the justice and love of God.[2]

The Sadducees

Like the Pharisees, the actual origin of the Sadducees is clouded. However, even though we do not have a specific literary reference to them in the time of the Maccabean revolt, their roots clearly lie in this era. As we have noted, it was in this time that the debate over the issue of life after death came to the front. The Pharisees believed in it. The Sadducees did not. This debate between them had become quite significant by the time of the New Testament.

Further, the Sadducees were generally made up of the wealthy aristocracy: priests, merchants, and government leaders. This party probably grew from the Tobiads of the Seleucid era. The new group was motivated by two major concerns. The first was pragmatic. They sought to make whatever accommodations were necessary in order to maintain their own power, prominence, and wealth. The second motivating concern of the Sadducees was their loyalty to the God of Israel. This primarily showed up in the temple cult. Thus they tried to be loyal to their past and its traditions while making such adjustments as were necessary to preserve the *status quo*.

The future disagreements between the Sadducees and Pharisees may have their roots far more deeply imbedded in their differences regarding accommodation than in their theological differences. This was clearly seen in the reign of John Hyrcanus (135/34-104 B.C.) At that time he sought to win the support of the Pharisees by assuring them of his commitment to the Torah. Not only were they not swayed by this, they actually sought to get him to resign the high priesthood because of a question as to the legitimacy of his birth. However, the Sadducees supported him, primarily because he kept them in power. From this time the break between these two groups never healed.

In the reign of Salome Alexandra (76-67 B.C.) the conflict between the Sadducees and Pharisees became violent. During the reign of her husband, Alexander Jannaeus, the Pharisees had suffered intense persecution. When she succeeded him, she sought to make peace with them and took a number of them as her advisers. This may even have been done upon the advice of her son, Aristobulus II, who was himself a Sadducee. However, as the Pharisees began to feel the freedom of power, they in turn incited her to acts of vengeance against the Sadducees. At this point, the Sadducees came before her with a plea that she end this bitter conflict, which she did. However, the seeds of party disagreement had now brought forth a flower of bitter hatred.

In the latter days of the Hasmoneans as well as during the early days of Roman rule in Palestine, the Sadducees fell upon bad times. They had supported the wrong side during the time of Roman conquest with the result that their numbers had been greatly reduced, particularly during the time of Herod the Great. However, they had not been eliminated. During the time of Jesus, they were still on the scene and were still obviously the party of power and wealth.

The Sadducees had learned to adjust to Rome and to utilize collaboration with Rome in order to maintain that power. They controlled the high priesthood during this era. Accepting the fact that Rome was on the scene to stay, they as always made the most of a bad situation. Clearly, they prospered from that policy. However, we must note that although the Sadducees were the party of power and wealth, they were never as numerous as were the Pharisees.

The Zealots

Another significant party within Judaism at the beginning of the New Testament era was the Zealots. Although we find no mention of them as early as we do the Sadducees and Pharisees, their roots probably go back at least into the Seleucid era. However, they are first mentioned in our sources during the reign of Herod the Great (37-4 B.C.). The one fundamental belief of the Zealots was that God alone was King over Israel. As an outgrowth of this belief, they were committed never to rest until every evidence of foreign domination was swept out of Israel.

Two different strands fed into the Zealot movement. This group first appeared in Galilee, which had been brought back into the Hebrew kingdom during the time of the Hasmoneans (142-63 B.C.). However, having been long separated from the people of Judea, their reunion at that time meant that the basic allegiance of the Galileans was more to the nation than to the law. They were more committed to Hebrew nationalism than they were to religious fanaticism. Furthermore, Galilee was subject during the entire interbiblical era to grinding, blinding poverty. In such situations, anything was viewed as being better than what they had experienced and were experiencing. Throwing off the Roman yoke might not help, but they believed that it certainly could not be any worse than what they were enduring at present. Many peasants' revolts have sprung from such roots.

The second major strand which fed into the Zealot party was found among the more fanatical members of the Pharisees in Judea. In contrast to their Galilean counterparts among the Zealots, the allegiance of the Judean Zealots was more to the law than to the nation. It is of note that this was so because they also believed that God alone was King. This allegiance to the law of God rather than to the nation placed them in violent opposition to King Herod's erecting the Roman eagle over the temple entrance. However, even though these two strands came together to make up the Zealots at the beginning, it was the basic difference of their commitments which meant that most Pharisees would have nothing to do with the Zealots throughout the ongoing history of the Palestinian Jews.

As the Roman oppression grew more intense during the New Testament era, the numbers and fanaticism of the Zealots grew as well. It was their growing strength which ultimately bred the Jewish revolts (A.D. 66-74, 132-135). As a result of these two fanatical but futile attempts to overthrow Roman domination, Palestine ceased to be a Jewish state until modern times. We perhaps ought to note that at least one of Jesus' disciples, Simon, is identified as being a Zealot (Luke 6:15).

The Essenes

One of the Hebrew sects which was on the scene at the time of Jesus was the Essenes, although until recently we have known little about them. We have no way of knowing the origins of the Essenes. However, most scholars now trace them back to the *Hasidim* of the Maccabean era. Essentially an ascetic sect, we know that there were several small groups of them scattered among the major cities of the region. A rather significant enclave appears to have been located in the barren hills above the western edge of the Dead Sea at a place called Qumran. (We shall deal with that specific group later in the chapter).

The Essenes were primarily concerned with both understanding and preserving their Scriptures, the Old Testament. A smaller sect of this group was known as the *theraputae,* a group of healers who were concerned with a healthy body and spirit. The Essenes were pacificists and celibates. As a result, they took no part in any plan which advocated military action against Rome. Further, because of their celibacy, their numbers had to be filled by converts rather than by the training of their children. Particularly in the period just before the death of Herod, they appear to have been quite missionary, reaching their time of greatest growth and influence.

According to Josephus, the Essenes were on the Palestinian scene as an organized group at least by the time of Jonathan (152-142 B.C.). Because of their desire to practice the teachings of the Scriptures, they were as strict about Sabbath observance as were the Pharisees. From what little we know of them, it is likely that they were descended from the nonmilitant part of the *Hasidim.*

Because of their nonmilitancy, Herod had no problem with them. He actually seems to have been quite favorable to them, particularly since an Essene is reported to have predicted to him as a boy that he would one day be king. The Essenes are not mentioned in the New Testament, though their influence may have been seen in a number of instances.

The Qumran Community

The Qumran community, a monastic-type enclave located in the hills above the western edge of the Dead Sea, was unknown to us until the explorations following the discovery of the Dead Sea Scrolls in A.D. 1947. Since the discovery of the remains of their community and the translation of the many documents which they produced, we now know a good bit about them. However, numerous tantalizing questions about these people remain unanswered.

Scholars debate whether or not any relationship exists between the inhabitants of Qumran and the Essenes. However, the evidence does appear to support the conclusion that the inhabitants of Qumran were a sect of the Essenes, if not Essenes proper. These people reacted with great disapproval to the priest-kings of the Hasmoneans and withdrew to their desert enclave as a political and religious protest. There they followed a leader known as "The Teacher of Righteousness."

Rather than confronting the issues of the turbulent times in which they lived, they chose to withdraw from the world and follow the teachings of the law and the dictates of their own consciences in a peaceful life of hard work and Bible study. They longed for the better days of God's ultimate kingdom but were willing to wait for it in patience. It was their expectation that God would inaugurate His reign of peace on earth in His own time and without any assistance from them.

The people of Qumran had little use for either the Jewish or Roman leaders. They were basically devout, pious, and good. Since they appear to have practiced celibacy, their numbers had to be filled by converts. This of necessity made them missionary. In those turbulent times, however, their isolation made them attractive to many who had grown tired of the tensions under which they lived. Attempts which have been made to tie the people of Qumran directly to Jesus or the early Christians have failed. On the other hand, John the Baptist may have had some indirect ties with the

Qumranians. At the very least, he and the early Christians were aware of the presence and significance of these people.

The Herodians

Another party which was on the scene at the beginning of the New Testament era was the Herodians. In fact, the only place where this party is mentioned in our ancient sources is in the New Testament itself (Matt. 22:16; Mark 3:6; 12:13). It is possible that this is the group to which Josephus referred to as "followers of Herod," although some would dispute this.

Nothing is known of the Herodians other than what can be deduced. They were apparently committed to following Herod's goals, even (or especially) after his death in 4 B.C. This would mean that they saw a political policy of being loyal and obedient servants of Rome as the only hope of Judea. Such a policy clearly put them in direct opposition to the Zealots and Pharisees. On the other hand, this policy would have meant that some of their goals would have coincided with those of the Sadducees.

The Scribes

The scribes were known as an apparently separate group as early as the time of Ezra and Nehemiah. Ezra himself is identified as "the scribe of the law of the God of heaven" (Ezra 7:12,21). At the same time, they apparently did not come into their own as a separate group of political and religious influence until the New Testament era itself. The Hebrew term for this group is *sopherim*.

Actually, anyone who could write was a scribe. However, by the time of Jesus, the term had a technical meaning which referred specifically to those who were involved in preserving, studying, and teaching the Word of God. At that time they were still distinct from the Pharisees, although they had much in common. In fact, it appears that many Pharisees were also scribes. The scribes also appear to be the group from which the rabbis of the synagogues arose. The scribes appear to have been more concerned with what their Scriptures said and meant than they were with God or the practical issues of daily life.

The Sanhedrin

Although the name was not actually used until about 63 B.C., the Sanhedrin first shows up in the Ptolemaic era in Judea (301-

198 B.C.). The Sanhedrin was not actually a party within Judaism, but it was of such significance by the time of Jesus that we at least need to consider it here. This was the Jewish high court. Located in Jerusalem, it was presided over by the high priest and apparently administered local Jewish affairs, at least in Jerusalem.

Throughout most of the interbiblical era, the Sanhedrin was made up of Sadducees, or at least of those who would have been more sympathetic to their views than to those of the Pharisees. However, during the reign of Salome Alexandra (76-67 B.C.) the Pharisees were given more power and influence within the court itself. The Sanhedrin considered that they had an authority over the actions of any Hebrew, including those who were in political power, such as Herod. It was only when they sought to convict Herod and sentence him to death that they discovered that their powers were far more limited than they had supposed (ca. 43 B.C.). During his reign, they almost lost all power and influence, but this began to be regained after his death, during the administration of the Roman procurators.

During the New Testament era, the Sanhedrin was apparently made up of senior priests who were generally Sadducees and scribes and elders, who were generally Pharisees. Since the high priest presided over it, it was generally controlled by the Sadducees. It could pronounce judgment upon both religious and civil matters. Though it could issue a death sentence, it did not have the authority to carry out such a sentence until it had been reviewed and confirmed by the Roman governor. As an indication of the wide range of their powers, the Sanhedrin appointed Josephus as general of the Jewish forces in Galilee during the First Jewish Revolt (A.D. 66-74).

The Diaspora

From at least the time of the beginning of the Babylonian captivity (586 B.C.), Jewish refugees had spread over the world of the eastern Mediterranean. They established centers wherever they went. These settlers came to be known as the Jewish dispersion or by the more technical term of the *Diaspora*. Among the many centers which were established, the most significant was at the city which in the Greek period came to be known as Alexandria. That center became almost as significant as Jerusalem itself.

Out of this center came the Greek translation of the Old Testament known as the Septuagint (LXX). That Greek translation gave the whole Mediterranean world the Old Testament in a language which they would be able to understand.

Furthermore, by the time of Julius Caesar, Judaism was given the status of *religio licta,* a legal religion. This meant that Jews, wherever they were within the empire, were at liberty to practice their religion. It was this freedom which allowed the communities of the Diaspora to thrive and prosper. Thus Judaism was recognized and accepted throughout the empire by the time Jesus was born. While not always popular, it was present in most metropolitan centers.

The Synagogue

As a part of the growth of the Diaspora, the synagogue became a major factor in the development of Judaism. With the destruction of the temple in Jerusalem in 586 B.C., the Jewish people lost the place of sacrifice and the sacrificial ritual for a time. Sometime during this era, the synagogue was born. These local congregations gave the Jewish people an outlet in which to practice their religion as well as a center in which to teach it to their children. Originally it appears to have been totally organized and led by lay people.

However, eventually it became obvious that such centers of religion needed someone who was in "authority" to pass on the teachings of their Scriptures as well as the traditions of the Hebrew people. It was in response to this need that rabbis began to be trained and associated with the synagogues. *Rab* means teacher, and *rabbi* means my teacher. However, with the passage of time *rabbi* simply became synonymous with teacher. The rabbis, in the tradition of the scribe and Pharisee, sought to learn the Scriptures and their interpretations and to teach these to others. It was the synagogue and its rabbinic leaders who allowed Judaism to live and survive as a living religion. This, too, was to have its impact upon the New Testament era and spread of the gospel.

The Faith

Judaism was the outgrowth of the religion of the Old Testament, but the faith of the Jewish people had undergone some transformation. By the time of the New Testament era, the faith of Judaism had several beliefs which were to be of major significance for the rise of the New Testament churches. First of all, Judaism had become quite ingrown in that they were not evangelistic, but they had a world outlook. The scattered congregations of the Diaspora had seen to that.

In addition, the synagogue movement itself had set the stage for the rise of churches. Judaism had ceased to be primarily a religion of one place—the temple—and of one city—Jerusalem. The Hebrews had discovered that people could worship God in many places and somewhat differing ways. Both the Diaspora and synagogues had given Judaism the awareness that God was not confined to one place or language.

Two other aspects of Judaism which were significant for the early Christians was its messianic hope and its awareness that faith had a dimension which was far more than political. The Hebrews were now looking forward to God's intervention on their behalf and His establishing His kingdom on earth. These concepts helped pave the way for their acceptance of the early Christian proclamation.

Finally, Judaism had led many of its adherents to look forward to life after death. Such a hope of ongoing life and the resurrection of the dead again paved the way for the proclamation of the first evangelists. While the idea of Jesus' resurrection was unbelievable to the Sadducees, it was not unacceptable to the Pharisees and many of the Hebrew people. Thus one more root leading to the nurture and growth of early Christianity had been prepared by the Lord God of Israel.

Notes

1. For details of this early conflict, refer to Robert Cate, *A History of the Bible Lands in the Interbiblical Period* (Nashville: Broadman Press, 1989), 88-104.

2. For a more detailed study of the growth of this idea, see Robert Cate, *Old Testament Roots for New Testament Faith* (Nashville: Broadman Press, 1982) and *A History of the Bible Lands in the Interbiblical Period* (Nashville: Broadman Press, 1989).

10
Summary

Throughout part 2, we have sought to examine the various roots by which the world had been prepared for the coming of Jesus and the spread of His kingdom. In looking back over these, a number of features have been identified which need to be brought together at this point. Reviewing these will help set the stage for beginning the actual study of the early years of Jesus of Nazareth and the world in which He grew up and ministered.

From a theological standpoint, the gospel of Jesus Christ can be said to begin with the statement: "In the beginning was the Word, and the Word was with God, and the Word was God" (John 1:1). However, theology is not our primary concern. Our concern here is with history, the history of Jesus and His followers in the New Testament era. From the larger historical perspective, therefore, we could begin by focusing upon the statement: "The book of the genealogy of Jesus Christ, the son of David, the son of Abraham" (Matt. 1:1). This, however, carries our historical interests back to the call of Abraham. As we have noted earlier, this is beyond the limits of this particular study, even though Jesus' historical roots plainly go that far back.

Luke grounds his Gospel in the more immediate past, with the introductory words: "In the days of Herod, king of Judea . . . ." (Luke 1:5). Simply put, what we are concerned with is an answer to the question: What was the world of Palestine like when Herod was king of Judea? What was the world like when Mary gave "birth to her first-born son"? (Luke 2:7).

A World at Peace

At the beginning of the New Testament era, the Mediterranean world was enjoying the famous *pax Romana,* the peace of Rome. Insofar as Judea was concerned, this was the first time real peace had settled over the region since the beginning of the Maccabean revolt (168 B.C.).

The peace of Rome also brought a certain degree of prosperity to the region. Highways allowed trade to flow and massive building projects were undertaken at the direction of Rome. Further, at least along the highways, Roman patrols kept outlawry under good control. Pilgrims, refugees, and merchants were able to travel from one end of the empire to the other with relative ease and security.

The peace of Rome was no gentle peace. Legions marched over the same highways that merchants and travelers used. Soldiers strutted up and down the countryside, and the presence of the occupying forces was always visible. Thus, the local people were never able to forget that they were a subservient people, not truly free in any sense of the word. People along the highways could be compelled to carry the baggage of an occupying soldier from one milestone to the next.

In addition, the occupying forces of Rome cost money. This meant that taxes were an ever present reality. If this were not enough, those taxes were collected by "tax farmers." These were natives who had bought the right to collect taxes by paying their overlords in Rome. In New Testament times, these people were called publicans and were considered to be traitors to their own people. They were hated by their own people and were simply endured by the Romans as a necessary evil.

Taken at its very best, the peace which Rome brought was that of a military dictatorship. Peace could be enjoyed only at the price of utter submission to the will and whim of the dictator. Even though Rome brought a rule of law to the world, it was a law which was partial to the Roman and often ignored by governors and soldiers who lived and served at the extremities of the empire. That was precisely where Judea was, at the outer edge of Rome's concerns, both geographically and politically.

A World United

The world in which the era of the New Testament was born was also a world which was outwardly united. It was united by a common language and culture. The language was Greek and the culture was Greek, although it had been adapted by the Romans. Because of this, merchants and travelers could journey from one end of the empire to another and be understood by those in distant lands. This made communication easy, preparing the world for the first missionaries who sought to tell people from all parts of the empire the good news about the Lord Jesus. Further, the common culture made it possible for them to be more readily understood because people were familiar with the same sorts of cultural experiences. Holding words and ideas in common, people could comprehend new ideas which were couched in the common vessels of communication.

Furthermore, the conquests of Rome had destroyed the barriers which existed between nations. People were able to move freely across such national boundaries and were seldom challenged as they did so. The Roman roads made travel possible. The elimination of national barriers made it easy.

Yet we must take another look here as well. The world of Greece and Rome was a world grown cynical. Having been exposed to everything, they believed nothing. Jesting Pilate's later question of Jesus, when he asked " 'What is truth?' " (John 18:38) was typical of the age. There were temples and shrines on every hand and gods aplenty claiming the worship of followers. Worship was so common and strange beliefs of the mystery religions were so ordinary that a new religion or belief hardly caused a raised eyebrow.

Further, the morals of the Roman world had sunk to an unbelievable low. Almost anything which satisfied the body or pleased the senses was acceptable. The wealthy grew in wealth, living in luxurious self-indulgence. The poor groveled in their poverty and found life unbelievably oppressive. Even in Jewry, many things were accepted as long as the proper rituals were observed. It was a godless time. The flames of faith burned low. Yet at the same time, faith was held onto tenaciously by a loyal few. We must also remember that as we look at the beginnings of Christianity.

A People with a Faith

We need to consider four or possibly five dimensions of Israel's faith at the time of the birth of Jesus. First, both in Judaism and throughout the world there was a note of expectancy; people were longing and looking for something which might change the state of the world. In Judaism, that was translated into a messianic hope. They were looking for the coming of God's long-promised messiah. Due to this, perhaps during the lifetime of Jesus, many people arose in various places in Judea and Galilee who called themselves "messiah" and gathered followers around them. In every instance, hope in such persons was quickly dashed.

Yet the basic hope did not die. Instead it grew in intensity. It matters not that those messianic hopes focused primarily upon a military deliverance from Roman oppression, it was a real hope nonetheless and must be considered as we seek to understand that time and its influence upon the development of Christianity.

Second, as we have noted, Judaism had essentially become a religion of the synagogue. This is not to minimize the great festivals which were held in Jerusalem, but because of the Diaspora, the real faith of Israel was being transmitted in small gatherings where the people came to hear their Scriptures taught and expounded in specific applications to the lives which they led. These communities served as the centers for faith and became the early centers to which and from which the first Christian missionaries went.

Third, because of the presence and influence of the scribes and Pharisees, Judaism had become a religion of the law, at least for many of the Jews. As a result, the law had become a loveless, oppressive burden which people had to bear in order to please God. Further, this meant that life itself was being lived under such a cloud that spiritual fear had become as great a load as the physical fear which had to be borne under the Roman oppression.

Fourth, in direct opposition to this idea, because of the long-standing influence of the Hellenists and Sadducees, there was also a mood among many of the Hebrews that accommodation and compromise with Rome ought to be the rule of the day. This had therefore led to a real sense of division among the people. Both sides believed themselves to be loyal to their God, but each side generally distrusted the other. At the worst, they despised one another.

Thus there was no unity either of aim or process among the leaders of Judaism. This certainly was disillusioning to its followers.

The fifth concept which possibly needs to be considered is the Diaspora itself. While plainly not a separate belief of Judaism, the Diaspora certainly introduced a new stream of thought and tradition into their faith. Throughout most of their history, the Jews had been a people basically turned inward upon themselves. With the Diaspora, at least a part of that changed. Living in many parts of the world, the Jews in those scattered centers had learned that it was imperative that they at least get along with their neighbors. Furthermore, they had also learned that there were things of value in cultures other than their own.

Because of the Diaspora, many Jews had actually forgotten how to speak Hebrew, or its daughter language, Aramaic. This meant that they could no longer read or understand their holy Scriptures. It was this development which necessitated the translation of their Scriptures into Greek. This translation came to be known as the Septuagint, abbreviated as LXX.

The Septuagint translation was significant for the early and rapid spread of Christianity. First, as Christians were converted from circles other than those of Palestine, they had the Scriptures of the Old Testament already available in a language which they could understand. Perhaps equally as important, when the missionaries began to spread over the Mediterranean world with their proclamation, they were able to refer to Scriptures already in a language which was understood in any country to which they came.

Another feature of the Diaspora may also have had significant overtones for the world in which Jesus lived and to which His gospel was proclaimed. In many of the centers of the Diaspora, the Jewish people became the victims of anti-Semitism. The most violent of these outbreaks occurred in Alexandria during the reign of Herod the Great. However, such outbreaks created an intense hostility between Jew and Gentile. This meant that since early Christianity was perceived as a sect of Judaism, it was also on the receiving end of some of this hostility from its earliest days. On the other hand, it also meant that since the official Roman position was that Judaism was a *religio licta*, a legal religion, Christianity enjoyed this recognition at the very first. Therefore the early evangelists had the legal freedom to proclaim their good news.

A People with a Hope

Although we touched on this in the preceding section, perhaps the most important feature of Judaism which was prevalent at the time of the birth of Jesus was that they were a people with a hope. Because of the forward look of the Old Testament at the beginning of the New Testament era, the Jews looked forward. The glorious days of their history were in their past. By any human measurement, the Jews had no future. In less than a century-and-a-half, the Jewish nation had wholly ceased to exist. They could look back to glorious days of the past. They had no reason to look forward.

However, look forward they did. They looked forward because of their faith in God and their trust in His promises. It was that forward look based upon their past experience with God which truly prepared the way for Jesus and His followers. Hope when there was no human reason to hope set the stage for Christianity and became the watchword of the early Christians. Thus Paul could write to a church in the very center of the empire, "For whatever was written in former days was written for our instruction, that by steadfastness and by the encouragement of the scripture we might have hope" (Rom. 15:4). On that note, the stage was set for the great drama of redemption which began with the birth of Jesus.

Part 3
The Word Became Flesh

"The past is prologue." Most historians do their writing as well as their research from this perspective. The study of any period of history is the means by which we can begin to understand those which immediately followed. This is certainly true of the New Testament era. All that we have done to this point has been for the purpose of setting the stage for understanding the times in which Jesus and His disciples lived and served. Further, as we understand those times, we are better prepared to comprehend many of His words and deeds. We are also better able to understand many of the features which characterized the early Christians, their ministries, and the churches which they established. We are also better able to understand their difficulties and failures.

The world into which Jesus was born was a Jewish world. He was born a Jew. His family members were Jews of Nazareth but with a Judean heritage. As such, they had inherited the Old Testament faith and hope of their ancestors. They also sought to serve God within the structure of first-century Judaism. As a child, Jesus would have been instructed in the Torah from that standpoint.

At the same time, the faith of Galileans was a simpler faith than that of their Judean cousins. Therefore the faith in which Jesus would have been instructed almost certainly would not have included the finer nuances understood and taught by the priests of Jerusalem. Also, it would clearly not have included the political sensitivities of the Jerusalem hierarchy. However, the Galileans were normally more patriotic than their Judean contemporaries. The people of the north appear to have been far more volatile in their attitude toward Rome. Jesus would certainly have seen the bitter hatred which his friends and their parents felt toward the occupying forces.

This brings us to the fact, however, that the world into which Jesus was born was a Roman world. Whatever else we may say about that time and place in history, the Jews of Palestine were a conquered people being ruled by an occupying force. This they were never able to forget. Roman laws governed their every move. Roman troops were present, compelling obedience. Roman justice was quick, harsh and always slanted to the side of the Romans.

The world into which Jesus was born was a human world. Jews and Romans faced the same problems which people of every age and place face. Love and hate, guilt and innocence, strength and weakness, and fear and trust were known by both Jews and Romans. Sickness and death saddened the people. Marriages and births brightened their lives. Hard work characterized their daily activities. Greed was experienced, oppression was felt, lust reaped its grim harvest, and hunger warped a person's outlook on life. Temptation confronted people at their points of weakness, and for some at least, a striving for righteousness motivated them to resist when they could find the inner strength.

In the light of the issues and facts with which we have dealt to this point, we are now ready to consider the New Testament era itself. The beginning place is obviously the life and ministry of Jesus. Were there no Jesus, there would have been no New Testament and no New Testament era.

11
Chronological Considerations

In beginning our study of the history of Jesus' life and ministry, once again we are brought face to face with a basic task of every historian: that of establishing, insofar as is possible, an accurate chronology for the period under study. Please note that I did not say that this is the *major* task of a historian. The *major* task of historians is not establishing dates but identifying meanings. Historians are basically concerned with what ancient events meant to those who participated in them and to us today. Before we can do this, we must seek to identify when the events occurred and in what relation to one another. No matter how much students may dislike the study of dates, history can neither be adequately nor accurately studied apart from dates. Dates are the cement which hold events together and relate them to one another.

Three significant problems confront us in relation to the identification of an absolute chronology for the life of Jesus. First, we need to try to establish the date for the beginning of Jesus' ministry. As part of this larger issue, we will try to answer a related question: When did John the Baptist begin his ministry? Obviously, he had to have begun his ministry in Judea before the baptism of Jesus. This brings us back to our primary question: When did Jesus begin His ministry? These two questions are clearly related and need to be established for us to be able to place the ministry of Jesus into its proper historical environment.

Establishing the date of the ministry of Jesus is of major significance for any attempt to understand what He did in light of the times in which He lived. It is equally as important for us as we try to discover the reactions of Jesus' audiences to Him.

However, our second major chronological problem is of almost equal significance for a historian. We also need to try to determine when Jesus was born. While the issue of the date of Jesus' birth is not of equal importance with the first one in regard to an understanding of His ministry, it is of historical significance for three major reasons. The first reason is the fact that all modern calendars are established around the supposed date of Jesus' birth. A second reason why the date of Jesus' birth is important is that it affects our understanding of some of the events which surround the nativity of our Lord.

The third and perhaps least significant reason for the importance of establishing the date of Jesus' birth is that it determines the age of Jesus when He began His ministry. When we have established the dates of His birth and baptism, we will have determined His age. While this in itself may not be of great importance, it could have affected how people related to Him. It may also have affected His stamina and general approach to life.

The final chronological issue related to Jesus' ministry is that of trying to date Jesus' death. This is more closely related to the ultimate understanding of that ministry than either of our other primary issues. Further, Jesus' death set the stage for the beginning of the mission and ministry of the New Testament church. It also establishes the ultimate length of Jesus' ministry as we relate His death to its beginning.

Having considered the reasons for trying to establish the actual dates for Jesus' birth, the beginning of His ministry, and His death, let us turn to the task. Clearly related to these tasks is that of attempting to determine the relationship of the relative chronologies of each of the four Gospels. In dealing with each issue, I shall summarize the available evidence. Following this, I will give my own conclusions. We shall begin with the attempt to identify the date of His birth. However, there is some basic data of which we need to be aware before we begin our task.

Basic Data

Roman Emperors

Obviously, since all of the territory in which Jesus lived was under Roman control, it is helpful to know who the people were in whom Rome's authority was exercised. The central government during this era was vested in two men. Octavian, who later came to be known as Augustus, was Caesar in Rome from 27 B.C. to

A.D. 14. He was succeeded in that position by Tiberius, who was Caesar from A.D. 14 through 37.

Roman Authority in Palestine

Throughout the New Testament era, Roman authority in Palestine was handled in several different ways. At the beginning, Herod the Great was king in Judea and Galilee. His reign extended from 37 to 4 B.C. Herod had actually become governor several years before this, but the title of king was only given to him by Augustus and the Roman senate in 37 B.C.

Upon the death of Herod, the authority in the region was shared among three of his sons. Herod Antipas became tetrarch of the region of Galilee and Perea, serving from 4 B.C. to A.D. 39. (This was the Herod before whom Jesus was paraded by Pilate immediately before His crucifixion. See Luke 23:6-12.) At the same time, Philip was made tetrarch over the region of Northern Transjordan. These two men with their long reigns gave their territories a great deal of stability.

The situation was quite different in Judea, however. Herod's son Archelaus was made ethnarch of Judea in 4 B.C. and served in that position only until A.D. 6. Because of consistent unrest in that area, the Romans decided to change its form of government, appointing procurators from Rome in an attempt to bring peace and furnish stability. The procurators were at first appointed for relatively brief periods of service under Augustus. However, these terms were lengthened under the reign of Tiberius.

Roman Procurators in Judea

Coponius	A.D. 6-9
Ambibulus	A.D. 9-12
Rufus	A.D. 12-15
Valerius Gratus	A.D. 15-26
Pontius Pilate	A.D. 26-36

Jewish Festivals

The major festivals of the Jewish religion are of significance for understanding much of the life and ministry of Jesus. However, to the non-Jewish contemporary reader, these are seldom understandable, particularly in regard to their place on the calendar. Therefore we also need to be aware of what they were and when they occurred. This table will help you to deal with these.

Annual Feasts of the Jews

January	
February	
March	Purim (late February or early March)
April	Passover (late March or early April)
May	Pentecost (fifty days after Passover)
June	
July	
August	
September	Day of Atonement (late September)
October	Tabernacles (five days after Atonement)
November	
December	Feast of Lights (late December)

Equally as important as knowing when these festivals occurred is knowing what each one commemorated for the Jews. Their significance frequently adds meaning to Jesus' words and deeds.

• *Purim* celebrated the deliverance of the Jews from the persecutions of Haman during the time of Esther. Its background is set forth in that book. This was probably the most joyous of all Jewish festivals and was frequently accompanied by a great deal of drunkenness.

• *Passover* is probably the most familiar of Jewish festivals, at least insofar as Christians are concerned. This originated in the deliverance from the slavery of Egypt. It was clearly the most important of all the Hebrew festivals, drawing the largest crowds of pilgrims to Jerusalem. In the time of Jesus, Jewish tradition held that the Messiah was to be expected to manifest Himself at a Passover festival.

• *Pentecost* was celebrated fifty days after Passover. The name actually comes from this, being derived from the Greek word for *fifty*. This festival is also known by the older name of "The Feast of First Fruits." Its purpose was to celebrate the harvesting of the first grain of the year. Those familiar with the early Christians will remember that it was at Pentecost that the Holy Spirit descended upon the Christians.

• *The Day of Atonement* was not really a festival. Actually, this was a fast. It was (and is) also known by its Hebrew title of Yom

Kippur. This was the only day when anyone could enter the holy of holies in the temple. On this day, the high priest, dressed as an ordinary priest, entered the holy of holies to make atonement for the sins of all the people of Israel.

• *Tabernacles* was also known as the Feast of Booths. It came five days after the Day of Atonement. It symbolized the people dwelling in the midst of their fields during harvest time. They dwelt there in booths or tents (tabernacles) for the purpose of protecting the harvest, being close to it in order to get the harvest done more quickly, and celebrating its abundance. It was essentially a celebration of thanksgiving to God for the harvest. It was also a celebration of God's provision for their ancestors during their wanderings in the wilderness. This usually occurred in late September.

• *The Feast of Lights* is also known by its Hebrew name of Hanukkah, or as the Feast of Dedication. This festival was a joyous celebration, commemorating the rededication of the temple under the leadership of Judas Maccabeus. This was the newest of the Hebrew festivals, having first been celebrated in 165 B.C.

Jewish High Priests

The final piece of general data which we need to have in front of us before we proceed with our studies relates to the Jewish high priests of the era. The high priest at any time during this period was the religious leader of the Jewish people. In addition, at least some of the time during the rule of the procurators, the high priest was granted a great deal of political autonomy. At such times, they appear to have been able to exercise total home rule with the exception that they could neither issue coins nor carry out a death sentence upon convicted criminals. Furthermore, the high priesthood was generally bought and sold during this era. The Romans pocketed the money as a form of tribute or taxation. For our purposes, the two men of major significance were Annas (A.D. 6-15) and his son-in-law Caiaphas (A.D. 18-36).

The Date of Jesus' Birth

With this general data before us, we are now ready to try to establish a basic chronology for the era. In the sixth century A.D., a Syrian monk by the name of Dionysius Exiguus calculated the date of Jesus' birth. He suggested that this was the appropriate place to begin counting years, both forward and backward. However, it took two-and-a-half centuries for his idea to win out. In the reign of Charlemagne the official policy was established of counting the years before the birth of Jesus as B.C. and those afterwards as A.D. (*anno Domini,* "in the year of our Lord").

Unfortunately, we now know that Dionysius made some mistakes in his calculations. Therefore we must try to identify when Jesus was actually born. In seeking to establish this date, several independent but related lines of investigation should be followed. These are:

(1) An attempt must be made to establish the date of the taxation census of Caesar Augustus. It was this which brought Joseph and Mary to Bethlehem (Luke 2:1). As a part of establishing this date, we must also determine when Quirinius was governor of Syria (Luke 2:3).

(2) If at all possible, we must try to establish the date of the appearance in the heavens of the star of Bethlehem (Matt. 2:2). Related to this issue is the visit of the wise men from the east. Perhaps we can date that as well.

3. An attempt must also be made to date the slaughter of the little boys of Bethlehem (Matt. 2:16). As in the above, a related issue is found here. The date of the death of Herod is also clearly involved at this point (Matt. 2:19). He could not have ordered this slaughter after his death.

The Census of Bethlehem

The historical setting for the birth of Jesus is given by Luke. He established the background of Jesus' birth with the following words. "In those days a decree went out from Caesar Augustus that all the world should be enrolled. This was the first enrollment, when Quirinius was governor of Syria. And all went to be enrolled, each to his own city" (Luke 2:1-3). Starting at this point, we can begin to close in on the date of Jesus' birth.

According to Luke, Caesar Augustus ruled over the Roman empire at the time of Jesus' birth. This means that, within the widest possible margins, Jesus must have been born no earlier than 27 B.C. and no later than A.D. 14. That leaves us with the choice of any date within forty-one years.

The next step in trying to narrow that gap is an attempt to date the taxation census or "enrollment" itself. We have no actual Roman records of a taxation program in the province of Syria in this period. However, Josephus describes a taxation which apparently took place about A.D. 6. Although this fits within the larger parameters of Augustus' reign, it does not fit in with other chronological data from the New Testament. Many people have concluded that there was a major discrepancy here between Luke and Josephus.

However, we now know that Roman taxation of the provinces usually went through two stages. First, there was a census of sorts where all persons and property were systematically listed. This was the catalog which served as the later basis for an actual assessment of taxes. Further, this first stage was not as precise as modern censuses. The one in Gaul, for example, took over forty years to complete. At the present time, however, we do not have sufficient information to give a precise date to the census which drew Joseph to Bethlehem.

The governorship of Quirinius also offers some problems. The Roman records indicate that Quirinius became governor of Syria at least ten years after the death of King Herod. Yet Herod was king when Jesus was born (Matt. 2:1). This difficulty, however, may not be overwhelming. Ethelbert Stauffer points out that Quirinius was apparently given power over the province of Syria in 12 B.C. and ruled over it until A.D. 16 with a brief interregnum.[1] Further, even though the powers may have been shared at times with both a military and political authority, this appears not to have been unusual for Roman rule in such provinces at such times.

However, we are still unable more closely to define the actual date of the census. We have only narrowed the possible date to the period beginning with Quirinius' authority from 12 B.C. to the end of Augustus' reign (A.D. 14).

The Death of Herod

Obviously, Jesus had to have been born during the reign of Herod the Great. Matthew gives us this bit of information, telling us that "Jesus was born in Bethlehem of Judea in the days of Herod the king" (Matt. 2:1). Further, we are told that Herod died shortly thereafter when Mary, Joseph, and young Jesus were refugees in Egypt (Matt. 2:19). The year of Herod's death has been identified as 4 B.C. If any date in the Roman history of this era is firmly fixed, this one is. Therefore we are now able to narrow the period in which Jesus had to have been born from to 12 to 4 B.C.

We earlier noted Herod's viciousness, especially whenever he suspected anyone of laying claim to his throne. The slaughter of boys in Bethlehem two years old and under certainly fits into what we know of his personality. If he suspected that a child in Bethlehem would one day lay claim to his throne, this was exactly how we would have expected him to act. Further, his desire to make the land mourn at his death also would fit in with this kind of act, particularly if he were nearing death.

Following his conversation with the wise men from the East, he ordered the execution of all male children two years old and under (Matt. 2:16). This may have been done to make sure that he had included every possible threat. On the other hand, this age may have been decided upon due to the information of the Magi. If this is so, then Jesus' birth should be dated at least two years before Herod's death. At the same time, the birth cannot be considered to be too far before that date or the age of the victims would have been higher. It appears then that we must place the date of Jesus' birth somewhere around 6 B.C. with it being no later than 4 B.C.

The Star of Bethlehem

Five major suggestions have been made as to the nature of the star of Bethlehem. First of all, it may have been a unique, miraculous occurrence which God placed in the heavens to announce the birth of His Son. If this is the case, then the only hope we have of establishing its date outside of the New Testament would be if some other people somewhere saw it and recorded it in their official records. Unfortunately, to this point in time, we have found no such reference. So at the present, this path of investigation leads up a blind alley.

Second, Chinese records reveal the appearance of a spectacular event in the heavens which has been identified as a supernova, the explosion of a star in its death throes. Some have questioned whether this might have been the star of Bethlehem. However, there is no record of this having been seen or recorded in any nation nearer to Judea, and its timing does not appear to fit within our basic parameters.

Third, again from China comes the record of a comet which approached the earth at about 6 B.C. Some scholars have identified that as the star of Bethlehem. However, no other record of this celestial event is found in the records of the nations nearer Judea. This, too, must be rejected as a possibility for Jesus' natal star.

Fourth, some scholars have suggested that the star of Bethlehem may have been Halley's Comet. In the year of 12 B.C., this comet made an approach to earth. During part of that time, it was extremely bright. At that same time, in early September of that year, it rose in the due east. This time of the year has been seen as explaining why Mary accompanied Joseph, since this was the time of the Feast of Tabernacles, a major pilgrimage festival. However, although this would fit within the larger period we have identified, it is too far before the death of Herod to be acceptable.

Fifth, Thomas Kepler suggested that the star of Bethlehem was the conjunction of Jupiter and Saturn in the constellation of the fishes. This conjunction occurs only once every 794 years and occurred in 7 B.C. However, we must ask if the people in the East could have predicted such an occurrence and why they would have come to Jerusalem if they had done so.

The Berlin Planetary Tables from ancient Babylon contain a list of the forthcoming movements of the planets from 17 B.C. through A.D. 10. The calculations for 7 B.C. are precise to the day. Further, as Stauffer points out, these astronomical features had specific meanings to the astrologers of the day. Jupiter was interpreted as being the sign of the Ruler of the universe. Saturn was considered to be the sign of Palestine. Finally, the sign of the fishes was understood as the sign of the last days. This conjunction would have plainly meant to these ancient astrologers that the Ruler of the universe was about to initiate the last days by appearing in Palestine. If this were happening, where else would He have been born other than in Jerusalem, the capital? Thus they went there first. Upon reference from the Scriptures, they went on to Bethlehem, where they found Him. If this is the true reconstruction, then Jesus' birth would have to be placed in 7 B.C.

Conclusion: The Date of Jesus' Birth

If the star of Bethlehem were a unique miracle, then the closest we can get to the date of Jesus' birth is to place it about or before 6 B.C. On the other hand, it may have been a miracle of a different kind. God may have established the miracle of the star of Bethlehem in the very movement of the planets from the moment of creation. That would show careful, divine planning of a sort beyond my comprehension. In addition, He would also have overseen the superstitions of pagan astrologers to bring them to interpret the sign in such a way as to send them to the right place at the right time. Such a miracle would not only show His sovereignty over the world of nature but over the minds of all peoples. To me that is equally as miraculous as a special star flung into the heavens at the right moment.

I conclude then that the birth of Jesus is to be dated in 7 B.C. If that is not correct, then it has to be dated around 6 B.C. and no later than 4 B.C.

The Date of Jesus' Death

The date of Jesus' crucifixion appears to have been far more narrowly confined by the study of historians but is more difficult to identify with precision. The most common dates suggested are A.D. 29, 30, 31, or 33.

Further, the difference between the dates usually suggested for Jesus' death is too slight to make it worth considering each position in detail for our purposes. Such discussions are extremely technical and not particularly profitable for a beginning student. What I propose to do is consider the basic evidence and then give my conclusion.

The first data which enables us to begin to focus upon a probable date for Jesus' death is the fact, witnessed by all four Gospels and the Apostle's Creed, that Jesus was crucified by the order of Pontius Pilate. Pilate was the Roman procurator of Judea from A.D. 26 to 36. Thus we must settle upon a date which fits within this time frame.

However, we search in vain for any other specific chronological reference within the Gospels relating to Jesus' death. Does this mean that we are at an impasse? Not quite. When we search the Roman records, we come across an interesting bit of information which seems to offer some help.

A Roman official under Tiberius Caesar by the name of Sejanus was executed on October 19, A.D. 31. What is significant here is that Sejanus was executed for anti-Semitic activities against the Jews. Furthermore, Pontius Pilate had been appointed as procurator in Judea at the instigation of Sejanus. Any time immediately after that, Pilate would have been quite fearful of being deposed, or even executed, as one of Sejanus' protégés. Furthermore, immediately after Sejanus' execution, Pilate would be extremely careful not to appear in any way to be anti-Semitic or hostile toward the Jews. Thus his attitude toward the Jewish leaders at the trial of Jesus makes more sense the closer we are to Sejanus' execution.

Before settling on a specific date for Jesus' death, we at least should note that many people have tried to identify the date based upon the data for the Jewish Passover in this era. While this sounds possible, the available data is so inconclusive, and the conclusions which have been reached are so diverse as to suggest the improbability of success, given the state of our knowledge at this point.

For the time being then, let us at least try to draw a tentative conclusion for the date of Jesus' death. In doing so, we need to recognize that we may have to return to this issue at a later time and modify our date in light of other evidence. Dealing with the chronology of Jesus and the New Testament era is like working a jigsaw puzzle. Every piece has to mesh precisely with every other piece.

Jesus was obviously crucified at a Jewish Passover. All four Gospels agree on this. Passover occurs in late March or early April. Since Pilate's attitude toward the Jews makes more sense the closer we are to the execution of Sejanus, I tentatively conclude that this occurred at the first Passover which followed it. This would date the crucifixion of Jesus as the first Passover following Sejanus' execution. This was late March or early April, A.D. 32.

The Date of the Beginning of Jesus' Ministry

Tradition has generally ascribed the length of Jesus' ministry to three years. Like most ancient traditions, this can only be accepted along with a question mark. If actual chronological data within and without the Bible conflicts with this, then we must be prepared to cast aside the tradition. A survey of the literature dealing with the subject shows that numerous historians have indeed rejected the tradition. The length commonly ascribed by New Testament scholars to Jesus' earthly ministry has varied from slightly more than one year to more than four or five. In order to deal with this issue, we need to consider the data which we have available.

Basic Data

The only actual piece of information which the Gospels give us relating to the date of the beginning of Jesus' ministry is connected with the ministry of John the Baptist. This tells us:

> In the fifteenth year of the reign of Tiberius Caesar, Pontius Pilate being governor of Judea, and Herod being tetrarch of Galilee, and his brother Philip being tetrarch of the region of Ituraea and Trachonitis, and Lysanius tetrarch of Abilene, in the high priesthood of Annas and Caiaphas, the word of God came to John the son of Zechariah in the wilderness (Luke 3:1-2).

The baptism of Jesus apparently occurred shortly after John began his ministry (Luke 3:21). Therefore if we can determine the date indicated by Luke's chronological data, we may have arrived at the approximate time for the beginning of Jesus' ministry. At the least, we will have the earliest time which could be assigned to it.

Unfortunately, the data given to us by Luke is not totally clear. The only specific item is the "fifteenth year ... of Tiberius Caesar." It seems that this ought to be perfectly straightforward, but it isn't. As Jack Finegan points out in *Handbook of Biblical Chronology*, this could indicate any one of three different dates.[2] If this reference relates to the time which had elapsed since Tiberius had begun his joint rule over the imperial provinces, then it would have been A.D. 26. However, if it refers to Tiberius' rule following the death of Augustus, it would be A.D. 28 by the Jewish method of counting years or A.D. 29 by the Roman method. Any one of these dates would fit with the other data which Luke gave us, so we are left at this point with three possibilities but no certainties or even probabilities as yet.

The only other possible help from the Gospels concerning the beginning date of Jesus' ministry is Luke's statement that He "was about thirty years of age" (Luke 3:23). We concluded earlier that Jesus was born before 4 B.C. and possibly in 7 B.C. Thirty years after these dates would be from A.D. 23 to 26. However, we are not told that He was thirty but was "about thirty." This would be reasonably true of any date from A.D. 26 to 29.

It is possible that the emphasis upon the fact of Jesus being "about thirty" may have had other overtones than those of chronology. In Jewish circles, a man was considered to be mature enough to serve on the Sanhedrin or as a priest after his thirtieth birthday. Luke's reference may have been aimed at showing that

Jesus had waited for that stage of maturity when people would have been willing to take Him seriously as a teacher. However, we still do not have a date for the beginning of the ministry.

The Relative Chronology of the Synoptics

The first three Gospels are called the Synoptic Gospels by serious students of the New Testament. This points up the fact that all three follow the same basic synopsis or outline of Jesus' life. Mark records the arrest of John the Baptist early in his narrative (Mark 1:14).

Shortly thereafter, Mark tells us of Jesus' disciples eating grain in the fields on a Sabbath (Mark 2:23). Grain began to ripen in the spring. Thus we can assume that this was a spring following John's arrest. This is the first actual season of a year which we can identify in the Synoptics. The next date which we can positively identify in Mark is the Passover when Jesus was crucified (Mark 14:1). Since Passover occurs in late March or early April, this had to be in the spring as well. The relative chronology of Matthew and Luke is identical to that of Mark.

This analysis of the chronology of the synoptics leaves us with a basic conclusion. The ministry of Jesus must have lasted at least a little over one year. It could have been longer, but it had to include two springs as a minimum.

The Relative Chronology of John's Gospel

When we turn to the Gospel of John, however, we come upon a different situation. A tradition which goes back at least to the time of Pappias in the latter part of the second century A.D. says that the Fourth Gospel was not written in chronological order. That tradition has normally been universally accepted. Modern scholars generally conclude that John's Gospel is a theological gospel with little or no interest in chronology. However, before we accept that conclusion, we need to consider the possibility that it may not be justifiable.

In reading John's Gospel, we begin to note that he gives a significant number of chronological references. The following serve as examples.

The Passover of the Jews was at hand . . . (John 2:13).

Now when he was in Jerusalem at the Passover feast . . . (v. 23).

> There are yet four months, and then comes the harvest (4:35).
>
> Now the Passover . . . was at hand (6:4).
>
> Now the Jews' feast of Tabernacles was at hand (7:2).
>
> It was the feast of the Dedication at Jerusalem; it was winter . . . (10:22-23).
>
> Now the Passover of the Jews was at hand . . . (11:55).

This unusual attention to chronological data implies that John, contrary to popular opinion, had a rather extensive interest in chronology. Therefore I conclude, at least until we see how other data coincides, that it is quite presumptuous to assume John's Gospel is not chronologically arranged. This does not mean that this Gospel was not also written from a theological perspective with a major theological purpose.

However, if the Fourth Gospel is chronologically arranged, then we must seek to establish its chronological framework. The following appears to be the minimum time period which we are given in John for the life of Jesus.

(1) The emphasis of John the Baptist upon Jesus as being the Lamb of God would be most understandable at a Passover (John 1:29,41). That was the time when they focused upon the lamb as the symbol of God's deliverance. This would have been the first Passover in Jesus' public ministry.

(2) Another Passover is clearly identified in John 2:13,23. Jesus visited Capernaum between these two, so this would have been the second Passover, the end of the first year of ministry.

(3) John the Baptist was still active after this, not yet having been imprisoned (John 3:24). Still later, Jesus pointed out that there were four months until the harvesttime. Harvest usually began in May or June. Four months before would thus have been in January or February of Jesus' second year of ministry.

(4) The next chronological reference is to the Feast of Tabernacles (John 5:1). This occurred in the fall, usually in September. This means that we have no identifiable reference to the third Passover. However, we would now appear to be in Jesus' third year of ministry.

(5) The fourth Passover of Jesus' ministry approached

while Jesus was involved in His Galilean ministry (John 6:4). This would have ended the third year of ministry and begun the fourth.

(6) At this point, events appear to have rapidly begun moving to their climax. At Tabernacles, the Jewish leaders sought to arrest Jesus (John 7:2,30,32,44; 8:59). They also sought to stone Him. This would have been in September of His fourth year of ministry.

(7) This was followed by a similar attempt to stone Jesus at the feast of Dedication in December (John 10:22-23,31,39). This, too, would have been during the fourth year.

(8) Finally, the fifth Passover came (John 11:55). It was at this one that Jesus was actually crucified.

Following John's arrangement, Jesus' ministry would have covered at least four years. It may have lasted longer, but if John is correct, it could not have lasted any less. As numerous biblical students have noted, the chronology of John does not match that of the Synoptic Gospels. On the other hand, the chronology of the Synoptics can quite easily be fitted into that of John.

Conclusion: The Date of Jesus' Ministry

At this point, we are ready to conclude tentatively that Jesus' earthly ministry covered at least four years. We earlier concluded that He was most likely crucified in A.D. 32. This would then mean that the latest He could have begun His ministry and gotten in all the time which John insists upon would have been at Passover in A.D. 28, which was four years earlier. We must now ask: How does this fit in with our other data?

We had earlier concluded that Jesus was apparently baptized shortly after John the Baptist began his ministry. We also concluded, depending upon the way Tiberius Caesar's years of reign were reckoned, that John's ministry had to have begun in A.D. 26, 28, or 29. Obviously the last date is impossible. The second one fits in precisely, and the first would also be a possibility. However, for the first to be accepted, we would have to assume at least two more years of ministry than what the Gospels appear to indicate. Therefore it appears to me that we can conclude with reasonable assurance that Jesus began His ministry in A.D. 28 and was crucified in A.D. 32.

Notes

1. Ethelbert Stauffer, *Jesus and His Story,* trans. Richard and Clara Winston (New York: Alfred A. Knopf, 1960).

2. Jack Finegan, *Handbook of Biblical Chronology* (Princeton, N.J.: Princeton University Press, 1964), 301.

12
The Background

John began his Gospel with the affirmation that "the Word became flesh and dwelt among us" (1:14). No statement could be more theologically profound than this. However, it is historically profound as well. With these words we are told that the Son of God, the Divine Word, God's ultimate message to all humanity, actually lived in this world. He lived at a real time, in a real place, among people who looked and spoke exactly like Him. Furthermore, the one who wrote those words had known and experienced Jesus as a real person.

Admittedly, Jesus was unique. Yet He lived in history. That being so, we must expect Him to be a person of His times. He was influenced by the same historical, geographical, physical, emotional, sociological, and religious forces which influenced His contemporaries. Therefore, if we are going to understand as fully as possible the life He lived, we must examine it against the background of the times in which He lived. There is no other adequate way to begin to understand Him.

Clearly, seeing Jesus as a man of His times, or even as *the* man of His times will not explain all that He did or said. It will help us better understand much of what He said and did. This fact is what makes the effort worth while. Anything which gives us a better understanding of Jesus' life and ministry is worth the effort we must make to attain it.

We have sought to describe what the world was like at the time Jesus was born. We must now direct our study to the examination of the world in which He lived, ministered, and died. Our primary concern will be with Palestine in the first three decades of the Christian era.

For the people of Palestine, whether Roman, Jew, Greek, Samaritan, Egyptian, or otherwise, it was an extremely turbulent time. The people were under the direct rule of an Ethnarch and five procurators, as well as by a number of high priests. At times, in fact for much of the time, the religious and political leaders were at odds with one another. In viewing the Roman officials, we see a succession of generally brutal, often venal, and frequently incompetent officials. The people of Palestine in this period were never exposed to the best Rome had to offer. Perhaps because of this, the government of the Roman empire never saw the best of the Jewish people either. The center of the empire viewed the Jews as revolutionary, disloyal, obstinate, unappreciative, and even atheistic, since they failed to worship the Roman gods.

Jesus grew up and ministered in such a world as this. It is the influence of these features upon His life and those of His disciples as well as upon the people to whom He ministered which we must seek to understand.

The Roman World

As we noted earlier, Caesar Augustus was ruler of Rome from 27 B.C. to A.D. 14. Thus he was not only the ruler who set the stage of Roman influence in Palestine prior to the birth of Jesus, he was also the one who led the Roman world during the years of Jesus' birth and childhood. A generally enlightened dictator, Augustus had been somewhat less than enthusiastic over the final days of the rule of Herod the Great over Palestine. We must remember that, although he was called "King," Herod ruled with the permission of and at the pleasure of the emperor. Again, as we noted earlier, Herod's will presumptuously provided for the division of his kingdom among three of his sons. These provisions were of no effect unless approved by Augustus. Thus the whole land was experiencing a time of great uncertainty in the period immediately following Jesus' birth.

A delegation of Jewish leaders from Jerusalem sought to get Augustus to reject the will of Herod. Their intent was to get the emperor to establish a Roman governor as the civil authority with the high priest as the religious authority. However, after considerable intrigue and debate, Augustus finally gave a partial approval to the will of Herod. He appointed Archelaus ethnarch of Judea and

Samaria. Philip was made tetrarch of the northern Transjordan, and Antipas was made tetrarch of Galilee and Perea (southern Transjordan). Each of these was made ultimately responsible for his administration to the Roman governor of the province of Syria.

Augustus recognized, as most astute politicians do, that it was important for his appointees to feel secure in their position. On the other hand, it was equally as important that they be both loyal and effective. The end result of their service to Augustus was that they keep the peace and keep taxes flowing steadily into the Roman coffers.

When Archelaus' rule proved so ineffective that a combined delegation of Jews and Samaritans pled for his removal, Augustus acted. Anything which caused Jews and Samaritans to unite forces had to be taken seriously. Archelaus was removed and Judea and Samaria were made into a third class province ruled by a governor or procurator appointed by the emperor. Since Augustus limited the terms of service of these appointees to three years, there was little continuity in the way Roman authority was experienced in the region. Even worse, these procurators had little opportunity to learn enough about these people to be able to govern them with anything like an adequate understanding. The end result was that the early years of Jesus' life were characterized by extreme unrest among the inhabitants of central Palestine, at least insofar as the leaders were concerned. Uncertainty appeared to be the rule of the day.

Upon Augustus' death in A.D. 14, he was succeeded by Tiberius Caesar, who ruled from A.D. 14 to 37. Tiberius, the adopted son of Augustus, had been associated with Augustus in ruling the eastern provinces for at least two years prior to his actual accession to the throne of Rome. No official path of succession to the throne had been established either by the Roman senate or Augustus himself. While the adoption of Tiberius as both son and successor took care of the issue for the moment, the failure to provide an official legal process was to bring a harvest of bitter fruit for Rome in the not too distant future.

While not directly involved in the internal affairs of Palestine during his reign, Tiberius made his influence felt at several significant places during this era. He was more enlightened than many Roman rulers and was especially concerned with the conditions under which Rome's subject people lived. This concern carried even to the remotest parts of the empire and clearly included the Jews of Palestine.

As an outgrowth of Tiberius' concerns, he sought to curb the expanding expenses of the imperial government. Under his leadership, the Roman government adopted an austerity program and was therefore generally able to reduce the burden of taxation upon the people. Also, Tiberius sought to establish a more stable government in the provinces, believing this affected the well-being of the subject peoples. To aid in this policy, his provincial appointees served for considerably longer periods of time than those of Augustus.

While his acts brought stability and even some personal popularity in the extremities of the empire, Tiberius became increasingly unpopular with the Roman senate. This led to a growing suspicion on his part of many of the leaders of Rome.

During this time, Tiberius placed much of the day-to-day operations of government in the hands of the prefect of the imperial guard, a man named Sejanus. To consolidate his power and favor with Tiberius, Sejanus brought numerous charges of treason against Roman officials and leaders to the attention of the emperor. As an outgrowth of this, it became quite important in the latter days of Tiberius' reign to become known as *amicus Caesaris,* a "friend of Caesar."

In order to further consolidate Sejanus' own power, he had encouraged Tiberius to move to the Island of Capri. This was done ostensibly as a means of self-protection on the part of the emperor. From that place, Tiberius ruled by correspondence, but Sejanus became the actual man on the scene in Rome.

The outgrowth of Sejanus' feeding Tiberius' fears of treason and disloyalty, coupled with his own increasing personal power was that the emperor ultimately became suspicious of Sejanus himself. Thus Sejanus was condemned and executed by Tiberius in A.D. 31 for treason. This was brought to a head in particular as an outgrowth of Sejanus' anti-Semitic policies. The final years of Tiberius are quite obscure, leading up to his death in A.D. 37. This clearly brings us beyond the time of the life and ministry of Jesus of Nazareth.

Judea and Samaria

As we have noted, Herod the Great had designated Archelaus to succeed him in reigning over the territory of Judea and Samaria. The very fact that Herod did not seek to leave all of his authority to Archelaus or any of his other sons showed that he did not believe that any one of them was fully capable of succeeding him. History proved his judgment to be wholly accurate. Be that as it may, Archelaus did succeed his father to authority in the central region of Palestine.

Upon the death of Herod, Archelaus wisely chose not to carry out his father's plans for executing many of the Jewish leaders of Judea. However, so great was the joy of the people that Herod was dead that celebrations began and turned into a major rebellion. Archelaus had to make two attempts before he finally succeeded in crushing it. When this had been accomplished, he and his two brothers, Herod Antipas and Philip, set out for Rome in an attempt to get Augustus to ratify their father's will, placing them in power over his kingdom. Unfortunately for them, two other delegations were also on the way to Rome with different pleas to place before the emperor. A Jewish delegation sought to get Herod's will wholly overthrown. They hoped to get the high priest appointed as civil ruler with military power resting in the Roman governor of Syria. At the same time, a delegation from the Greek cities of Hippus, Gadara, and Gaza sought for their cities to be excluded from either Jewish authority or Herodian authority. They wished to be regarded as independent cities, being directly responsible to the Roman governor of Syria alone.

It was against Roman policy for a son to succeed his father to power in any of the provinces. However, Herod had been an able ruler and loyal subject of Rome. Thus Augustus gave his wishes serious consideration. While the various delegations waited and Augustus sought to make up his mind, another major rebellion broke out in Palestine. Varus, the governor of Syria marched into the region, quelled the insurrection, and left a legion behind to maintain the peace. Due to the harshness of its commander, a new rebellion erupted. Varus returned and once again crushed the outbreak. In an attempt to ensure a more permanent peace, the Syrian governor crucified about two thousand of the rebels.

These events show the inherent instability of the region and the difficulty which Rome had in dealing with it. Augustus realized that Herod had at least maintained some semblance of peace. The emperor hoped that Herod's sons might be able to do the same. However, the Roman emperor could not take lightly the desires of the citizens of the region to be rid of a Herodian king.

Augustus compromised by appointing the three sons to power, but made none of them a king. Further, he did grant the request of the three Greek cities, assigning the three petitioning cities directly to the province of Syria. Archelaus became ethnarch of Judea, Samaria, and Idumea with the promise that he might be made a king later if he did a good job as ethnarch. An ethnarch had less power and independence than a king but more than a tetrarch.

As a ruler from either the Jewish or Roman standpoint, Archelaus was a miserable failure. He appointed and deposed high priests at will, thus scandalizing the citizens of Jerusalem. His marriage to Glaphyra was even more scandalous. She had been married to his half-brother and then to the king of Mauretania, who later divorced her. Archelaus divorced his own wife and took this woman as his wife in a marriage with no semblance of legality from the Jews' perspective.

Archelaus followed in Herod's footsteps with several major building projects. He was also as harsh as his father had been without the political wisdom to allow him to come close to getting by with it. His cruelties were a byword in Judea and Samaria, uniting those bitter racial enemies in their hatred of him. They jointly pled to Augustus for relief. Because of his failure to keep the peace and maintain the steady flow of taxes, Archelaus was banished to Gaul. He probably was not executed only because he was Herod's son.

Since his experiment with Archelaus had failed, the Roman emperor reorganized that part of the empire into a subdivision of the province of Syria, appointing procurators to rule over this region. These procurators were supposedly responsible to the governor of Syria, but in actual fact were relatively independent in matters of both civil government and military activity. Their official residence was established at Caesarea, but they moved to Jerusalem during times of real or threatened danger, such as the great Jewish festivals. Augustus also decided that keeping the terms of these procurators brief would prevent them from becoming susceptible to bribes and would increase both their loyalty to and dependence upon the emperor himself. (A table listing these procurators and their terms of service is given in the preceding chapter.)

The coming of the period of the procurators made two major differences in the way this territory was governed. Perhaps the most significant of these was that the Roman procurators could directly impose the death sentence. No longer did the permission of the emperor have to be sought for executions. The second difference is found in the fact that the procurators were Romans. Though they were specifically ordered to be as sensitive as possible to the beliefs of the inhabitants of the land, they acted out of ignorance. If they did not have good advisors, which they generally did not, they often acted in such a way as to create problems which kept many people almost always ready to break forth into open and immediate rebellion.

The reigns of the early procurators were not of great significance for our purposes here. The procurators' presence simply reinforced the fact that the Jews were constantly made aware that they were a conquered people. Their short terms of service led to a genuine instability in the government of the land. Policies were not consistent. Thus there was no feeling among the people that the rules by which they lived one day would be the same on the next.

When Tiberius succeeded Augustus these things changed. Tiberius was aware of the failures of the system of government in Samaria and Judea and sought to correct them. He extended the terms of service of the procurators in an attempt to achieve a greater stability in the government of the provinces.

Tiberius' first appointment as procurator of Judea and Samaria was Valerius Gratus who served from A.D. 15 to 26. Gratus apparently made a significant increase in the taxes which Rome collected, because an appeal was made to Tiberius for relief in A.D. 17. We do not know how this was settled, but the taxes were apparently reduced. Tiberius had a basic policy of reducing taxes, and since there is no record of any further appeal being made, we can probably assume that he overruled the policy of his appointee. The only other thing we know for certain about the rule of Gratus was that he appointed four different high priests. The fact that this was done with such rapidity and without the death of the incumbent high priest probably indicates that Gratus was accepting bribes as the basis for such appointments. This obviously says something about him, as well as about those who served as high priests.

Gratus was succeeded by Pontius Pilate, who served as procurator from A.D. 26 to 36. This period covers the entire ministry of Jesus. Because he was the one who ordered the execution of Jesus, he has become the most familiar of all Roman procurators. The Apostles' Creed, recited regularly by millions of Christians, memorializes this otherwise inconsequential Roman bureaucrat with the statement that Jesus "suffered under Pontius Pilate, was crucified, died and was buried."

According to the report of Josephus, Pilate was utterly despised by the Jews. This needs to be understood in the light of the fact that they would have probably despised any ruler who represented the hated Roman forces of occupation. Be that as it may, two acts show why Pilate was so hated. Early in his rule, Pilate brought the shields of his troops into Jerusalem. These bore the image of the emperor and such an image in the holy city was an outrage to the Jews. Pilate did this in direct disobedience to a standing imperial order. However, it was probably done at the instigation of Sejanus, Pilate's friend in power who was later accused of being anti-Semitic. The Jews immediately appealed to Caesar, and Pilate was ordered to remove the shields.

Pilate later tried again, this time using shields with only the emperor's name inscribed upon them. Again Pilate was ordered to remove them, although this time he was allowed to hang the shields in Caesarea. This compromise saved the Jewish feelings but also saved the imperial honor.

At a later time, Pilate sought to ease the constant problem of the water supply of Jerusalem by building an aqueduct to furnish water to the temple mount. Because of its purposes, Pilate confiscated temple treasures to pay for this. The Jews were incensed at his high-handed action. Recognizing their surging tempers, Pilate sent his soldiers into the temple area in disguise. When he went there to meet with the Jewish leaders, the people lashed out at him. At that point, the soldiers retaliated with great violence, quelling the revolt in a brief blood bath. The open resistance was crushed, but the Jewish hatred was intensified. Against this background, we must understand the undercurrents and interactions at the trial of Jesus.

Pilate's downfall came when a Samaritan prophet called for a gathering of his followers to Mount Gerizim, claiming to be about to restore the sacred vessels which had been stolen from the temple in the time of the Babylonian exile. Pilate, knowing of the gathering, suspected that an insurrection was being planned. He and his soldiers attacked the defenseless crowd, slaughtering many people. This act was reported by the Jewish leaders to Vitellius, the legate of Syria, who ordered Pilate to report to Tiberius in Rome. It was Pilate's good fortune that Tiberius died before he arrived. Nothing else is really known of Pilate. He apparently avoided execution because of the death of the emperor. According to an unsubstantiated legend, he was removed from government service and banished.

Galilee and Perea

The inhabitants of Galilee and Perea were more fortunate than those in Judea and Samaria when the kingdom of Herod the Great was divided. Herod Antipas was appointed tetrarch there by Augustus. His reign basically covered the entire life-span of Jesus because he ruled from 4 B.C. to A.D. 39. That continuity alone gave a stability to the region which the more southern territory of Palestine lacked.

Galilee was far more fertile and productive than the territory of Judea. The people there were farmers, and like most small land holders were fiercely independent. Further, they were rarely involved in world affairs and thus were on the sidelines of the issues which threatened the very existence of Judea.

Herod Antipas is known in the New Testament simply as Herod. Like his father, Herod was a builder. Also like his father, he was a schemer of the first order. His reputation for cunning was memorialized in the New Testament when Jesus referred to him as "that fox" (Luke 13:32). However, Herod was more sensitive to the feelings of his people and joined the citizens of Jerusalem in their appeal to Tiberius to force Pilate to remove the shields from Jerusalem. That may have been the beginning of the bad blood which existed between Herod and Pilate (Luke 23:12).

Herod's most outstanding building project was the city of Tiberias on the edge of the Sea of Galilee. During its construction, it was discovered that the city was being built on the site of an ancient cemetery. Due to its ceremonial uncleanness, no Jew could live there, and Herod had to populate his city with foreigners. That fact may have helped him escape many of the conflicts which befell his counterparts in Judea.

The personal life of Herod was as entangled as that of his father or brothers. His wife, Herodias, had been married to his half-brother, Philip. This scandalized the very orthodox among his Jewish citizens and ultimately led to his arrest and execution of John the Baptist. Further, the fact that Herod divorced his first wife, daughter of Aretas, king of the Nabateans, in order to marry Herodias, created international entanglements for the region of Galilee and Perea. A long and ongoing series of border disputes disturbed the peace of the region where Perea touched the kingdom of Aretas.

Herod's ambition, fueled by his wife Herodias, proved to be his ultimate downfall. Near the end of his rule when he sought to be elevated to the title of king, his act was viewed with additional suspicion by an already suspicious Caligula, the new emperor of Rome. As a consequence, Herod was banished to Gaul in A.D. 39.

Northern Transjordan

When Augustus ratified the will of Herod the Great, Philip was appointed tetrarch of the several small provinces situated northeast of the Sea of Galilee. As far as the records indicate, he was unlike his father or any of his brothers. Not one single harsh or disapproving judgment is recorded against him. No complaint to Rome was ever lodged against him by his subjects.

Unlike other members of his family, Philip lived a quiet life. His wife was Salome, the daughter of Herod Philip, his half-brother, and later step-daughter to Herod Antipas. Her dance led to the beheading of John the Baptist. Philip almost never traveled outside the boundaries of his assigned region but traveled through that region extensively. He sought to take justice to his people, rather than forcing them to come to him at his palace.

From all outward appearances, Philip's major purpose in life was to keep his people happy and contented. Carrying a portable throne with him on his travels, whenever he found a case which needed judgment, he would set up his throne, hear the case, and pass judgment. Of major significance is the fact that no charge of bribery or injustice was ever leveled against him.

However, when it came to the matter of building, Philip was obviously his father's son. He is credited with rebuilding ancient Panias for his capital, naming it Caesarea Philippi. He also built a city near the fishing village of Bethsaida, which he named Bethsaida Julias in honor of Augustus' daughter. This was a border city, located just across the Jordan River from the major Roman customs post of Capernaum.

The territories under Philip's rule were far more peaceful than those assigned to his two brothers. This was probably due to the fact that they had never been a part of Jewish land and were primarily populated with Gentiles or at least non-Jews. Thus they were not nearly as sensitive to religious matters as were the citizens of the rest of the region. Philip had the images of both Caesar and himself stamped on his coins, and no one seemed to care. This clearly would not have been the case in either Judea or Galilee. The region was generally quite peaceful and offered a place for Jesus and His disciples to escape from the tensions of the Jewish homeland as well as from the pressures of opposition, hostility, or attack on the part of the Jewish leaders.

Again, unlike his father or brothers, Philip was deeply loved by his people. His death in A.D. 34 brought a period of genuine grief and mourning to the people of the region.

Judaism in Palestine

Two major factors shaped the world in which Jesus lived and ministered. The first of these was the Roman domination. The other major force which molded Jesus' world was Judaism, the religion of the Jews. These two shaped the world of Palestine in that day both from the political and religious standpoints.

Jesus was born a Jew. The Judaism of His day established the religious faith of those with whom He worked and to whom He ministered. He was a child of the synagogue, worshiped at the temple in Jerusalem, and celebrated His faith as those around Him did. However, the Judaism of His day did not differ in any significant way from that of the years immediately before His birth. Therefore we do not need to reconsider in detail the material which has already been presented in chapter 9, where the Judaistic root of the world of the New Testament was discussed. A few summary features should perhaps be repeated in order to get the full picture before us again.

The major features of Judaism which impinged upon the ministry of Jesus, other than the basic faith which permeated the everyday lives of the people, can be effectively considered under three basic headings.

The High Priest and the Sanhedrin

All the religious authority of the day rested in the Sanhedrin and its president, the reigning high priest. In addition, this group also had almost all authority over the internal governmental affairs of Judea. The only three real limitations on their power was that they could not issue coinage to be used outside of the temple area, they could not assign the death penalty to a convicted felon, and they could not enter into any treaties with other provincial rulers or countries.

Rome had learned that the high priesthood was a valuable commodity. Leading Jews were quite willing and even eager to pay for the privilege of serving in that office. It was a political appointment and carried a great deal of power. Thus the reigning high priest was usually more of a politician than a religious leader. The same could also be said of the concerns of the Sanhedrin. Although its members were not political appointments of Rome, they were quite aware that their power was a gift from Rome.

The Parties

Most people familiar with the New Testament are familiar with the Pharisees and Sadducees. These were the two major parties of Judaism. However, as we have noted, large numbers of people were never involved directly with them. The Pharisees were primarily concerned with righteousness and thus with obedience to the Law. The world has probably never known a group of people who were morally better than these people. However, their extreme legalism made life miserable for themselves and all those whom they influenced through the official regulations of the Judaism of their day. While numbers of the Pharisees were involved in the Sanhedrin, they seldom controlled it or the Judaism of their day.

The Sadducees, on the other hand, were generally representative of the more wealthy and powerful segments of Jerusalem. The high priest during this time always appears to have been a Sadducee. The Sadducees seem to have been primarily concerned with maintaining their power and thus their position. Collaboration with

Rome was high on their list of priorities. "Peace at almost any price" appears to have been their motto. Their actual numbers were even smaller than the Pharisees, but their influence over life, at least in Jerusalem, appears to have been far greater than their relative numbers.

The other parties, the Herodians, Essenes, and Zealots, all appear to have been of smaller numbers, less organized, and only occasionally of any real influence. The agenda of the Zealots was throwing the Romans out of Palestine at any cost. Thus their presence was always a threat to the peace. Further, they were always looking for a leader or "Messiah" to lead them in a military assault upon the hated Romans. They kept the hatred of the Romans alive and were more influential among the Jewish people the farther away from Jerusalem one got. The Herodians apparently sought for a return to the days of the rule of the Herodian family and were supporters of collaboration with Rome at any price, as long as it kept them in power. The Essenes apparently were very other-worldly, seeking to withdraw from the miseries of present life by moving into monastic-type communities. Their influence upon Judaism might have been felt in some of their hopes and their disgust with life as it was.

Finally, the last major influence of Judaism upon the world of Jesus might be best described as geographic. This focuses upon the difference in outlook and life-style between the Jews of Galilee and those of Jerusalem and Judea. Because of their very distance from Jerusalem, the Galileans were far less concerned with the worship of the temple or with the concerns of orthodoxy voiced by the Pharisees. They were also far more nationalistic and individualistic. These people were more likely to explode at any moment in open rebellion against Rome.

On the other hand, the people of Judea saw the Roman troops more often and felt their occupying power more frequently but also realized that open rebellion was less likely to succeed. They were far more concerned with the issues of temple ritual and the "business" of the temple. They were also far more involved with trade and the concerns of economics. Finally, their peace was more often disturbed by the throngs which came to Jerusalem for the annual festivals.

This, then, was the kind of world in which Jesus grew up, ministered, and died. It was a world in turmoil. It was a world where people had little real hope and looked for the intervention of God to deliver them. It was a world burdened down by the cares of life and cruelties of existence but which was almost waiting in expectancy for something significant to happen. It did.

13
The Obscure Years

Descriptions of the life of Jesus often seem to demand more of human language than it is capable of delivering. His has been called "the greatest story ever told" and "the greatest life ever lived." These seemingly extravagant titles trivialize a life which is beyond comprehension. On the other hand, students of history must seek to comprehend His life as best we can.

Whatever else we may say about Jesus' life, it was begun in relative obscurity, and the formative years were lived in almost utter oblivion. The only two events of Jesus' life before His actual ministry of which we have any record are his birth, including the events surrounding it, and the visit to the temple with His parents at the age of twelve. Other than this, we can only make educated deductions from the records of the four Gospels. Let me plainly say that I discount any of the non-Gospel records of His childhood which show Him as a miraculous prodigy. This presentation of His formative years is so foreign to what the canonical Gospels show of the rest of His life as to reveal them to be demonstrably false.

Jesus' Birth and Infancy

We concluded earlier that Jesus' birth most likely occurred about 7 B.C., possibly 6 B.C., but in no way could it be any later than 4 B.C. He was clearly born in the last years of the reign of Herod the Great. This was a time of great unrest within the regions over which Herod ruled. This region included both Nazareth, the home of Joseph and Mary, and Bethlehem, the birthplace of Jesus. Not only was there an ongoing conflict between Herod and the Pharisees, Herod himself was torn by insecurity and suspicion of treason on every hand as well as a sense of frustration at his failure to win the support of the people of Palestine for whom he had really done so much. He would tolerate no opposition to his policies or authority, nor would he any longer deal in patient understanding with those who distrusted or disliked him.

The birth of Jesus shows up in no record outside of the New Testament, nor should we expect it to do so. Our records are not all that good for the births in families of major leaders of the Roman world. Why should we expect anyone to have noticed or to have made an official record of the birth of a son to a man and his wife who had journeyed to Bethlehem for the taxation census?

The family into which Jesus was born had a regal heritage, being of the line of David. As such, they were part of Israel's messianic hope. That hope had been long deferred and most people of the day probably thought little about it. At the same time, Mary and Joseph had been forced to deal with the issue of God's miraculous intervention into their lives. Both of these people deserve a serious look by any historian.

Mary was probably about fifteen years of age. That was the normal time for Jewish girls of that day to be married. We might think she was extremely young to be assuming the responsibility of a home and family, and she was. Consider the fact that she had been additionally blessed and burdened by being singled out to be the mother of the Son of God. From the beginning she had to have been aware of the fact that hers was a story which none of her friends, family, or neighbors would believe. How could she expect Joseph to accept her tale, glorious though it was? She had to have known that she faced months and years of gossip, snide remarks, disapproval, and outright hostility. That was the best possible outcome. Society's judgment would have branded her an adulteress, which was punishable by death. While trusting God to protect her and His Son, she also had to have faced the very human fears which would have accompanied her pregnancy.

Joseph also faced grave difficulties. His fiancée came to him with an unbelievable story of a virgin conception. The law demanded her exposure and death, but his love for her made him seek to avoid that path (Matt. 1:19). To that end, in a dream he was led to the prophecy of Isaiah (7:14).

The most interesting fact here is that if the original Hebrew text of Isaiah had been the one to which he turned, he would have found no help. The original indicates a birth but not necessarily a virgin birth. When the LXX translated this passage into Greek, the words were carefully chosen to show a prediction of a *virgin birth*.

The Isaiah passage gave Joseph hope. This, coupled with his gentle but courageous love of Mary, led him to proceed with his plans for the marriage. However, he too had to be aware of the consequences. At the best, people would think that Mary's pregnancy was the result of Joseph's immorality. At the worst, they would accuse him of being a fool to have been misled by his young bride or to have accepted her as an "immoral" woman.

We know nothing else of Joseph. Tradition describes him as being somewhat older than Mary, perhaps even a widower. However there is no evidence for accepting the latter judgment, unless you wish to believe that Mary was forever a virgin. Then the other children of the family would have been his by a former marriage. Joseph's age may be indicated by the fact that he disappears from the Gospel narratives even before Jesus began His ministry. This probably means that Joseph was dead by that time, which might be evidence of his more advanced age. Certainly Jesus would not likely have been so concerned about His mother at the crucifixion if Joseph had still been alive (John 19:25-27).

When Mary and Joseph arrived at the small town of Bethlehem in response to the imperial census, they found the town bursting at the seams with others who arrived there for the same purpose. People who had close relatives or friends there would have been staying with them. Others would have been staying in the open fields nearby. Mary needed better than that because the time of her delivery was at hand. Motels or hotels in our sense of the term would have been nonexistent. The only possible accommodation would have been the local caravansary, or inn (Luke 2:7).

A normal caravansary was simply a large, walled enclosure. The camels and donkeys of travelers would have been tethered in the center with the travelers sleeping around the walls with small fires for cooking and warmth. Only the most luxurious of these would have had low walls separating each group of travelers from the other, thus affording some rudimentary kind of privacy. Even at the best, such an "inn" would have afforded poor accommodations for a woman giving birth and no privacy at all. The innkeeper assigning Mary and Joseph to a stable may have been offering them the most private place he had, particularly with the crowd of pilgrims present at that time. Further, the stables of that region were normally caves, not small outbuildings.

Following Jesus' birth, He went through the normal things in the early days of His infancy which would have been done with any Jewish child born in those times and at that place. He was circumcised on the eighth day, according to the law (Luke 2:21; Gen. 17:12; Lev. 12:3). This was the outward symbol of Israel's covenant relation with God. In addition, Mary and Joseph took Jesus and made the short journey to Jerusalem forty days after His birth for His dedication and her purification.

We do not know why Joseph did not take his family back to Nazareth. It may be that he simply hated to face the remarks and attitudes of the people there. For whatever reason, the family remained in Bethlehem for some time following Jesus' birth.

In the days of Jesus' infancy or early childhood, the Magi came to Jerusalem seeking "the King of the Jews." If we are correct as to their interpretation of signs in the heavens, their reason for going to Herod in Jerusalem is easily understood. Where else would they look for the king of the Jews other than in the palace of the reigning king, Herod? Not knowing what they were talking about, Herod sought his councilors' advice. From the scroll of Micah they found the prophecy which sent the Magi on to Bethlehem. Having found the young Jesus, they then went home without reporting back to Herod.

Herod's response to the threat of a rival King was swift, cruel, and quite in character. In 7 B.C., Herod had executed two of his sons because he suspected them of treason. In 4 B.C., he did the same with another. In between these times, he executed three hundred leaders of his army who were suspected of supporting his sons and a large number of Pharisees who were involved in a rebellion. He had planned the execution of a large number of Jewish leaders at his death so that the land would mourn.

The slaughter of the male children of Bethlehem who were two years old and under was quite in character for this bloody leader. However, we must not overemphasize what was done. Bethlehem was not a large town. The number of such children would not have been great. To the parents involved however, even one child would have been too many. Herod's wrathful outburst failed to achieve his ends. Before his soldiers arrived to carry out his despicable orders, Mary, Joseph, and Jesus had fled to Egypt (Matt. 2:13). An exile from His own land, Jesus found safety among foreigners when there was no safety among His own people.

Herod the Great died in 4 B.C. Sometime thereafter, Mary and Joseph took the boy Jesus and returned to Nazareth. There he grew and was nurtured in a poor home but one where He was assured of love and care.

Jesus' Visit to the Temple

At the age of twelve, Jesus accompanied his parents on the pilgrimage from Nazareth to Jerusalem for the Passover celebration (Luke 2:41-50). This was a time of great significance in the life of any Jewish boy because it was at that time that he became a "son of the law." For Jesus, it would have had that same significance.

If we are correct in dating Jesus' birth, then the year of His pilgrimage would have been A.D. 6. For the Jews of Judea, A.D. 6 was a year of destiny. That was the year when Augustus deposed Archelaus, changing the official status of Judea and placing Roman authority there in the hands of a procurator. So the first Roman procurator with his marching soldiers would have been parading the streets of Jerusalem at the time Jesus and His parents arrived there.

Six A.D. was also the first year of the high priesthood of Annas. He would have been officiating at his first Passover, making it a significant moment both for him and the Jews. At the annual celebration of the Passover, the Sanhedrin frequently held public meetings in the temple, allowing the bystanders to question them over interpretations of the law. It is fascinating to consider that Jesus was there, listening to and learning from the one who would years later be the first to interrogate Him following His arrest (John 8:12-14).

The fact that the boy Jesus was left behind in the temple when Mary and Joseph started their homeward journey is not as much an indication of their parental failure as it might first seem (Luke 2:44). For safety, pilgrims usually made such journeys in large companies. At such a time, the women usually started out ahead of the men, who followed later with the entire company joining together at the first night's camp. Each parent could easily have assumed that Jesus was with the other until they got together and discovered otherwise.

Upon the return of Mary and Joseph to Jerusalem, Jesus was finally found in the temple after a long search. They probably initially sought for Him among friends and in the places where an adolescent boy might be expected, such as the markets with all of their multitudinous attractions. We should not misinterpret what Jesus was doing in the temple courts. He was not putting the priests and members of the Sanhedrin "through their paces" as some have often suggested. The words describing what He was doing, "listening to them and asking them questions" are those normally used of a pupil learning from his teacher (Luke 2:46).

The Home in Nazareth

Following the episode in the temple, Jesus went back to Nazareth with His parents. There He grew up in a home where He was taught to love and live as a part of the "chosen people" of God. Admittedly, we know very little of Jesus' childhood or adolescent days. However, from His later words and things we are told about His home life we can deduce a number of features about that home and the community in which it was located. We can at least describe a number of Jesus' boyhood experiences with a fair degree of certainty.

Later in His life, when Jesus was teaching in the synagogue of Nazareth, the bystanders who questioned His authority identified Him as the "carpenter's son" (Matt. 13:55). Over the centuries, artists, teachers, and preachers have described Him as growing up learning the skills of a carpenter from His father. This may be correct. However, this has also raised a number of questions due to the fact that Jesus regularly took the subjects of His parables from agriculture rather than carpentry. The only reference we have from Him in the Gospels which could be interpreted as being from a carpenter's background is His reference to an easy yoke (Matt. 11:29-30). This could also be from the field of agriculture.

However, an eminent archaelogist, the late Professor Joe Callaway, has offered an interesting observation relating to this issue. (This was done in a private conversation with the author.) The normal meaning of the word translated here as *carpenter* is precisely that. There are at least three references found in ancient papyri where the context clearly requires the meaning of *farmer*. The word apparently originally meant "to cut" and was normally applied to the cutting of wood. However, it apparently could also mean the cutting of soil with a plow, thus referring to a farmer. If this is correct, then Joseph may have been a farmer, and Jesus may have been a "farmer's son." This would then give the perfect background from which He could have gotten the subjects for His parables.

In addition, we know something about the family in which Jesus grew up. At least seven children made up the circle in which Jesus was nurtured. There were four brothers, James, Joseph, Simon, and Judas (Jude), making a total of five boys (Matt. 13:55). Furthermore, since those who knew Jesus referred to His "sisters," there had to have been at least two of them (Matt. 13:56). In such a family, as the older brother, Jesus may have learned quite early the value of telling good stories. He certainly developed that ability at home before setting out on His ministry.

In that family circle, Jesus clearly learned responsibility. As we have noted, His mother Mary was apparently widowed, since the Gospels make no mention of Joseph during Jesus' ministry and He was so concerned for her care at the time of His crucifixion (John 19:25-27). This may also be hinted at when Mark points out that some of the people simply identified Jesus as "the son of Mary" (Mark 6:3). This may offer an additional basis for understanding the tender compassion which He showed for widows and orphans. He was also quick to see the widow casting in her offering in the temple treasury (Mark 12:42; Luke 21:2). Further, in that family circle Jesus must have learned and demonstrated many of the things which made up a great part of His later teachings because the Christian ideals point to obedient sons and loving brothers and sisters.

In that Nazareth home poverty must never have been very far away. There He learned the value of work and money. The least expensive sacrifices permissible by law accompanied His infant dedication (Luke 2:24). Jesus also knew the cost of the cheapest meat, "five sparrows sold for two pennies" (Luke 12:6). His awareness of the fact that no one patches an old garment with new cloth, lest it be torn by the shrinkage of the first washing, reflects the kind of knowledge gained only through bitter experience (Matt. 9:16; Mark 2:21). He also showed knowledge of children beset by hunger asking for fish, eggs, and bread and knowing that a loving father, even if he cannot supply such requests, will not respond with stones or scorpions (Luke 11:11-12). Finally, He knew that oil lamps had to be put where they would give the best light, for no one wasted even the dim light which they provided (Matt. 5:15).

Jesus also showed His knowledge of the panic accompanied by the loss of one silver coin and the serious searching until it was found (Luke 15:8). He was also aware of the seriousness with which the destruction of moths and rust was taken and the horror at having something stolen by sneak thieves (Matt. 6:19).

In that family Jesus learned the heartache of children who would promise to work and later fail to do it (Matt. 21:30). Either in His own home or that of a neighbor He learned the heartache of a willful son who left home for a "far country" (Luke 15:13).

Jesus also knew the bitterness of Roman occupation. Their soldiers marched all over His homeland, and He knew that any native could be compelled to carry a soldier's baggage for a mile (Matt. 5:41). It is even probable that He had learned this by firsthand experience. Further, He had seen the wealthy merchants travel along the highways of His land, realizing the utter emptiness of the glories of this world.

His childhood shows through the words of His manhood. He had wandered over the hills of Nazareth where He had learned about the holes of foxes and the nests of birds (Matt. 8:20; Luke 9:58). The echoes of childhood games with His playmates of Nazareth are found in words telling of "let's pretend" weddings and funerals. We can even hear His memories of a sulking child who refused to play (Matt. 11:16-17; Luke 7:32).

Jesus was also obviously a student of the synagogue school of Nazareth. He spoke three languages—Aramaic, Greek, and Hebrew. Aramaic was the native language of His people at that time. Greek was the official language of the provinces of the empire. We cannot expect Pilate to have understood Aramaic, so for Jesus to have later been able to converse with him must mean that Jesus spoke Greek. Further, at the beginning of His ministry, Jesus *read* from the Scriptures in the synagogue at Nazareth. Although the Old Testament had been translated into Greek, the synagogues would have only used the Hebrew text. Jesus' ability to read makes Him quite unusual, because this was a skill not normally held by Jewish youths of that time.

Jesus' later knowledge of the sacred Scriptures shows that He had pondered them long and seriously. However, the questioning of those who later wondered where He got all His knowledge may imply that His education had been interrupted before it was completed (Matt. 13:55). This could be an additional piece of evidence for the earlier death of Joseph. Such an event would have forced Jesus to assume the responsibility of breadwinner for His family. That may also explain why He was so long in beginning His ministry. He could have been waiting for the other sons to reach the place where they could assume this responsibility, leaving Him free to begin His main task.

In addition to the experiences of His home, Jesus was also a child of His times. The death of Augustus and the accession of Tiberius may have led Him, along with others of His people, to hope for better times. Tiberius was a more lenient ruler, but he was still the dictator of a foreign power nonetheless. Further, with each new procurator there was also renewed hope for better times. These hopes were always dashed on the rocks of actual experience. Jesus was aware that there were those of His people, publicans and high priests alike, who were willing to sell out their people in their own quest for power and wealth.

All of these things together shaped the training and experience of Jesus. He brought the influence of a godly home and parents, the training of a beloved rabbi at synagogue school, and the devotion and problems of living within a family to the tasks of His ministry. These years have often been called His years of preparation. They were. They have also been called the "silent years." This they were not. These years later spoke through Jesus every time He acted or taught. Obscure they were, but they shaped the man He became and the ministry He rendered. He was a child of history. Those days passed, and He stepped from their obscurity onto the stage of history.

14
The Early Ministry

In the early years of the second quarter of the first century A.D., in an obscure region of a border province on the eastern edge of the Roman Empire, a life was lived which transformed the empire, the world, and all history. The only real sources for a study of that life are the four Gospels: Matthew, Mark, Luke, and John. While these books are not history writing as we know it, these books are certainly rooted and grounded in history. Their message is clearly theological, yet they set forth the meaning of a life which was lived in a real place, at a real time, and by a real person: Jesus of Nazareth.

The Gospels are not biographies of Jesus in any sense of the term. Further, they are just as clearly neither the diaries of Jesus nor of His disciples. However, all four of the Gospels deal with a common theme: the life, death, and resurrection of Jesus. That is just the point. They are gospels, the "good news" of what God was doing in, through, and with Jesus. However, to understand much of what that good news is, we must first understand these books and their message against the background of the time in which He lived. For the study of this background, we do have other sources as we have noted earlier.

To understand the nature of the four Gospels as well as the other books which comprise the of the New Testament, a diligent student should study several good introductions to the New Testament. To profit most fully from this study, I recommend that a good synopsis or harmony of the text of the Gospels be used along with this book. This kind of book seeks to put the texts of the various Gospels in parallel columns so that one may have insofar as is possible a connected story of the life of Jesus. Most scholars will probably use a harmony of the first three Gospels and refer to John separately.

However, I find it more valuable to use A. T. Robertson's *A Harmony of the Gospels* which includes all four together.[1] Every student needs to recognize that *any gospel harmony* is simply an attempt by its editor to organize the texts of the four Gospels into a consistent, chronological pattern. We must not allow ourselves to become a slave to anyone else's attempt at organization. Instead, we shall use it where it is helpful and abandon it where it isn't.

Tentative Outline of the Early Ministry

To keep us on track in our consideration of the historical background of that ministry, it will be helpful to get the proposed basic outline of the early part of His ministry before us again at this point.

Early Chronology

A.D. 28	Mar./Apr.	Passover, Jesus baptized (John 1:29,31)
	(Summer?)	Jesus' visit to Capernaum
A.D. 29	Mar./Apr.	Second Passover (2:13,23)
		John the Baptist still active (3:24)
A.D. 30	Jan./Feb.	Four months before harvest (4:35)
	Mar./Apr.	Third Passover not mentioned
	September	Feast of Tabernacles (5:1) (John the Baptist may have been arrested shortly before.)
	Fall	Jesus back in Galilee
A.D. 31	March	Five thousand fed
	Mar./Apr.	Passover (6:4)

In the early fall of Jesus' third year of ministry, events began moving toward their conclusion with rapidly increasing speed. Therefore we shall break our study of His ministry in the late summer of that year (A.D. 31). Before this time, we are dealing with what I call the period of His early ministry. After this, as tensions mounted and threats of death became ever more real, we are in the period of the final days of His life. Against the historical period described by this rough outline then, we will seek to understand and visualize His life and ministry.

The Beginning of Jesus' Ministry

As we have noted, Luke sought to place the beginning of the ministry of John the Baptist on the stage of history with a series of six very precise historical references. It was

In the fifteenth year of the reign of Tiberius Caesar, Pontius Pilate being governor of Judea, and Herod being tetrarch of Galilee, and his brother Philip tetrarch . . . of Iturea and Trachonitis, and Lysanius tetrarch of Abilene, in the high priesthood of Annas and Caiaphas (3:1-2).

This was apparently A.D. 28. It was at that time that the word of God came to John in "the wilderness" (3:2). The wilderness of Judea was a rough, rocky, barren territory in the hills stretching southward from Jerusalem. John apparently came from there to the Jordan Valley, thundering his call to repentance like the prophets of old.

John's message was proclaimed at a place where many people could hear him, very likely on the highway at the fords of the Jordan where pilgrims and travelers from Galilee crossed from Perea into Judah near Jericho. This was the normal crossing place for those who made the journey between Galilee and Judea and did not wish to travel through the territory of the hated Samaritans. As John's fame spread, additional crowds made the journey from Jerusalem to join the Galilean pilgrims in hearing this new prophet from God.

Much of John's message sounds like that found in documents from ancient Qumran. Further, the people of Qumran practiced a baptism for those who became a part of their community. On the other hand, a great deal of John's preaching is quite different from the Qumranian beliefs. We suspect that during John's formative years, he lived near their monastery in the wilderness. During that time, he apparently knew of the inhabitants there and may have assimilated some of their ideas into his own thinking. Be that as it may, it was at least in that environment that he heard God speak and from that environment that he came to proclaim God's new day for the people of Israel. He not only called his people to God, he gave them very down to earth advice on how to live according to God's expectations, urging tax collectors to be fair and soldiers not to grumble about their pay (Luke 3:12-14).

At such a site as John had chosen, a steady stream of pilgrims would have passed at any time. However, at festival times, the throngs of pilgrims from Galilee would have swelled to unbelievable proportions. At such a time, Jesus appeared at the river, requesting baptism at John's hands.

We do not know how long John had been preaching when Jesus

came to him. However, we do know that just before this particular time he had been dealing with questions regarding whether or not he was the Messiah ("Christ") (3:15). Such would have been a legitimate question at any time. However, the Jewish people of that era had a greater hope at Passover than at any other time. There was a current tradition that the Messiah would come at the Passover season. Thus at Passover their hope for the Messiah was kindled to a fever pitch. This was one of the reasons why Pilate moved his troops into Jerusalem at Passover time, just to be ready in case a revolt broke out.

John's sensational rise to prominence also gave pause to the Sanhedrin in Jerusalem. They, too, feared someone who might claim to be Messiah arousing Rome's wrath. (This same fear later led them to crucify Jesus.) So they sought to find out who John really was (John 1:19-28).

Somewhere in the midst of all those crowds, John baptized Jesus, his cousin from Nazareth. We do not know for certain if they had ever known one another. It seems highly likely that not only had they known one another as boys, but that John's parents would have shared with him the strange stories about both his and Jesus' birth. However, their paths had clearly parted during the intervening years.

Following the baptism of Jesus, John identified Him to some of his disciples as "the Lamb of God" (vv. 29,36). This obviously could have been done at any time. The large crowds make a festival time very likely. Further, the emphasis upon the lamb appears to make the Passover the most likely festival (Ex. 12:1-13). It is unlikely that John thundered his announcement to the multitudes as some interpreters make it appear, for there was no serious reaction from the crowd. Instead, it appears that he simply pointed Jesus out to some of the closest of his disciples. The second announcement was only made to two of his disciples. It was they who became the first followers of Jesus (John 1:35-38).

If Jesus' baptism and His first gathering of followers were at Passover, A.D. 28, it was almost certainly at the end of the festival; because following His baptism, Jesus and those early followers headed northward into Galilee (John 1:43). Since they were already at the Jordan, they apparently went northward on the traditional route of that day, following the road up the east side of the Jordan in Perea until they drew near to the Sea of Galilee. There they would have crossed over at the Valley of Jezreel and journeyed northward to His home in Nazareth.

Following a brief interlude at a wedding in Cana, where He went along with His disciples and His mother, Jesus made a visit to Capernaum. There he was also accompanied by the first disciples and His family (John 2:12). We do not know why Jesus visited Capernaum at that time. Probably he was seeking a new home from which He might begin His ministry.

Capernaum is the Greek spelling of an Aramaic name, *Kepher Nahum,* meaning the village of Nahum. We cannot definitely tie the village to the Old Testament prophet of that name, but the tradition of that heritage was obviously there. This would have offered a rich sense of history to Jesus. Further, the site is quite close to the major east-west highway which is just to the north of the Sea of Galilee. The location made travel easier. It offered Jesus a base of operations with exposure to more people, and it did not have all the inherent dangers of Jerusalem or some major Roman city. However, He did not settle there at that time.

We cannot even guess as to what Jesus and those first disciples did in the next few months. He apparently still dwelt with or near His family in Nazareth. It was obviously a time of quietness and consolidation. It has long been supposed that Jesus had waited until His brothers were old enough to assume the family responsibilities before He began His ministry. If that is so, this first year may have been spent close to home to be sure that they were adequately caring for her. However, the days moved swiftly, and before long that first year had passed. The Passover of A.D. 29 drew near. The time for the real ministry was at hand.

Days of Popularity and Outreach

If the first year of Jesus' ministry had been overly quiet, the second began with a bang. Jesus and the disciples came to Jerusalem quietly, probably following the traditional route through Perea along with the multitudes of other pilgrims from Galilee. Upon arriving in Jerusalem, He was overcome with anger at the merchants and moneychangers in the temple. In anger he overturned their tables, driving them and their animals from the precincts (John 2:13-22). This episode raises two significant issues.

The first of these issues relates to the fact that the Synoptic Gospels seem to place this same event in the last week of Jesus' life

(Matt. 21:12-13; Mark 11:15-18; Luke 19:45-48). Numerous commentators consider that the incident is misplaced in John's Gospel and that the Synoptics have it properly located. However, there is no real difficulty in assuming that Jesus performed the same act on two occasions. It is not at all unlikely that Jesus would have begun and ended His ministry with the same kind of protest, making the same kind of demands.

The second issue related to Jesus' cleansing of the temple raises the question of why He did it at all. In the temple of Jerusalem, Gentiles were not allowed into the inner courts, being relegated to the outer areas only. According to Jewish belief of the time, this court of the Gentiles was the only place in all of Jerusalem where a Gentile could appropriately make an approach to the God of Israel. Furthermore, no animal could be offered as a temple sacrifice which was blemished in any way. The priests themselves had to certify that an animal was fit for sacrifice.

Beyond this, the Sanhedrin did not allow Roman coins to be used in the temple precincts. Only Jewish coins could be used there. However, at this time Jewish coins were not legal in the Roman province of Judea. Thus pilgrims to Jerusalem had to change their Roman coins into Jewish ones and then use those to buy their sacrifices. The pilgrims could not be assured that any animal they brought to the temple would be approved by the priests. Thus the safest thing was to buy "preapproved" animals. All of this took space, and the space which was used was the only place in all the city where a Gentile could worship God.

We cannot assume that Jesus' anger was aroused because the priests were stealing. They are not charged with this. What did arouse His anger was the fact that they were more concerned with their orthodoxy than with helping the Gentiles to worship. They were also concerned with personal profit. These concerns had led them to shut the Gentiles out from God. Instead of bringing people to God, their actions forced the Gentiles away. It was that hardhearted callousness which aroused Jesus' wrath.

As we noted in the preceding chapter, it was customary at the great Passover festival for the Sanhedrin to hold public meetings in the temple courtyard. At such times they would become involved in discussions with one another and with passersby regarding the interpretation of the Torah (law). As a boy of twelve, Jesus had become involved in such discussions. Is it possible that He again did such at this Passover in A.D. 29? If not, He at least attracted the attention of the crowds because of His signs and teachings.

If Jesus did not have direct contact with the Sanhedrin at this Passover, His reputation certainly reached their ears. They were quite concerned with knowing what was going on in their city. This concern would always have been heightened at Passover time due to the throngs, the popular expectations of a Messiah, and the inherent volatility of the pilgrims from Galilee. At the Passover, the Roman troops and the Roman governor were always present in Jerusalem in order to be able to deal quickly with any kind of unrest or outbreak, lest it get out of hand.

Thus the Sanhedrin would surely have been quite aware of Jesus and His activities during His visit to the city. What they heard must have aroused curiosity on the part of some. It clearly aroused intense interest on the part of one, Nicodemus. He sought Jesus out to get his information firsthand (John 3:1-21). Coming to Jesus by night was obviously intended to keep down the curiosity of the Jews, the antagonism of the other members of the Sanhedrin, and above all the suspicions of the Romans. They would have been intensely suspicious of any activities which might have looked like sedition or revolution.

We need to remember that this was Passover time, the time of the new moon. The nights would have been dark in Jerusalem. The hillsides outside the city would have been even darker, as there would not even have been house lights there but only the scattered glow of dying camp fires. When we also consider that it was the time of the new moon, we recognize that the darkness would have been quite intense because there would not even have been any moonlight. Thus Nicodemus' journey by night was truly under cover of darkness, intended to prevent anyone being aware of it.

When Jesus left Jerusalem after the Passover, He made a dramatic alteration in the normal pattern of Galilean pilgrims. Although the most direct route from Jerusalem to Galilee was along the water-parting route through the central hill country, this was not normally followed by the Galileans because it led through Samaria. The Samaritans were hated and despised by the Jews, a feeling fully reciprocated by the Samaritans. Thus Galilean pilgrims regularly took the far longer route of going from Jerusalem to Perea through Jericho and across the Jordan. There they would have turned north until they reached the valley of Jezreel where they would again have crossed the Jordan and proceeded on into Galilee.

In His earlier travels, Jesus had followed the traditional route. On this occasion, however, He led His disciples through Samaria. In itself this would have been amazing to them, but when He spoke with a Samaritan woman along the way, they were shocked (John 4:5-42). This was done at Jacob's well near Sychar. The location tied the episode tightly into the common heritage of the two peoples.

The conversation between Jesus and the woman of Samaria showed that Jesus was not only unafraid to break barriers, He aggressively assaulted them. Note how openly He attacked them. First, He went through Samaria itself. Second, He had public dealings with a Samaritan. Third, He publicly talked with a woman. This was simply not done in those days. And fourth, He openly talked with a woman of dubious reputation. The fact that she had come to draw water in the heat of the day showed that she was an outcast to the other women of the village. They would have drawn water in the cool morning or just before dusk in the evening.

By all of His acts, however, Jesus showed that He was breaking several barriers which people had built between themselves. Jesus taught by His actions as well as by His words and miracles. After a brief stay in Samaria, Jesus and the disciples proceeded on their way to Galilee (4:43-45). The journey *through* Samaria had been startling enough. Jesus' stay in Samaria was the most startling thing of all. By that final act in this series of surprising acts, He showed that He was primarily concerned with establishing bridges between peoples, not with observing barriers.

Somewhere about the same time as Jesus' journey through Samaria, John the Baptist was arrested. During Jesus' visit to Jerusalem, John's ministry was centered near Aenon, a distinctly northward move on his part (3:33). He may have moved there to escape the wrath of the Sanhedrin. His blunt attacks on the social ills of his day could not have long been ignored by them. However, that same bluntness became his downfall. Preaching in the territory of Herod Antipas, John attacked Herod for his violation of Jewish law in marrying Herodias, his brother's wife (Luke 3:19-

20). John had also reproved the tetrarch for other lawless acts.

Josephus added that Herod had arrested John because he feared a potential revolution. While John himself was no revolutionary leader, both Herod and John were aware that the tides of nationalism ran quite deep among the Galileans. Because of this, they were always on the verge of a revolt against Rome or anything which smacked of foreign domination. Herod acted with haste, arresting John and transporting him to the far south of Herod's territories. There John was imprisoned in Machaerus, Herod's southern fortress on the eastern side of the Dead Sea. Meanwhile, Jesus began what has come to be called His great Galilean ministry. God's work goes on regardless of what happens to God's workers.

In Galilee Jesus first visited Cana and Nazareth (Luke 4:16; John 4:46). In Nazareth we see Him attending a regular synagogue service on the Sabbath, "as his custom was." In the synagogues of that time, there was usually a locally elected president, but seldom a permanent rabbi. Scripture texts were read by a member of the congregation and then the text was discussed. When a visitor or visiting rabbi was present, he was asked to lead this part of the service. This was the role which Jesus filled at that time (Luke 4:17-27).

The people of Nazareth were amazed at Jesus' wisdom. Their surprise might indicate an awareness that His education at the synagogue school had been interrupted, as it perhaps had been at Joseph's death. On the other hand, they might simply have been amazed that anyone whom they knew could know so much and speak with such ability. At a later time, people were surprised at the authoritative manner with which He spoke. Regardless of the reason, the inhabitants of the little village of Nazareth were offended by Jesus and sought to kill Him. This appears to have been an extreme reaction, but to them what He had done was both heretical and blasphemous. It may have been that this was Nazareth's last chance to have Jesus in their midst.

Jesus did not fight back at His rejection by the people of Nazareth. Instead, He simply moved on, locating His base of operations to Capernaum (Matt. 4:13). From that point on, that little fishing village on the northwest shore of the Sea of Galilee became Jesus' new home. It was from Capernaum that His ministry extended into the surrounding regions. Nazareth had missed its chance.

Days of Teaching and Training

Obviously, Jesus had already done some teaching and performed some miracles. The Gospels note a few of these prior to the beginning of Jesus' residency in Capernaum. However, we have little information regarding those early days of His ministry. At the very least Jesus had attracted some attention, had gathered some of John's followers, and was gaining a reputation both among the people of Galilee and Jerusalem.

After Jesus moved to Capernaum, He began seriously to gather some specific followers who would become His intimate disciples. This had apparently been a pattern established by the prophets of the Old Testament. It was clearly a pattern followed by the rabbinic teachers of Judaism. In some instances, such as that of Simon and Andrew, these were people who had become associated with Jesus as early as the time of John the Baptist. He had sensed their hunger, need, commitment, and surrender to His will and purposes.

With these first fully committed followers, Jesus set forth on a preaching-teaching-healing mission throughout Galilee (Matt. 4:23-25; Mark 1:39; Luke 4:44). He focused His attention on the synagogues. His fame went throughout the region, and people came to hear Him from outside Galilee itself.

His first specific disciples were typical, hard-working laborers of Galilee. Nothing would have attracted much attention to Peter and Andrew or James and John. The latter two may have been persons of some significance. At least they were from a family sufficiently wealthy to have servants (Mark 1:20). This was not common among the fishermen of Galilee. Even so, they were obviously workers on their own part.

However, when Jesus singled out Matthew the publican, otherwise known as Levi, He placed one among His disciples who could have been a stumbling block to other people. Again, as when Jesus went through Samaria, He placed the need to reach people and break down human barriers on a higher plane than the need to have public approval.

Publicans were just as much despised by loyal, patriotic Hebrews as were the Samaritans. Publicans were tax collectors for Rome. They were believed to have sold out their fellowmen to the hated occupying power. They made sure that Rome got her tax dollars, and this was the ultimate humiliation to the occupied people. When Jesus called Matthew, that choice would have immediately alienated large numbers of the Jewish people. It would have been assumed that no one could have been the Jewish Messiah who associated with publican traitors.

Not only did Jesus call a publican to be one of His closest associates, He went to a party with other such people (Matt. 9:10). This act of acceptance on His part alienated the Pharisees and the scribes (Mark 2:16). This may have been the real beginning of open hostility between Jewish leaders and Jesus. At least it accelerated the process. Even John's disciples joined the Pharisees in criticizing Jesus for His open celebration of life (Mark 2:18). They demonstrated their religious devotion with fasting, while Jesus led His disciples in celebration as they enjoyed the good things of life.

This entire year of Jesus' ministry had a Galilean emphasis. It was characterized by the gathering of large crowds wherever He went that they might hear Him. But it was also characterized by the first thunderclouds of opposition. It began to be obvious that all was not going to be peace and light for Jesus. The son of Mary was attracting the attention of some powerful opponents.

The great Galilean ministry was interrupted by Jesus' journey to Jerusalem for "a feast of the Jews" (John 5:1). Some ancient manuscripts say "the feast of the Jews." The former expression could apply to any of the major festivals. The latter one most likely applies either to Passover or Tabernacles. Most commentators interpret this to be a Passover. This would have been the one in A.D. 30. On the other hand, Jewish tradition says that the waters of the pool of Bethesda (Bethzatha) were normally stirred at the time of Tabernacles. If this is true, then this journey of Jesus to Jerusalem would have occurred in the fall of A.D. 30 as I conclude. If this is so, then the third Passover is not mentioned in the Gospels.

During the visit to Jerusalem, Jesus healed a paralytic on the sabbath day. This so aroused the anger of the Pharisees that they "sought . . . to kill him" (John 5:18). The hostility which had been aroused in Galilee was beginning to take concrete form. It is important to note that the opposition toward Jesus at this point was being justified on the basis of His being a lawbreaker. Once again, however, its focus really seems to have been the fact that He was compassionate, being more concerned with the welfare of outcasts (cripples were outcasts from the congregation) than He was with the keeping of the Law. That being so, sabbath controversies continued to follow Him.

Upon His return to Galilee, the Pharisees constantly watched Him for Sabbath violations. He seems to have steadily gone out of His way to confront them at this point (Mark 2:23-24; 3:1-2). The end result of these episodes was a steady hardening of their resolve to destroy Him (Mark 12:14). So great was their hatred that they even consorted with the Herodians, their bitter enemies, in making these plots (Mark 3:6).

It was obvious to Jesus and any careful observer that affairs could not keep on this way. From a human perspective, He knew that He had to have trusted followers to carry on His ministry if or when His enemies decided to crush Him. So He completed the task of appointing the twelve. These were called "apostles" (Mark 3:14; Luke 6:13). This word comes from a Greek word which means to be sent. The term derived from the Latin word with the same meaning is *missionary*. These were the people entrusted with carrying on Jesus' mission.

Although Jesus began seriously to direct His attention to the preparation of the twelve, He also continued to carry on His mission to the multitudes in Galilee. The Sermon on the Mount is apparently typical of His teaching. His powerful words were coupled with deeds of love and mercy. These were even extended to a Roman solider (Luke 7:1-10). Again, such an act had to arouse bitter feelings on the part of the Pharisees and Zealots.

During this time, John the Baptist remained in Herod's clutches in the prison at Machaerus. There he had obviously been receiving word of the ministry of Jesus. From there John had sent some of his disciples to question Jesus: "Are you he who is to come, or shall we look for another?" (Matt. 11:3). Most interpreters have always assumed that John, under the duress of his imprisonment, was beginning to wonder if Jesus were really the Messiah. If that were the issue, it is certainly understandable given what had happened to him and what he apparently had expected from Jesus.

However, if we are correct in believing that John was at least aware of the teachings at Qumran, his question may have had a different focus. At least some of the people of the Qumran community were looking for *two* messiahs. They were looking for a king from David's line and a priest from Aaron's. If John was aware of that, he might have been asking Jesus: "Are you the only one who is coming or is there going to be another in addition to you?" Such an understanding would be far more in line with the portrait we were earlier given of the bold prophet of the Jordan. Jesus' answer might make more sense as well. John had already identified Jesus as Messiah, the King. Jesus pointed out to His disciples that He was also carrying on a priestly ministry. He was both King and Priest.

Following that episode, Jesus continued His ministry in Galilee (Luke 8:1-3). Once again, we see Him breaking the barriers which the society of that day had established. Not only did He carry the twelve with Him, but He was also accompanied by some women disciples as well. This simply was not done by a rabbi. However, Jesus numbered among His closest followers "Mary, . . . Joanna, . . . and Susanna" (vv. 2-3). It is worth noting that one of these, Joanna, was the wife of Herod's steward. His disciples came from unexpected places.

At the same time, the opposition continued to be active (Mark 3:22; Matt. 12:22). In the face of this opposition, Jesus' mother and brothers sought to get to Him, probably trying to deliver Him from real and anticipated attacks (Mark 3:31-32). Jesus, however, would not let either the hatred of His enemies or the love of His family turn Him aside from His mission.

As we note the rising tide of opposition during Jesus' Galilean ministry, we should note that this was not universally true. At least one synagogue president, Jairus, sought Jesus' help. Even though this was motivated by the serious illness of his daughter, he recognized the compassion of Jesus and sought His help at that critical time (Luke 8:41). Also, during that time, the multitudes who sought to be with Jesus forced Him to journey back and forth across the Sea of Galilee on several occasions, simply to escape them. Jesus also at that time made what was apparently His final visit to Nazareth (Mark 6:1-6). Instead of facing either welcome or opposition, Jesus almost seems to have faced indifference. They knew Him. They could identify His heritage; they expected nothing from Him. That is precisely what they got.

At that point He once again set forth on a tour of Galilee. This time, however, He sent His disciples on a ministry apart from Him. He had trained them, and now they had to see what they could do without Him (Luke 9:1-6). His commission to them was quite simple. "You have received what you did not pay for. Give without expecting recompense" (Matt. 10:8, author). This was truly a Great Commission.

At some time during this era, Herod had executed John the Baptist (Mark 6:21-29). However, he was not altogether conscienceless about it. When He heard about Jesus and His ministry, Herod fearfully assumed that John had come back to life. He was wrong about that. However, what he was right about was that you cannot silence God's message by executing God's messengers.

The one miracle of Jesus' Galilean ministry which is recorded in all four Gospels is the feeding of the five thousand (Matt. 14:13-21; Mark 6:30-44; Luke 9:10-17; John 6:1-13). This was clearly done at the time of the Passover, probably in A.D. 31. The multitude had come to hear Him and had outrun their provisions. Realizing their need, Jesus set about to meet it with His power and their meager resources. For our purposes, two features stand out. First, in preparation, they sat down in companies of fifty. This sounds like an army.

Second, when they had been fed, the multitude sought to take Jesus and force Him to become their king (John 6:15). How wonderful it would be to have a king who could feed an army without carrying provisions, heal the wounded, and raise the dead, even the disciples seem to have been swept up in this. So Jesus had to send them and the crowd away in order to break up the coronation (Matt. 14:22-23). That was the beginning of the end of the Galilean ministry of Jesus.

The crowds followed Jesus for a little while longer (John 6:22-71). However, they had discovered two things about Him which were steadily confirmed. He was not going to be what they wanted. Rather, they were going to have to accept Him or reject Him as He was. Being unable to control Him or use Him for their own purposes, they went on their way to find some other Messiah (John 6:66).

Almost wistfully, Jesus sought to see if the twelve were also going to turn away, bluntly asking, "'Do you also wish to go away?'" (John 6:67). But they didn't. Obviously they had not understood much of what He had done and less of what He had said. However, they recognized that He was what they needed as well as what they wanted. So they clung to Him. Yet the days of throngs and multitudes had passed. A darkening shadow comes over the Gospel record from this point onward.

Jesus' Ministry Outside of the Land of Promise

As tensions built up around His ministry in Galilee during the latter part of His early ministry, Jesus made several journeys into regions outside of Galilee and Judea. His purposes seem to have been at least three-fold. First, He was apparently seeking to escape temporarily from the press of the crowds and their varying moods, demands, and expectations. Second, He also seems to have been avoiding a showdown with the Sanhedrin at least until a time of His own choosing. Third, being quite aware of the interest of Pilate in keeping the peace at whatever price, He also appears to have been avoiding any kind of direct confrontation with Rome. As He later said to Pilate, " 'My kingship is not of this world' " (John 18:36).

Added to these purposes we may also see an inherent desire on Jesus' part to minister to others outside the nation of Israel. Primarily, though, Jesus appears to have been seeking release from immediate stress. This may have been as much for the disciples as for Himself. However, He and the disciples seem to have needed a regrouping, a reassessment, and the re-creation of their spiritual and physical resources.

Two regions were available to Jesus for retreats from the territory controlled by Pilate with some delegated assistance from the Sanhedrin (Judea) as well as from that controlled by Herod Antipas (Galilee, Perea, and Iturea). The first of these were the regions of the Decapolis and Gaulanitis, both being part of what is more familiarly but less precisely known as northern Transjordan. This territory had been assigned to Philip, who served as tetrarch there.

Philip's region of authority had not been a part of the original promised land. Further, many of the cities there, particularly those of the Decapolis, had been either settled by Greeks or they had so moved into them that the Jewish influence was relatively insignificant. This meant that when Jesus was there He was away from the immediate threats and pressures which were so continually present in the other parts of the land. For Jesus, these regions were readily available, as they touched upon the eastern shore of the Sea of Galilee. Among the other places Jesus visited was Gerasa in the region of Gadara where Jesus healed the demoniac (Mark 5:1-20).

The second region into which Jesus and His disciples went was designated as the "district" or "region" of Tyre and Sidon (Matt. 15:21; Mark 7:24). This territory was under the direct control of the Roman governor of Syria. As such, it had no direct ties with any of the regions of Jewish influence. If there were any questions as to why Jesus went into such a place, Mark's careful record of the fact that when He left there He went to the Sea of Galilee by going through the region of the Decapolis shows that He was avoiding the territory under the control of Herod Antipas.

He apparently made a brief visit across the sea into Galilee but quickly retired again to Philip's territory, crossing the border into Bethsaida (Mark 8:22). From there He turned northward to Caesarea Philippi, still carefully avoiding Herod's territories (v. 27). It was apparently somewhere in that region that Jesus was transfigured (9:2-4). The fact that Peter suggested making three booths may indicate that this was near the time of the Feast of Booths, probably in A.D. 31.

After that retreat into Philip's territory, Jesus came back into Galilee, stopping first at Capernaum. It was there that they paid the temple tax (Matt. 17:24-27). This was levied for the support of the temple in Jerusalem and was supposed to be paid by every Jew. It was normally collected at the Passover time. It appears that the tax collectors for the Sanhedrin began this process in the outlying regions about six weeks before Passover. However, it also appears that those whose taxes were missed at that time were asked to pay later, and the final ingathering was sent to Jerusalem at the time of the Feast of Booths.

In any case, the Feast of Tabernacles was at hand in A.D. 31 (John 7:2). Jesus was urged to go to Jerusalem but at first refused to do so. At least, He did not wish to do so openly. The whole land was apparently aroused by His words and deeds, but He was still not ready for the great confrontation. When His friends and family had left for the journey to Jerusalem He made a secret and hurried trip by way of Samaria (v. 10). The point at issue was that Jesus had not yet wished to be a victim of someone else's plan. He stayed in control of His own fate.

However, away from the pressures and advice of friends and companions, He finally decided that the time had come to begin to force the issue. Luke described it simply; Jesus' "face was set toward Jerusalem" (9:53). From that point on, the story builds in intensity. Note that Jesus once again did not follow the regular pilgrim route. Instead, He journeyed through Samaria. This was more quickly done, as it was shorter, but it also allowed Him to avoid the publicity of the crowds of excited pilgrims from Galilee. With the transition in His purpose, Jesus' ministry took on a new tone. His later ministry had begun.

Note

1. A. T. Robertson, *A Harmony of the Gospels* (New York: Harper and Brothers, 1950).

15
The Later Ministry

While the early years of Jesus' ministry had some moments of real danger and many times of great stress, they were generally a time of preparation. For Jesus, those years gave Him the opportunity of facing the ultimate issue of what "kind" of Messiah He was going to be. This was first faced at the time of His temptation (Matt. 4:1-11). However, that was not the last time that He had to deal with this issue. His victory at that time was only temporary. Following the description of that victory, Luke asserted simply that "the devil . . . departed from him until an opportune time" (Luke 4:13).

In addition to His own preparation, Jesus also used those early days to prepare the people of Judea and Galilee for dealing with Him. He made sure that they saw Him, heard Him, heard about Him, and were forced to consider who He was and what He was about. At times, He acted just as any of them did. At other times, He did the startling and unexpected. He intentionally crossed barriers which His people believed were uncrossable, either by God or by God's people Israel. He refused to be what they expected Him to be and sought to force them to see Him as He really was.

Jesus also used those early days to prepare His disciples. He dealt with them in the midst of crowds. He also withdrew with them so that they could be alone with God. He sought to help them begin to learn how to function on their own without Him. That preparation, however, was intensified as He moved into this latter part of His ministry.

It is at this point that we pick up our narrative. Jesus is portrayed in the New Testament as being in control of His own life and own fate. He chose the time when the Jewish leaders were finally forced to act. They ultimately had to decide either to accept His words or reject Him. From the midpoint of His ministry on, Jesus began to apply pressure to His opponents. He began to pressure them to make a decision. They were forced to see that He would not go away and leave them alone. From this point on, the intensity of the Gospel records increases, especially in Luke and John. Perhaps the best way to see this growing pressure is to follow the words of Luke.

When the days drew near for him to be received up, he set his face to go to Jerusalem. . . . his face was set toward Jerusalem. . . . As they were going along the road, . . . as they went on their way, . . . As he went away from there, . . . He went on his way . . . journeying toward Jerusalem. . . . "I must go on my way today and tomorrow and the day following; for it cannot be that a prophet should perish away from Jerusalem." . . . On the way to Jerusalem . . . he said to them, "Behold, we are going up to Jerusalem," . . . As he drew near to Jericho, . . . He entered Jericho and was passing through. . . . he went on ahead, going up to Jerusalem. . . . When he drew near to Bethphage and Bethany, . . . As he was now drawing near, at the descent of the Mount of Olives, . . . he drew near and saw the city . . . And he entered the temple . . . (9:51,53,57; 10:38; 11:53; 13:22,33; 17:11; 18:31,35; 19:1,28-29,37,41,45).

These words focus upon a major issue of the later ministry of Jesus. He was on the move, going up to Jerusalem, and pressing toward the final goal of His life. Jesus chose the time. He forced a decision from the Jewish leaders, as well as from everyone else who was involved with Him. He still does. He did not and does not allow people to ignore Him. Let us then examine this deliberate march by Jesus toward the holy city—and ultimately toward the cross.

The Final Autumn

The Feast of Booths in A.D. 31 found the crowds in Jerusalem seeking for Jesus and debating about who He really was (John 7:11-12). We need to be careful in understanding who it really was leading the opposition against Him. This is set forth in the words: "for fear of the Jews no one spoke openly of him" (v. 13). However, it was also Jews who were talking privately about Him and were afraid of other Jews. Thus, this is not a blanket condemnation of all Jews but of the Jewish leaders, the Sanhedrin and those closely related to it.

In the midst of the feast, Jesus appeared at the temple and began to speak to the crowds who were gathered there (v. 14). Jesus informed His hearers that His life was in danger, but they did not yet believe Him (vv. 19-20). However, in one way or another many began to accept His words concerning this threat (v. 25). They may even have become aware of some of the growing intrigue on the part of the Jewish leaders, culminating in the Sanhedrin's sending some officers from the temple police to arrest Jesus (v. 32). The temple police found Jesus not in hiding but openly teaching in the temple. As they listened, however, they discovered no grounds for arresting Him (v. 46).

Through all of this, the multitudes continued the debate as to Jesus' identity. Their views went all the way from some thinking that He was demon-possessed to others believing that He was the Christ (vv. 20,27). The basic point is that the multitude was confused by Him and about Him (vv. 40-43). He was not the kind of Messiah which they had expected. Neither was He from the place that a prophet normally came. Further, the things which He did and said were equally surprising.

The Sanhedrin itself entered into that debate, but privately. At one of those meetings, Nicodemus sought to defend Jesus from unfair and illegal condemnation. For his defense, however, he himself was severely criticized by his fellow members of the council (vv. 47-52). It is important to note that this was the first open support for Jesus from anyone with any official capacity.

In the midst of all of this turmoil at and around the activities of the feast, Jesus made one of His more startling pronouncements. The Feast of Booths was one of the more joyous festivals in the Jewish religious calendar because it celebrated the abundance of the harvest. As a part of its ritual, the priests daily poured water upon the altar, acknowledging by that act that without God's gift of water there would have been no harvest. On the last day of the feast, this ceremony was even more dramatic because the priests circled the altar seven times before pouring out their water pots upon the altar. Jesus took this as an opportunity to try to help the people understand who He really was.

"On the last day of the feast, the great day, Jesus stood up and proclaimed, 'If any one thirst, let him come to me and drink'" (v. 37). This was a claim which could not be misunderstood. He obviously was claiming to be God's gift to the people of Israel. It was

He who would bring ultimate life and fruitfulness. That was a claim which could hardly be misunderstood. It could be disbelieved, but not misunderstood.

Furthermore, each evening throughout the feast, the priests brought out four great menorah into the temple courts, and these were lighted for the joyous celebration of the people. Though the nights in Jerusalem were normally quite dark, during this feast the temple mount would be aglow during the night and shed its light throughout the city from that mountain height. Against that backdrop, with light from the temple scattering the darkness of the city, Jesus proclaimed, "'I am the light of the world; he who follows me will not walk in darkness'" (8:12). Again, this could hardly be misunderstood, even though it, too, could be disbelieved. Jesus clearly used the events of that joyous celebration to help the people to understand who He really was. They were debating His identity. He gave them guidance.

Having failed in their attempt to arrest Jesus, the Jewish leaders next sought to destroy His ministry in other ways. They began to attack Him personally, calling Him both a Samaritan and one who was demon-possessed (v. 48). Such methods have been used before and since to destroy the work of those trying to alter the paths of life.

Not content with these personal attacks, the leaders of the Jews also sought to entrap Him by His own compassion. They brought to Him a woman who had been caught in the act of adultery, a crime which was punishable by stoning, to see what He would do with her (vv. 1-11). (I am quite aware that this is not in the oldest manuscripts of John's Gospel, but it sounds so much like Jesus and like the Jewish leaders that I do not question its authenticity.) It is obvious that the leaders were prejudiced both against the woman and Jesus. We note that they did not bring the man involved, whom they would have also captured. It appears that they had chosen to let him go.

The priests' concern was straightforward: destroy Jesus. They thought that if He agreed with the stoning of the woman the people would no longer believe in His compassion. On the other hand, they thought that if He let her go, then they could have accused Him of rejecting the Old Testament law and so destroyed His credibility. However, once again Jesus outsmarted them. He was compassionate and forgiving, but he also upheld the law. In the face of His command, the leaders departed quickly and quietly. Their defeat, however, only intensified their anger toward Him because of their public humiliation. Having failed to destroy His reputation, they next sought to destroy Him physically. Laying in wait for Him, they prepared to stone Him. Priests, Pharisees, and Sadducees—all those entrusted with upholding justice and righteousness in Israel—were about to become a lynch mob (v. 59). Jesus, however, avoided them and left the temple in safety.

Jesus' victories and the Sanhedrin's defeats had merely further solidified their opposition. In addition, a new step in their hostility had been taken. They had obviously decided that Jesus had to go. His presence was no longer going to be tolerated by the members of the Sanhedrin.

Since the Sanhedrin had failed to destroy Jesus Himself, their next step was an attempt to intimidate those who believed in Him. Shortly thereafter Jesus healed a blind man (9:1-41). By making a poultice of clay and anointing the man's eyes, Jesus deliberately broke the Sabbath Law. This was an act of healing, not simply a spoken word. Such an act on the Sabbath was punishable by death. However, this time instead of attacking Jesus, the leaders attacked the man and his parents. Knowing the ultimate cost for themselves, the parents of the man refused to take a stand, but the man himself would not be intimidated. As a consequence he was excommunicated (v. 34). Jesus was becoming dangerous to know and even more dangerous to follow.

At the same time, Jesus' teachings became even more frustrating to those who heard Him. His message on the good shepherd, probably an interpretation of Psalm 23, gave at least two parts of His audience great difficulties (10:1-21). His references to the "hireling" would most likely have been heard by the common people as referring to the high priest, for this was precisely what he had become, a hireling of Rome. It surely would have antagonized the priests and Sanhedrin because they would all have felt the sting of those words. On the other hand, Jesus' words concerning His death and resurrection led to the judgment on the part of some that He was either insane or demon-possessed. This conclusion was hard for others to accept in the light of His miracles of healing.

Apparently, sometime after the Feast of Booths, Jesus sent seventy disciples on another preaching mission (Luke 10:1-24). The most significant thing here from the historian's standpoint is that

Jesus obviously still had a significant number of committed followers. Further, these were committed enough to be willing to leave their homes and businesses to follow and serve Him. Although opposition to Jesus was building, some were still willing to face it with Him. Though debate raged as to whom He was and what He was about, some had clearly made up their minds about Him and remained unswayed by the uncertainties of others.

Yet we must not allow the commitment of some people to obscure the fact that the opposition to Jesus was growing in intensity. Furthermore, throughout these latter days, Jesus appears not only not to have done anything to ease this hostility but to have actually sought to force it upon those who opposed Him. When a lawyer sought to test Jesus' knowledge and judgment, as well as to demonstrate his own spiritual attainments, Jesus bluntly insulted him and punctured his pride by making a despised Samaritan the hero of His parable of compassion (vv. 25-37).

Further, it was during these days in Judea that Jesus made His temporary headquarters in the home of Mary and Martha in Bethany (vv. 38-42). Jesus always seems to have felt more at home with the common people than with the religious experts. At the same time, Jesus did not avoid friendships with the Pharisees. He simply wanted them to see themselves as they really were. Thus He confronted them with their own folly (11:37-54). We need to recognize that He saw their goodness—and they were very good! Jesus also saw that they did have a problem of the heart, and He sought to force them to see that.

In addition, Jesus continued to teach the crowds who gathered around Him. Yet in so doing, He continually refused to be what they wanted Him to be (12:13-15). While eagerly seeking disciples, Jesus never lowered the demands He made upon those who would follow Him. They had to accept Him as He was. This is still true.

We have noted that the Galileans were especially volatile. Pilate, the Roman governor, had sought to raise the money to pay for an aqueduct to bring water to the temple by taking money from the temple treasury. This aroused the populace, and as a result some of the Galilean pilgrims in the temple were slaughtered by Pilate and his soldiers. This word quickly reached Jesus and His followers, and Jesus referred to it in one of His sermons (13:1-3). These rising tensions in Jerusalem had to create problems for Jesus. The Sanhedrin had to become even more concerned with preventing anything which might lead to an uprising with which Rome would have to deal. As the tensions grew, the warmth of autumn gave way to the approaching desolate cold winter. Bitter winds began to blow throughout the land. It was growing cold in Judea.

The Final Winter

The depressing cold of the Judean winters was alleviated for the Hebrew people by the celebration of the Feast of Dedication or the Feast of Lights. This was the joyous commemoration of the rededication of the temple following its restoration under the leadership of Judas Maccabeus. The cold damp weather of Judea did not in any way hinder the exuberance of this celebration.

As should have been expected with Jesus still in Judea, He appeared again in the temple during this festival (John 10:22-39). Once again the Jewish leaders sought a means whereby they might legally arrest Him. Some of them directed a conversation specifically to the issue of His identity. Their questions were more blunt than ever before. In response to them, however, His answers were the same.

Finally, lest they fail to hear and understand Him clearly, Jesus said both abruptly and unequivocally, *"I and the Father are one'"* (v. 30, italics mine). This claim was more than their religious sensibilities could stand, so these defenders of the faith took up stones to kill Jesus. He had again driven them to the point of the loss of self-control. So once again the Jewish high court became a lynch mob. To these men, for anyone to claim to be identical with God was the height of blasphemy.

Jesus challenged them to judge Him on the basis of His deeds, not His words. This, however, they refused to do. In the meantime they must have calmed down a bit and recognized that they did not have the authority to carry out a death sentence under Roman law. However, they did seek to arrest Him. Once again, He eluded them and departed from the temple, Jerusalem, and Judea (v. 40). The long cold winter settled upon the land. By our reckoning, the year changed from A.D. 31 to 32, the year of destiny.

Jesus would have found greater safety from the wrath of the Sanhedrin if He had gone northward to Galilee. At least He was a Galilean and would have found refuge there. That, however, would have put Him too far away from Jerusalem, and He had come south specifically to be in that region. So Jesus settled for simply retiring across the Jordan and going into Perea for a season.

The region Jesus chose for this period of retreat was the same one in which John the Baptist had begun his ministry. As we noted then, it was on the major east-west highway leading up to Jerusalem and was well traveled by both merchants and pilgrims. The word of Jesus' ministry there once again spread and curious crowds sought Him out. Although in Perea Jesus was away from the territory under the direct control of the high priest and his cohorts, Pharisaic representatives of the Sanhedrin kept Him under observation (Luke 15:1-2). We need to note that Jesus, while engaging in direct confrontation with the Pharisees, had not shut them out. He still associated with them when they allowed Him to do so (14:1). It is clear that while He was their enemy, they were not His enemies. At the same time, Jesus never lowered the demands He made of those who would become His followers (16:14-17).

However, some of the Pharisees do seem to have been friends with Jesus. During Jesus' Perean ministry, Herod's anger was aroused. He may once again have suspected that Jesus was John the Baptist come back from the dead. However, some of the Pharisees warned Jesus of Herod's growing anger, urging Him to flee for His life (13:31). We may take their warning at face value. They may really have been concerned for Jesus' welfare. However, some interpreters suggest that they were simply trying to deceive Jesus, with the purpose of getting Him back into Judea and therefore under the jurisdiction of the Sanhedrin. Regardless of which is true, Jesus was not impressed. It is clear that He was going to remain in complete control of the issue of His fate. He expected to die in Jerusalem, and it was only going to happen when He was ready for it (v. 34).

During that winter, word came to Jesus of the serious illness of His friend Lazarus, the brother of Mary and Martha (John 11:1-3). Jesus tarried a few days longer in Perea before responding and then announced to His disciples that He was ready to return to Judea for the sake of His friends in Bethany (v. 8). The disciples tried to dissuade Him because of the danger there.

However, when it became obvious that Jesus had decided to return, Thomas became the leader of the disciples and boldly said, "'Let us also go, that we may die with him'" (v. 16). Twice in the preceding six months the Jewish leaders of Jerusalem had sought to stone Jesus. Within four months they succeeded in having Him crucified. Thomas' assessment of the danger was not pessimistic but realistic. Yet with more courage and greater boldness than any of the other disciples, he was willing to face that danger with Jesus.

Upon His return to Bethany, Jesus again revealed His humanity by grieving with His friends (v. 35). He also responded with power by raising Lazarus from the dead. This was an act of compassion for His friends. The leaders in Jerusalem also perceived it as an act in the line of prophetic-symbolic acts. By that act, Jesus made a bold claim that He was the author of life and death. It was an announcement that they could receive life from His hands, but they would not.

In immediate response to His act, the Jewish elders once again met to decide how to respond to Jesus. It was at that time that the final decision was made that Jesus had to die (vv. 45-53). No longer did they debate if He should die. From that point on, the only issue for the Sanhedrin was where and when Jesus would die.

The Final Spring

Jesus, however, was not yet ready to die. With hindsight, we know that He had determined that the time of His death would be the forthcoming Passover. Therefore He led His disciples on one last trek through the neighboring regions in order to avoid the Sanhedrin's wrath. So He made His way to Ephraim in northern Judea, Samaria, and southern Galilee and there apparently joined the thronging pilgrims journeying from Galilee through Perea to Jerusalem for the Passover celebration (John 11:54; Luke 17:11).

Two events along the way to Jerusalem stand out as moments of sadness for Jesus. The disciples clearly realized that there was something different about Jesus. They knew that a crisis was coming, but they were blinded to what was going on. Thus expecting the kingdom to be established soon, James and John sought to out-maneuver the others and gain the places of chief responsibility for themselves (Mark 10:35-45). They were clearly assisted in this by their mother (Matt. 20:20).

The other sad event of this journey was the visit of the rich young ruler. He was apparently one of the Jewish leaders who believed that Jesus really had something to offer. By addressing Jesus as "'*Good* teacher,'" he caught everyone's attention (Mark 10:17, italics mine). For the very orthodox, that adjective was reserved for God alone. Yet, even though he recognized something unique and godly about Jesus, he found Jesus' demands too strenuous and turned away. Jesus allowed him to go, proceeding on his own chosen path.

Finally, the journey south through Perea ended, and Jesus and His disciples, together with their fellow pilgrims, turned westward. They forded the Jordan and came to Jericho.

The throngs of Galilean pilgrims brought a sort of built-in tension with them. The excitement of Passover was always significant, particularly when it was coupled with the then current hope for the coming of the Messiah at Passover time. When all of that was added to the fact that Jesus was in their midst and their awareness of the growing tensions between Him and the Sanhedrin, the atmosphere must have been almost like a powder keg waiting for a spark.

The first spark was not long in coming. Blind Bartimaeus, hearing that Jesus was near, gave Him a messianic title, calling Him " 'Son of David' " (Mark 10:47). That would have been shock enough in that expectant crowd, but the real surprise came when Jesus allowed him to say it. By not denying that title, Jesus accepted it. The Sanhedrin surely heard of that event quite quickly.

Passing on through Jericho, Jesus saw the eagerness of Zacchaeus, a publican, and invited Himself to dinner (Luke 19:1-6). That, too, was noted by the crowd. It was just as certainly noted by the Sanhedrin's spies. The tensions were rising to a fever pitch. To heighten them even further, Jesus told a parable about a ruler whose citizens sought to have his authority denied to him (vv. 13-14). This was a clear reference to one of the sons of Herod the Great. Although this was not the main point of the parable, the people were reminded that they had once before taken matters into their own hands to determine those who would rule over them. This was the kind of thing which the Jewish rulers could not allow to happen again. Jesus had clearly moved on the attack. He was going to force the Sanhedrin and high priest to act. Everything He was doing was leading the people to believe "that the kingdom of God was to appear *immediately*" (v. 11, italics mine).

Meanwhile, in Jerusalem tensions were also building. Even before Jesus arrived, people were beginning to ask for Him (John 11:56). At the same time, the chief priests and Pharisees were already trying to find someone who would let them know where Jesus would be staying in the city whenever He arrived. They were at last prepared to arrest Him (v. 57).

However, although Jesus was seriously pressuring His opponents, He was still not ready for the final confrontation. So when He drew near Jerusalem, He stopped at Bethany to stay with Mary, Martha, and Lazarus. Tensions continued to build. Not only were the people wondering about Jesus, they were talking about Lazarus, newly raised from the dead. This, too, was a threat to the Sanhedrin. To prevent the situation from getting any further out of hand, they decided that Lazarus also had to die again (12:10-11). The warm spring of Judea was giving way to the hot wrath of the Jewish leaders. Not only was Jesus dangerous to know, it was dangerous to have been ministered to by Him.

The Final Week

The last week of Jesus' life could be described as being the intersection of several different lines, all of which met at Jerusalem at that particular time. First, there was the matter of the Jewish religious observance. They had been observing the Passover ever since their deliverance from Egypt in the exodus experience. For the faithful, this celebration looked back to God's great deliverance and forward to a new deliverance; all built upon trust in Him. Passover had been celebrated for more than a thousand years. The second line which led to Jerusalem was that of Old Testament messianism. Often misunderstood or hardly understood, the hope for a coming Messiah was the product of centuries of prophetic preaching. Many had claimed to be the one, but the faithful were still looking for Him.

The third line which led to Jerusalem at the Passover of A.D. 32 was the life of Jesus Himself. Threatened shortly after birth, His life had been preserved by God until He had arrived at Jerusalem—the place and time of His own choosing. A fourth line was that of the Jewish religious officials. Having once sought for freedom from any foreign entanglements, for many of them their only concern had become the keeping of their positions of power. This could only be done by collaborating with Rome. That meant getting along with Rome's representative, Pontius Pilate. Their concerns were no longer so much with what was right as with what was expedient.

The final strand which met at Jerusalem at that time was the Roman domination, exemplified by Pontius Pilate. Representing the world's most powerful government, he trembled at the thought of displeasing His masters at the center of the empire. He had been brought to power as the protégé of Sejanus, the chief of staff of Tiberius Caesar. However, Sejanus had been executed as a traitor in October of A.D. 31, and this brought fear to anyone who had been his loyal supporter. It also brought terror to the heart of any of Caesar's officers because if the powerful appointee in Rome could be executed so could any of the lesser ones.

It was at such a time and in such a place that Jesus approached Jerusalem on the first day of His last week. The throngs were awaiting Him, ready to acclaim Him Messiah, King, offspring of David. The Sanhedrin and Roman officials were also almost surely waiting for Him as well. We know that the Sanhedrin was ready and waiting. The Roman governor was always present at the Passover, accompanied with his troops ready to deal ruthlessly and immediately with any threat to Rome. From what we know of Pilate, it is inconceivable that he would not have been aware of all of Jesus' movements in the preceding few weeks. He would certainly have been waiting for His arrival at Jerusalem at that Passover. What has come to be known as the triumphal entry was carried out under the watchful eyes of everyone and anyone who had anything to gain or lose by Jesus' actions.

In the manner by which He entered the city, Jesus once again demonstrated that He was in charge of the situation. He came into the city, accepting the acclaim of the crowds and refusing the demands of the Pharisees that He calm His followers down (John 12:39-40). At the same time, entering into the city on a donkey spoke clearly to the Jewish rulers and the Roman governor. Conquerors come riding on white stallions, not upon donkeys. Rome might have been forced to act if Jesus had come on a stallion, but He entered Jerusalem on a donkey. That was the way a pilgrim entered. Thus Rome's hands were tied. Pilate would have made himself a laughingstock to have reacted with force to Jesus' entry.

The chief priests and Pharisees understood Jesus' act. They remembered the prophecy of Zechariah (9:9). Jesus' deliberate act of riding into Jerusalem on a donkey prevented Rome from acting, and yet it was a clear claim to the Jewish religious leaders that He was God's Messiah. These latter ones thus had to take Him seriously. They could not ignore Him. Jesus had seized the offensive and was backing them into a corner.

Following the events of this first day, Jesus went back out to Bethany (Mark 11:11). He was still making it a point to spend the nights in a place where He was secure among friends. He knew that the Sanhendrin, at this point, would not dare act against Him in the midst of the throngs, but they could act at night under cover of darkness unless He were in a place where they could not easily get at Him.

We are not wholly clear as to what events took place on which days for the remaining days of that week. Jesus apparently came back into the city each day, while spending the nights at Bethany. During that time, Jesus again entered into the temple and drove out those who bought and sold (vv. 15-18; note the discussion in the previous chapter as to the relationship between the Synoptics and John as they record these events). This, too, was an act which the Sanhedrin could not misunderstand. Jesus was claiming to be the Lord of the temple.

At the Passover celebrations, the population of Jerusalem was swelled not only by pilgrims from Galilee but by pilgrims who had come from all over the world. These would have been both Jews of the Diaspora as well as people of Gentile birth who had become converts to Judaism. In addition, others may have come who were simply seeking to find out more about the God of Israel. Among these were some Greeks who, after hearing about Jesus, wanted to see Him for themselves (John 12:20-22). They were apparently asking for permission because they knew (or had learned) that not all Jewish teachers would welcome the opportunity to talk with Gentiles.

On another day, Jesus was directly confronted by some representatives of the Sanhedrin. We have noted that the Sanhedrin was regularly in the temple during the Passover, teaching and answering questions. As a part of that process, apparently some of them came to Jesus, seeking to point out to the people that Jesus had no authority to teach or to act as He was doing (Mark 11:27-28). To them, the issue of authority was foundational. Jesus, however, dealt with them strangely. Instead of answering their query, He asked them a question: "'Was the baptism of John from heaven or from men?'" (v. 30). Both Jesus and the elders knew what He was getting at. If they agreed it was divine, He would ask why they had not accepted it. Yet if they claimed it was only human, they would fall into disfavor with the people who had followed John, so they refused to answer. They were not willing to take a stand on either side of the issue.

For Jesus that was just the point. Jesus apparently would have been willing to enter into a discussion with the Jewish leaders if they had been serious enough to make a decision, but they were not. They were not looking for truth. They were merely trying to entangle Him. So He did not waste His time dealing with them further (v. 33). Their defeat embarrassed them and further inflamed their hatred. Jesus, however, was still on the offensive. Although they had tried, Jesus had not allowed His opponents to seize the initiative.

The Sanhedrin next sought to trip Him up by sending representatives of other groups who were hostile to Jesus. In fact, they were now so determined to destroy Him that they appear to have become almost frantic. The next deputation which approached Jesus to question Him was made up of Pharisees and Herodians (12:13). A fascinating sidelight to this episode is the fact that the Pharisees and Herodians were normally bitter enemies. Their enmity stretched back to Herod the Great's attacks upon the Pharisees in the latter days of his life. Yet their common hatred of Jesus and desperation to discredit Him led them to unite for a time.

Jewish hatred of the Romans was palpable at any season. It normally reached fever pitch at Passover time. For the Jews, the most hateful evidence of Roman suzerainty over them was the payment of Roman taxes. Against that background, Jesus' enemies sought to discredit Him with the question of the legality of a Jew paying Roman taxes (12:14). They had figured that any answer He gave would be to their advantage. Agreement would alienate the multitudes who followed Him. Disagreement would leave Him open to charges of sedition by Rome. Once again, Jesus outsmarted His opponents. Holding up a silver coin imprinted with Caesar's image, He retorted, " 'Render to Caesar the things that are Caesar's, and to God the things that are God's' " (v. 17). Amazed by His shrewdness and their defeat, that group also slunk away. But they, too, had been made more bitter by His victory. Public humiliation was something which they could not stand.

The Sanhedrin still had other arrows in their quiver. Next came the Sadducees with a question about the resurrection (Luke 20:27-

40). Jesus also easily put them to an embarrassed if not hostile silence. Because of their disagreement with the Sadducees over the resurrection issue, the Pharisees found themselves in the position of having to agree with Jesus. Yet they still wished to discredit Him. Once again, He showed His knowledge of the Scriptures and of the Pharisaic teachings when He identified the greatest commandment for them (Matt. 22:34-40). However, taking a second verse from the Old Testament law, He pointed up their failure in keeping the whole law. They had rightly emphasized love of God while ignoring the love of God's people.

At this point Jesus apparently tired of His enemies playing theological and political games with Him. In anger He lashed out at the self-righteous attitudes of the scribes and Pharisees (23:1-39). While He condemned both their heartlessness and self-righteousness, He commended them for the good things which they did in meticulously keeping the law.

Jesus did not spend all of His time during that last week in debate with the Jewish leaders. He also spent some time continuing to teach His disciples. He had to remind them that they, too, were concerned with the wrong issues. Instead of being preoccupied with the cataclysmic end of the world, Jesus reminded them that their task was to carry the gospel to all nations (Mark 13:4,10). He also reminded His disciples of the difficult times which were coming upon them (vv. 11-13). Jesus continued to teach His disciples to the very end (Matt. 24:43 to 25:46).

For Jesus and His disciples it was a week of intense pressure. They should have suspected that the crisis was coming, but He clearly knew that it was. Yet He did not allow the coming crisis to turn Him aside from His basic purposes with them. In fact, its approach seems to have provided the awareness that this was the last real chance He might have with them. For Jesus, these last days were His final opportunity to get them ready to go on without Him. So His major focus throughout these days was upon His followers, not upon His enemies.

Thus the days dwindled down. The shadow of the cross loomed ever larger. The ministry of Jesus was drawing to an end. But was it really the end or a new beginning?

16
The End and the Beginning

The central focus of the proclamation of the New Testament and the early church was the death, burial, and resurrection of Jesus of Nazareth. It is also the central focus of the history of the divine drama of redemption. Interpreters sometimes disagree as to precisely when that drama began. Some suggest its origins are to be found in the garden of Eden or the flood. Others suggest the origin may be found in the call of Abraham or the covenant of Sinai. No student of Christianity doubts that the central and culminating point of that redemptive plan can be found at the cross and the empty tomb.

We could wish that we had more external information concerning the events of Jesus' death. We do not. Thus we can only study the Gospel record, the sermons of Acts, and the Letters of Paul and his compatriots to gain our historical background. We need to recognize that here, as everywhere in the New Testament, we are dealing with faith statements. The task of the historian is to compare these records with what we know of Roman and Jewish practices of the time.

What we need most to beware of in doing this is evaluating modern traditions as if they were ancient records. They are not. Contemporary Christian sermons may lead us to faith. They do not lead us to the historical realities which we are trying to find. We need to recognize and accept that we are treading upon holy ground as we deal with these final events in the life and ministry of Jesus of Nazareth. At the same time, we also need to acknowledge that history does not prove faith.

If I could actually point to the tomb where Jesus was buried, it would not prove that He had been resurrected. Let me remind you again that we are not seeking for proof but for illumination. In seeking to describe the historical background of these final days of Jesus' life, we are trying to shed light on those events which have become central to the faith of all Christians everywhere.

Preparation and Betrayal

Twice in less than a year, the Sanhedrin or at least representatives of it had given way to passion and sought to stone Jesus. Jesus had escaped their violence on each occasion. We need also to note that the only thing which kept them from seizing Him on other occasions was their fear of the violent reaction of the general populace.

In spite of Jesus' narrow escapes from arrest or violent death at the hands of the Sanhedrin, He kept the pressure on them. We do not often think of Jesus being on the offensive, but to read the Gospel narratives in the light of what we know of the times we must conclude that this was actually the case. In response to His constant and increasing pressure upon them, the Sanhedrin finally decided that they had to take action against Him. There was no longer enough room for Jesus and them in the center of Judaism. Jesus had to go.

> Then the chief priests and the elders of the people gathered in the palace of the high priest, who was called Caiaphas, and took counsel together in order to arrest Jesus by stealth and kill him. But they said, "Not during the feast, least there be a tumult among the people" (Matt. 26:3-5).

Luke added a more blunt, but probably more realistic reason for the nature of their plot, saying simply, "for they feared the people" (22:2).

At last the Sanhedrin had taken the fatal step which led to the final solution. Pressured by Jesus, frightened by the possibilities of a peasant's revolt, terrified of the potentialities of Pilate's precipitate action, and fearful of the loss of their authority over a disillusioned public, the normally cautious Jewish leaders threw caution to the wind. In deliberate haste they arrived at the ultimate decision: Jesus had to die. They knew that He had to be taken quietly, but at the same time it also had to be done quickly. From the Sanhedrin's perspective, further delay would accomplish nothing and risk everything. All that was left for them was to discover the means of finding Jesus alone at a time and in a place where they could seize Him without the Passover pilgrims being aware of it. The plot had been set afoot and the crime of eternity was underway.

The means of locating Jesus at a time when He might be arrested quietly was soon presented to the priests and their cohorts. One evening about midweek, Jesus and His disciples were having the evening meal in Bethany at the house of Simon the leper (Mark 14:3). As was the custom of the time, those eating the meal were reclining at the table. Mary approached Jesus and anointed Him with a very precious oil (John 12:3). Jesus' reclining position made it easy for her to anoint both His head and feet.

It was customary for a host to put a few drops of perfume on the head of a guest, but what Mary did was extravagant in the extreme because the value of the ointment she used was the equivalent of a year's wages. Her act clearly flowed from the extravagance of love.

In response to Mary's act, the disciples were indignant, proclaiming their concern with the needs of the poor (Matt. 26:8-9). Judas was apparently the leader of this outburst, but others joined in, including some who were outside the twelve (Mark 14:4; John 12:4-6). Jesus, however, rebuked Judas and the others because they lacked both sensitivity and real compassion (Mark 14:6-7).

Apparently as a result of the rebuke of Jesus, Judas shortly thereafter sought out the priests and their officers for the purpose of betraying Jesus. There he began to bargain with them to help them accomplish their desires (Mark 14:10; Luke 22:3-4). It is wrong, however, for us to try to place the full reason for Judas' betrayal upon the rebuke of Jesus. Others received that rebuke as well, and they did not enter into the Sanhedrin's plot. Other issues certainly had to be involved in Judas' twisted thinking. At this point, however, we can never recover the reasons for his treachery.

Neither do we know if the world of the priestly plot had made its way to Judas. If he knew about it, he may also have been thinking about it. On the other hand, he may simply have realized that sooner or later they were going to be forced to take such an action. Either way, the traitor sought the priests out. It was not they who sought him. They had been looking for the means of seizing Jesus, and it had been dropped into their laps. So they agreed with Judas to pay him thirty pieces of silver for his treachery (Matt. 26:15). A fascinating feature of this agreement is that this amount was the value fixed in the law as the price of a crippled slave (Ex. 21:32).

When the Sanhedrin had arrived at their original decision to kill Jesus, neither opportunity, time, nor place presented themselves. Almost immediately, however, the opportunity provided itself. To religious people such as they, it must have seemed that God was smiling on their plans. They were surely convinced that their course of action was right, but history has judged them wrong, dead wrong.

Though Jesus had apparently chosen *this* Passover as the time of His death, He was still not ready for it. He had some last things which He wished to do with and say to His disciples. So He did not let them know in advance where they were going to eat the Passover meal, although He had apparently made arrangements in advance.

When Thursday morning came, in response to the disciples' questioning about where they would observe the Passover celebration, Jesus sent two of His disciples into the city with instructions to follow a man carrying a water pot whom they would meet as they entered the city. He would lead them to the place (Mark 14:12-16; Luke 22:7-13). The man was apparently unknown to the disciples, but they were clearly known to him. This appears to indicate that he had been close enough to them at sometime to be able to recognize Jesus' disciples. Tradition says that this final meal was eaten in the home of John Mark, thus this man would probably have been one of the family servants. What made him stand out to the disciples was the fact that he was carrying a water pot. This was a job normally reserved for women in those days.

The disciples did as Jesus commanded, found the upper room, and prepared the Passover meal (Luke 22:13-15). At this point we are confronted by what some have suggested is an impossible contradiction between the Synoptic Gospels and the Gospel of John. This revolves around the issue of when the Passover meal was actually eaten.

To begin with, we need to remind ourselves that for the Jews a day begins at sundown and not at midnight. Thus a meal eaten on what we would call Thursday evening would actually be on Friday by Jewish calculations. The Synoptics are quite clear that Jesus ate the Passover meal with His disciples (Matt. 26:17-20; Mark

14:12-17; Luke 22:14-16). The problem arises with John's Gospel. The issue is first raised with the statement: "Now before the feast of the Passover, . . . during supper . . ." (John 13:1-2). This appears to be a direct contradiction. However, from what we know of biblical narratives, there may be more than twenty-four hours between verses 1 and 2. Furthermore, the expression "the feast of the Passover" could apply to the entire feast and not just to that one meal.

A more serious problem is found, however, in John's description of Jesus' trial before Pilate. There the priests refused to enter into Pilate's judgment hall, "so that they might not be defiled, but might eat the passover" (18:28). This was certainly after the supper described in John 13. This expression is found five other times in the Gospels, but in every case it is in the Synoptics. In all of these it clearly refers to the Passover supper itself. On the other hand, the word *Passover* in the New Testament has three meanings: the Passover supper, Passover lamb, and Passover festival. It occurs nine times in John's Gospel, and in every case but this one, it clearly refers to the entire festival. Thus John's usage would force us to conclude that the priests were concerned with their ability to celebrate the entire festival rather than with their ability to eat the initial meal.

The last related issue is raised by the statement, "Now it was the day of the Preparation of the Passover" (John 19:14). Some have concluded that the day of Jesus' crucifixion was the day before the Passover supper was eaten in the evening. That is simply untrue. All four Gospels use this term to refer to a day of the week, not to a day of a festival. It always refers to the day before the Sabbath, thus Friday. "The Preparation of the Passover" was the Friday of the Passover festival. Thus the end result is that there appears to be no contradiction between the descriptions of the Synoptics and that of John. Jesus ate the Passover meal with His disciples on Thursday evening by our reckoning and was crucified on Friday.

The details of the Last Supper are too familiar to need to be considered again here. However, one feature which is sometimes missed is the seating arrangement, or better, the reclining arrangement around the table. Contrary to most medieval paintings, the tables were probably arranged like a large *U*. The servant(s) would thus have been able to move freely within the "U," waiting upon the diners. Each one eating would have been lying on his left side, supporting his head with his left hand, and eating with his right. Jesus, as host, would have been in the center of the head table, the bottom of the *U*.

It is against this background that we need to understand the words from John's Gospel which describe what followed the disciples' consternation after Jesus' announcement that one of the disciples would betray Him.

> One of his disciples, whom Jesus loved, was lying close to the breast of Jesus; so Simon Peter beckoned to him and said, "Tell us who it is of whom he speaks." So lying thus, close to the breast of Jesus, he said to him, "Lord, who is it?" Jesus answered, "It is he to whom I shall give this morsel when I have dipped it." So when he dipped the morsel, he gave it to Judas, the son of Simon Iscariot (13:23-26).

The disciple whom Jesus loved was obviously lying in front of Jesus. That is the only way he could be "lying close to the breast of Jesus." However, for Jesus to be able to hand the sop to Judas, he must have been immediately on one side or the other of Jesus. This means that Judas must have been to Jesus' left, the position of honor at any meal. This makes our understanding of Judas' treachery even more heinous, because at that Last Supper, even after he had agreed to sell Jesus out, Jesus had given Judas the most honored place at the meal.

This may be seen as even more poignant when we realize that, as the disciples gathered, they had been questioning as to whom was the greatest among themselves (Luke 22:24). The one who was actually accorded the position of most honor at the supper became the one who ultimately perpetrated the darkest deed.

An equally fascinating sidelight to Judas' betrayal is seen in another part of the report of the evening's events.

> Jesus said to him [Judas], "What you are going to do, do quickly." Now no one at the table knew why he said this to him. Some thought that, because Judas had the money box, Jesus was telling him, "Buy what we need for the feast"; or, that he should give something to the poor (John 13:27-29).

First, Judas was the "treasurer" for the disciples. He carried the money box containing gifts from generous and loyal supporters, and from it he paid for anything which they needed. Whatever else we may say about Judas, no one is ever entrusted with other persons' money unless he is fully trusted by those people. Thus it is obvious that, from the beginning, Judas had the full trust of the other eleven disciples. The second feature, however, is even more striking. At the moment of the supper, the disciples still did not suspect Judas as being the betrayer. They simply assumed that he was being sent by Jesus on some needful errand. These features even further heighten the treachery of Judas. Not only did he betray Jesus, he betrayed the absolute trust of all the rest. He had not given even the suspicion of disaffection, much less of treachery to any one of them. No one was suspicious of him.

Following Judas' departure, Jesus took the few moments which remained to share His final admonitions with the eleven disciples who remained with Him. It was at that time that Simon Peter protested that he would be more faithful than the others, even to prison or death (Mark 14:29; Luke 22:33; John 13:37). Further, Jesus realized that the disciples themselves might be in danger that night, so he checked that they had at least some means of self-defense (Luke 22:38). He had plainly determined that this night was His hour; it was not yet theirs.

Following the conclusion of the meal, Jesus led His disciples over the Brook Kidron, up the Mount of Olives, and into Gethsemane (Mark 14:26,32; Luke 22:39; John 18:1). Until this night, Jesus had carefully hidden Himself from the priests and the Sanhedrin. But on this night He went to the place where He customarily went. Judas would have known precisely where to find them. And he did, accompanied by the officers of the temple and a "band" of Roman soldiers, armed with swords and clubs (Mark 14:43; John 18:2-3). The word translated *band* is an official designation, referring to a cohort, a military unit normally comprising three to six hundred soldiers. Although the Sanhedrin had taken every precaution, they were still prepared for armed resistance or a riot. Swords are military weapons. Clubs were for crowd control.

Judas' kiss of betrayal stands among the greatest acts of treachery in human history (Mark 14:44). The kiss could have been the kiss of friendship, given on both cheeks. It could have been the kiss of a servant, kneeling before his Master and kissing His hand. Most likely, since Judas addressed Jesus as Rabbi, it was the kiss of a student for his revered Teacher, being placed on the forehead or the top of the head. In any case, it was a symbol of love and respect hiding the darkest deed of an even darker heart.

At first, the disciples did not wish to yield Jesus up, but at His admonition they did so. Jesus was the towering figure of the entire episode. He had agonized in prayer, seeking a last way out of the events which He knew were necessary and had actually precipitated (Luke 22:42). We hear His humanity crying out for deliverance from the agony which was before Him. When the moment finally came, He stood calmly with the disciples, betrayer, and armed soldiers, submitting to their authority—and ultimately to the will of God. They did not take Him; He yielded to them.

Arrest and Trial

The arresting officers were surprised at the ease with which they were able to take Jesus. At first, they were even taken aback (John 18:2-9,12). However, their amazement did not last long. They quickly bound Jesus and led Him back into the city, to begin the long ordeal which they all knew was to result in His death. Jesus was first led to Annas, a former high priest and father-in-law of Caiaphas, the presently reigning high priest.

Many volumes have been written about both the Jewish and Roman trials of Jesus. We can only point to several significant details here. The procedural rules of the Sanhedrin required that a person accused of heresy must first be tried by two lower courts and found guilty before charges could be brought against him to the Sanhedrin. (These rules are found in the Talmud.) However, in Jesus' case, the Sanhedrin was clearly operating under great pressures of time. So they compromised and sought to follow a semblance of the law by having at least one of these preliminary hearings, the one before Annas (John 18:12-14,19-23). During this inquisition, Peter in the outer court made his three infamous denials of Jesus. It is intriguing to compare the fact that while Jesus was being interrogated about His disciples, one of those disciples was also (though less formally) being interrogated about Jesus and the other disciples. The contrast between the two makes the denial of Peter even more striking.

Following the inquisition by Annas, Jesus was led to the hearing before the Sanhedrin over which Caiaphas presided. This was the informal hearing, held before dawn. Witnesses were brought to testify against Jesus. The law required that for anyone to be convicted of a capital offense, the testimony of at least two witnesses must agree (Deut. 17:6). However, the attempt to find witnesses whose testimony against Jesus would agree foundered (Mark 14:56-59).

Up to this point, Caiaphas had simply sat and presided. However, he suddenly arose, along with the rest of the Sanhedrin who were required to stand whenever the high priest stood (Mark 14:60). This was an obvious attempt to intimidate Jesus, but He was unthreatened and remained silent. Caiaphas finally lost control and lashed out, asking: "'Are you the Christ, the Son of the Blessed?'" (Mark 14:61). He apparently began this question with the admonition, "'I adjure you by the living God'" (Matt. 26:63). These introductory words were believed to require a defendant to speak out. In this instance, that requirement would not have been necessary. The question alone would have elicited a response from Jesus because that was the whole purpose of what He was doing. He apparently did not intend to be crucified as Messiah, a political savior in the terms of that day. However, He did intend to die as the Son of God. At long last the question had been asked directly.

Jesus simply responded, "I am'" (Mark 14:62). The meaning of these words to the Jewish consciousness probably goes back to the call of Moses, where God revealed Himself as "I am" (Ex. 3:14). They were also repeated in the hope of a divine deliverance in the message of the Book of Isaiah (43:13). Caiaphas and the entire Sanhedrin were shocked at Jesus' words. The high priest tore his robe, the official sign of having heard words of blasphemy. He cried out for a verdict of condemnation, and it was immediately forthcoming (Matt. 26:65-66).

At this point the informal hearing broke up, and Jesus was turned over to the guards to be held for the formal trial. During this period He was abused and reviled. If we can excuse them for holding Him, we cannot excuse them for the manner in which they treated Him (Luke 22:63-65).

After dawn, the final and formal Jewish trial was held (Matt. 27:1). At this point each member of the Sanhedrin was required to cast a vote, beginning at the youngest and moving to the eldest, with the final vote being cast by the high priest. The verdict was a foregone conclusion, for Jesus had been heard by everyone of them to claim to be the Son of God. That was blasphemy by their standards and required the death sentence. They had accomplished their goal—the condemnation of Jesus. However, there was still one hitch in their plans. Under the authority granted to them by Rome, they could not legally execute anyone. Only the Roman governor had that authority, so the Sanhedrin still had to deal with that issue.

Somewhere in the darkness and early light of that morning, Judas had been standing by, watching the events. We will never know what he had expected to happen to Jesus. It is obvious that he had not expected Jesus to die as a result of his treachery. So he sought out the Jewish leaders and tried to undo what he had done (Matt. 27:3-5). However, it was already too late. In grief and remorse, Judas rushed forth and committed suicide. On the other hand, members of the Sanhedrin showed no remorse. In an outward demonstration of pious self-righteousness, those who had paid Judas the betrayal price refused to take it back. Instead, they sought to use it for a charitable purpose, providing a burial place for those who had no one to provide them with a last resting place (Matt. 27:6-8).

As soon as the priests and elders felt that they could, they lead Jesus to Pontius Pilate, the Roman governor, seeking to get a quick ratification of their death sentence on Jesus. It is significant that they had condemned Jesus on a purely religious charge, that of heresy. Knowing that Pilate would be unimpressed with that charge, they made a subtle change in it, charging Jesus with political aims at overthrowing the Roman rule (Luke 23:1-2). That was an issue which Pilate had to take seriously and with which he must deal. His previous record showed that he did take that kind of activity very seriously and normally dealt with it in swift and arbitrary measures.

However, the entire trial before Pilate reveals a different man from the one who had reacted with brutality when the Galileans and Jews of Jerusalem had sought to prevent his getting money from the temple to pay for the aqueduct he had built for Jerusalem. Instead of being the arrogant and confident autocrat of earlier days, he was tentative and conciliatory. As a background for this, we need to note that there appears to be no question that Pilate knew Jesus was innocent of the Sanhedrin's charges.

However, note that Pilate made every effort to keep the Jewish leaders happy. Further, He sought to avoid having to make a decision, seeking to turn his decision-making responsibility over either to the Sanhedrin or Herod Antipas (Luke 23:6-7; John 18:31). The Sanhedrin refused to accept the responsibility because they wanted Jesus to die and could not execute Him themselves. Herod mocked Jesus a bit and finally sent Him back to Pilate. The decision was to be Pilate's and his alone.

Why did Pilate act so differently here from the way in which he normally exercised his power? The answer may lie in the statement of the Jewish representatives, "'If you release this man, you are not Caesar's friend'" (John 19:12). When they said this, Pilate's resistance caved in, and he sentenced Jesus to be crucified. As we have noted, Pilate apparently received his appointment to govern Judea from Tiberius as the protégé of Sejanus, Tiberius' chief of staff. If our dates are correct, about seven months prior to the time of Jesus' trial Sejanus had been executed as a traitor. Pilate knew that he had to be quite cautious so that he did not fall with his master. He could not afford to have any enemies at that point in time. He certainly could not afford any Jewish enemies, since one of the charges leveled against Sejanus was anti-Semitism.

Equally as important, during the latter days of Tiberius, those Roman officials who especially pleased the emperor were designated *Amicus Caesaris,* "friend of Caesar." Without that designation, careers came to an ignominious end. With it, advancement and success were assured. The Jewish leaders and Pilate aware of this practice, and their implied threat to see that he was never given this title caused him to cave in before their wishes.

So Jesus died on the altar of the political ambitions of both the Jewish leaders and Roman governor. Fulfilling the letter of the law he had failed to uphold, Pilate had the condemned Jesus scourged and sent forth to be crucified.

Crucifixion and Burial

Again, the cruel sport of soldiers played a role in the final hours of Jesus' life. Hardened by the life which they lived, the soldiers taunted Jesus, even mocking Him with a crown of thorns and the reddish-purple robe of a Roman lictor (Matt. 27:27-30; Mark 15:16-19). With silent dignity, Jesus endured it all.

Tiring of mocking a man who would not strike back verbally, the soldiers finally led Jesus forth to be crucified. Almost certainly, Jesus and His two companions in death were laden only with the crossbeams of their crosses. The uprights were normally left standing at the place of execution. Jesus stumbled along under the leaden weight of the massive crossbar, weakened by the night's ordeal and the morning's tortures. When He stumbled and fell, a by-stander was conscripted to help by carrying the crossbar (Mark 15:21). This, too, was a normal practice when a condemned man was too weak to carry his own cross. That was a burden which no soldier would bear for his victim.

After the soldiers nailed Jesus to the crossbar, they would have lifted it in place on a notch of the upright, nailing the victim's feet to the upright. Finally, they nailed the governor's charge to the top of the cross and then sat down to cast lots for the garments of their victims. This was one of the normal "perks" for soldiers on such duty.

The place where Jesus was crucified was so cosmopolitan that the charge against Jesus had to be written in three different languages, Hebrew (Aramaic), Latin, and Greek (John 19:19-20). Having ultimately yielded to the Sanhedrin's demand in crucifying Jesus, Pilate refused to budge any further before their pressure, maintaining the title he had prepared rather than one which they wanted (vv. 21-22).

Crucifixion normally was a long, drawn out affair. Sometimes it took the victims several days to die. However, since it was the eve of the Sabbath, the Jewish leaders requested that the Roman soldiers break the legs of the victims after a few hours, so that they would die more quickly. This they did. Death from crucifixion normally came by strangulation, when the chest muscles became paralyzed under the strain upon the arms. This could be put off by the victim by standing upright and taking the strain off of the arms and chest. Broken legs prevented them from doing this. However, when the soldiers came to Jesus, they were surprised to find Him already dead (vv. 31-35).

The entire event was one sorry, sordid episode. Jesus' mother and disciples stood by in grief. Some of the priests and elders mocked. Curious passersby stopped to watch as the victims writhed in agony. It seems as if Jesus decided to die. His life and ministry had come to an end.

Normally, the burial of a loved one was carried out carefully. Much time was usually spent in preparing a body for burial. On that afternoon, however, time was a luxury which no one had. Apparently two members of the Sanhedrin, Nicodemus and Joseph of Arimathea, stepped forward to request that Jesus' body be turned over to them. In haste they prepared it, wrapping enormous amounts of spices in the winding cloths and placing it in Joseph's own tomb which was located nearby.

Family tombs were normally a cave with a stone slab in the center. The newest body would be laid out on that slab. When it came time to use the grave again, the remains would be swept aside or placed in a small alcove along the side, and the new body would be laid on the slab. Jesus' body, however, was placed in a new tomb. There was no evidence of former occupants. And as the stone slab was rolled along its groove to close the opening, the sun began to set in Jerusalem.

Resurrection and Ascension

For the priests and elders who made up the Sanhedrin, it appeared that with Jesus dead and buried they had been successful and totally victorious. However, they wished to take no chances. Thus they sought authority from Pilate to seal the tomb and place a guard at its entrance (Matt. 27:62-66). They feared that someone would steal the body of Jesus. Guarding the tomb was not a totally unique event. This had been done on other occasions. Only one thing was wrong, however, they were guarding the wrong side of the entrance.

From an historical perspective, when we consider events surrounding the resurrection of Jesus, we are treading on holy ground. Here we are dealing with issues of faith. To one who does not wish to believe on other grounds in the resurrection of Jesus, there is no proof which will convince. To those who have experienced the risen Lord, however, no other proof is necessary.

A feature about the resurrection records of the Gospels which is of importance to a historian is the fact that not a single one of the first witnesses was ready to believe what faith proclaims had happened. Mary thought Jesus' body had been stolen (John 20:15). The two disciples who raced to the tomb at her report saw that it was empty but had no idea what had happened. The two disciples on the road to Emmaus did not believe in the resurrection until the end of their journey (Luke 24:31). Along with other disciples, ten of the eleven who were gathered in the upper room did not believe until late in the evening when Jesus appeared to them (John 20:19-20). Finally, Thomas with neither more nor less faith than the others, refused to believe in the resurrection until a week later when Jesus appeared to him (vv. 27-28).

Following those initial appearances, other appearances of Jesus were seen by the eleven as well as by larger and smaller groups. Time was apparently allowed for them to absorb the idea that Jesus had conquered death. Finally, Jesus gathered the disciples together, giving them His final earthly challenge. Even then, some still doubted what they were seeing, but they were to remember and cherish His words.

> All authority in heaven and on earth has been given to me. Go therefore and make disciples of all nations, baptizing them in the name of the Father and of the Son and of the Holy Spirit, teaching them to observe all that I have commanded you; and lo, I am with you always, to the close of the age (Matt. 28:18-20).

> You shall receive power when the Holy Spirit has come upon you; and you shall be my witnesses in Jerusalem and in all Judea and Samaria and to the end of the earth (Acts 1:8).

So the life and ministry of Jesus came to an end. Or did it? The testimony of faith and the New Testament is a resounding, "No!" The early church carried on His ministry as they sought to obey these final words of commission. This leads us to the next section of our study.

17
Summary

The Christian faith has proclaimed with steady conviction that Jesus of Nazareth was the Christ, the Son of God, the Lord. However, with equal conviction, this itinerant Rabbi of Nazareth has been proclaimed with less vigor but with equal certainty to be a Jew of the first century. The Christian community has consistently branded as a heretic anyone who denied that Jesus was human as well as divine. Further, in doing this, it has insisted that He was *fully* human, as well as being *fully* divine. As I have pointed out earlier, my purpose here has not been and still is not to focus attention upon the Christ of faith. That is the task of biblical theology. Rather, my purpose is to direct your attention to the Jesus of history.

What I have sought to do in the chapters which make up this part of our study is to help you see that Jesus of Nazareth, the first Son of Mary, was a man of His times. To fail either to see or try to understand this is to fail to deal properly with His humanity. To fail to deal properly with His humanity is to fail to deal properly with Him.

Jesus was born just before the end of the reign of Herod the Great in Palestine and in the last half of the reign of Augustus Caesar over the Roman Empire. In contrast to what we might have expected, He was born into poverty, the child of peasants from Nazareth. Further, in addition to the normal dangers of the tragically high infant mortality rate of that day, Jesus was threatened shortly after birth by the wrath of one of the more vindictive rulers who ever reigned in Palestine. As a consequence, at least a part of His childhood years found Him growing up as a refugee in a foreign land. It was there that He escaped the political vendetta of a ruler who, like so many others before and since, sought to destroy any threat to his power.

Sometime during His childhood years, Mary and Joseph returned to their home in Nazareth, bringing the young Jesus with them. There He grew up in a loving family, but one which was apparently always on the edge of poverty. During those years, He obviously was a dutiful son and a diligent student. However, not only did He study the spiritual dimension of His Jewish heritage, He also studied human nature with careful observation motivated by a consuming curiosity. Nothing existed in God's world about which He seemingly did not care, as is exemplified by the breadth of references found in His later teachings. In addition, during those childhood years Jesus at least added the ability both to read biblical Hebrew and speak Greek, along with His native Aramaic, the language of the Jews in that time.

During His childhood and adolescence, Jesus also learned the importance of fulfilling duties at home. He obviously would have to assist in the care of younger brothers and sisters, as well as to assume the heavier responsibilities of being the oldest son when Joseph died and Mary became a widow. At the same time, His later stories reveal that He had had time to play with other children and wander the hills around Nazareth. There He would have observed foxes and birds, merchant caravans seeking the riches of this world, and arrogant and strutting soldiers of Rome as they brought their hated power to bear upon the Galilean countryside. Also, either through observation or personal experience, Jesus would have seen just how difficult it was for a poor widow to find anyone who would care what happened to her and her family.

During Jesus' maturing years, the emperor changed in Rome, and the form of government changed in Judea. Neither of those changes would have had much immediate impact upon His life, but His sensitivity to the issues which concerned His people coupled with His far-ranging curiosity would have made Him aware of those changes. He would have pondered their consequences. Later He was to experience them firsthand.

We will never know for sure why Jesus waited so long to begin His actual ministry. It may have been due to the fact that He had to wait for His younger brothers to be old enough and be willing to assume the responsibilities for Mary and the family. It may also have been that He was waiting for some divine signal of the fullness of times. If that were the case, the signal came with the ministry of His cousin John. Regardless, it was at that time that He severed the ties with home and stepped forth upon the stage of history.

The ministry of Jesus began with a nonremarkable baptism at the hands of John the Baptist. It was nonremarkable to the extent that He was only one among the throngs who were baptized by John. Jesus certainly attracted early attention to Himself with His cleansing of the temple, but then He almost seems to have faded from the major focus of the Jewish priests and elders for a season. It might have appeared that Jesus' ministry was going to be nonsensational, although His miracles certainly would have caused some local sensation.

Even though there were periodic visits to Judea and Jerusalem, Jesus' early ministry had its basic focus in Galilee. During those days He was gathering disciples around Him, like an Old Testament prophet or a contemporary rabbi. He sought to teach them not so much doctrine as a way of life. During those days, Jesus' fame began to grow. This was at first a localized phenomenon, drawing crowds from Galilee. However, Galilee had always been an explosive region, and its citizens were always, at least during this era, on the verge of revolt. Thus any sensation in Galilee soon attracted the attention of the Sanhedrin in Jerusalem. It was their task to maintain the peace so that they could maintain the authority which Rome had left them under the governorship.

So the crowds began to gather. Some came to learn. Others came seeking miracles. Still others came seeking answers to the deeper issues of life. Some came seeking the words of life. There were also those who came simply to investigate what was going on. Some sought to entrap Him, trying to render His ministry ineffective. Already some were beginning to suspect the way of Jesus and the way of the Sanhedrin could not coexist in their world. For them, it became obvious even in the early days that, one way or another, Jesus had to go.

During those days, Jesus was gratified by the attention of the crowds but was not deceived by them. He was also well aware of the strengths, frequently all too few, and weaknesses, generally all too obvious, of His more intimate disciples. Although seeking to attract crowds, Jesus never lessened His demands of what was expected of those who followed Him. On occasion, He simply withdrew from the crowd to their consternation and that of the disciples. Also, on occasion, He led His disciples away from the crowds into the safer regions outside the territory of Judea and Galilee.

Throughout this period, Jesus consistently revealed His awareness of the ongoing history and political realities of His time. He never allowed others to force Him into issues with which He did not wish to deal. Neither did He allow Himself to be entrapped by either the theological or political issues which might alienate those whom He sought to reach, or distract Him from His primary purpose.

As His final months drew upon Him, Jesus' attitude appears to have changed entirely. No longer did He seek to avoid confrontation with the Jewish leaders. To the contrary, Jesus suddenly began to appear to be forcing the issue. He moved onto the offensive and forced them ever more severely into a position where they had to deal with Him directly. In both September and December of His final year, the chief priests and elders sought to stone Him, although they could not legally do this under Roman law. Jesus pressured them so intensely that they became little more than a lynch mob on those two occasions.

On each of those occasions when death threatened, Jesus managed to escape from the clutches of His adversaries, to their dismay and chagrin. Although He left Judea at such times, He neither seems to have gone far away nor left for any extended period of time.

Finally, though, the Passover of destiny drew near. Once again, it becomes obvious that Jesus was the One in control. He clearly seems to have chosen the time and place of His death. Again, apparently being quite aware of both the national and international situations, Jesus forced the hand of the Jewish aristocracy and ultimately the Roman governor. When He arrived in Jerusalem, He entered the city in a manner to force the Sanhedrin to act in haste while preventing the Roman governor from taking Him at all seriously. Further, this time when He cleansed the temple He did not fade away into Galilee but stayed on the scene, appearing daily in the temple.

Although Jesus had forced the Sanhedrin to decide that He had to die, for the first part of the final week He kept Himself either in crowds where they dare not arrest Him or safely among friends at

Bethany from which they could not take Him. However, the decision had been made, and the answer to the Sanhedrin's dilemma presented itself when Judas showed up with his offer of betrayal. All that lacked was the time and place, yet to be arranged.

Still in control of the situation, Jesus provided both time and place. He did not let Judas know where the last supper was to be held. Following that, though, He and the disciples went to Gethsemane on the Mount of Olives, a place of regular retreat with which Judas was wholly familiar. It was there that Judas led the armed soldiers sent by the elders and chief priests and where Jesus was finally seized.

With the time of the Passover celebration drawing inexorably nearer, the pressure of time forced the hands of the Sanhedrin. In haste and with only a passing attempt at legality, Jesus was tried, convicted by His own words, and condemned. Once again, however, it appeared that the Sanhedrin's inability to carry out a death sentence might thwart their plans. However, they made their case sure by twisting the charges and adding veiled but real threats against Pilate. The Roman governor was finally forced to accede to their wishes.

Although there is no indication of it, the high priest and the Sanhedrin had to feel an immense satisfaction as Jesus was led forth to be crucified. The end of all their plans had come to a successful fruition. Judas' attempt to try to undo his act of betrayal was met with pious disdain. Pilate's discomfort at their political pressure was of even less concern. Only two things bothered them. The first was Pilate's subtle joke at their expense in the title which he placed upon the cross. Although they did not like the wording, they were so pleased at Jesus' sentence that they did not press the issue lest they lose what they had gained. The second fear of the Sanhedrin was that some of Jesus' disciples might steal the body. So they pled for and received a Roman guard at the tomb. From their standpoint, it was all over.

However, the chief priests and the elders were wrong. The Roman seal upon the tomb and Roman guard before it would have prevented the theft of Jesus' body. It did not prevent His resurrection. The tomb was opened from within, not without.

From the Sanhedrin's standpoint, the morning after the Sabbath brought catastrophe. Everything which they had nailed down suddenly came loose. The Jewish leaders had thought that the crucifixion and burial of Jesus had brought an end to all of their problems with Him, but they were wrong. It wasn't the end. It was only the beginning.

And Pilate, what of him? He had bought some time by yielding to the pressure of the Sanhedrin. He had betrayed his commission to uphold the law and maintain the peace by sacrificing both upon the altar of his political ambition. Yet within a few years he was recalled to Rome and apparently banished. All his machinations had accomplished nothing for him. He washed his hands of the affair, but that accomplished nothing either. Rome's problems with Jesus and His followers were only just beginning. That brings us to the next part of our story. What had appeared to be bad news for the followers of Jesus became good news for all people, in all times, and at all places.

Part 4
Witness in Jerusalem, All Judea, and Samaria

When Jesus was crucified, the chief priests and elders thought they were rid of Jesus. By all rights, they should have been. The death and burial of an itinerant rabbi from Nazareth should have put an end to Him and the influence of His followers. If the disciples' fear of ending up the same way as their Teacher had not scattered them, their disillusionment with the failure of His claims should have. But it didn't because the cross was followed by the empty tomb. The resurrection was followed by Jesus' ascension. The story didn't end with the crucifixion.

Thus the cowed, frightened, grieving disciples who hid in the upper room following Jesus' death turned into the bold witnesses who dared to preach to the Sanhedrin. This was something which caught both the Jewish leaders and Roman authorities by surprise. Further, no threat on the part of the Jewish leaders seemed to have any influence upon the once terrified disciples.

Slowly, but inexorably, the influence of those first followers of Jesus began to be felt. It was first felt in Jerusalem. Surprisingly, at least to the Jewish rulers, the spread of this new faith was not confined to the ignorant and excitable Galileans. Among the early converts were priests and Pharisees; Jews from the Diaspora; and some people of wealth, power, and influence.

The facts were indisputable. People began to listen both to the preaching and stories of those first witnesses. But listening was not all they did. Some among them began to believe. Even worse, at least from the standpoint of the Jewish leaders, those new converts became witnesses on their own part.

No question was left on the part of the Sanhedrin. The movement of the followers of Jesus had to be stopped. Threats were made. They were also ignored. Threats turned into open and violent opposition. Thus the religious leaders of Judaism, men who ought to have been followers of peace, began an all out war on those early followers of Jesus of Nazareth.

Whatever else we may think, the primary, overarching feature of the historical background of the early days of Christianity was the consistent, unswerving hostility of the leaders of Judaism toward the first Christians. We should not let this blind us to another equally as important fact. This is that the ordinary Jewish people were not so disposed. This is obvious because they listened, and some of them believed. The first Christians were all Jews. Even to the end of the New Testament era, when Christian missionaries arrived in a new community the first place they usually went to proclaim their message was the synagogue. Admittedly, they were frequently forced out by the leaders. On the other hand, the first converts in those new communities were usually still Jews.

In seeking to follow the spread of Christianity in those first days, for the sake of convenience, we shall again deal with it in two parts. The break I shall make is artificial but is intended to get the material into more easily manageable blocks. A number of more or less possible breaking points suggested themselves. For me, the most obvious place to break our study is at the place where the Christians deliberately began to move out of the normal ways of spreading their faith by adopting a deliberate missionary strategy. This occurred when Paul and Barnabas were sent forth from the church at Antioch. (See the Book of Acts.)

Once again, as with the study of the background of the life and ministry of Jesus, our resources are limited. We know little about how Christianity spread into most of the ancient world. We do not even know a great deal about the main theme of Acts, how the gospel spread from Jerusalem to Rome, the heart of the empire. We shall seek to place as best we can the information to be gleaned from Acts and the Epistles against the background of what we know about the first-century history of the Roman Empire and the Mediterranean world.

18
Chronological Considerations

As we noted in the introduction to this part of our study, I am dividing our consideration of the spread of Christianity and the birth and planting of the early churches at the point where Paul became a significant influence. However, this creates difficulties as we seek to establish the chronology of this era.

The chronology of the life of Jesus clearly gives us the beginning point for the era of the early church. On the other hand, most of the chronological data which we possess that relates to the early churches applies directly to Paul's life and ministry. Thus, the dates of Paul's ministry must be established, at least insofar as it is possible, in order for us to have any clear concept of just how long this early period was. Furthermore, we must know these limits before we can seriously evaluate the effects of their contemporary history upon the Christians of that era. In this chapter, therefore, we must begin by dealing with the chronology of all the remainder of the New Testament era. Then we shall back up and confine ourselves to the period which we are studying here: the pre-Pauline spread of Christianity.

One additional feature which we need to consider before actually proceeding with this study is the nature of chronological studies of the early church. Obviously, the period which we are considering covers a narrow part of human history. Thus, regardless of the approach made to it, the dates which various historians assign to the major events within it do not differ very widely. On the other hand, the reasons for the conclusions reached and the presuppositions upon which those conclusions are based vary considerably. The sources from which I gather my evidence here are the New Testament, particularly Acts and the Epistles of Paul, contemporary documents, and archaeological remains.

Basic Data

As always is the case in the attempt to reconstruct any historical period, the basic data which we already possess must first be identified and then kept in front of us. The student should refer to the earlier tables of Jewish festivals because these festivals continued to be of major significance throughout much of this period. This is especially so since most of the early missionaries and many of the early Christians were Jews.

In addition, other kinds of basic data need to be placed before us. All of the places told about in the narratives of Acts were within the boundaries of the Roman empire. As such, they were subject to Roman laws and policies, were ruled by Roman administrators, and were policed by Roman soldiers. This means that the Christians there were also subject to these same forces. Thus, the first group of basic data which we need to know is who the Roman emperors were as well as the time periods during which they exercised authority. The following table sets forth this information as it now appears from our best assessment of the evidence.

Roman Emperors

Tiberius	A.D. 14-37
Caligula	A.D. 37-41
Claudius	A.D. 41-54
Nero	A.D. 54-68
Galba	A.D. 68-69
Otho	A.D. 69
Vitellius	A.D. 69
Vespasian	A.D. 69-79
Titus	A.D. 79-81
Domitian	A.D. 81-96
Nerva	A.D. 96-98
Trajan	A.D. 98-117
Hadrian	A.D. 117-138

In addition to knowing these emperors, since a great deal of the focus of the Book of Acts was upon the church of Jerusalem and its relationship with the Jews there, the second kind of data of which we also need to be aware are the Roman rulers who exercised authority over Judea. For the period in which we are primarily interested, these were procurators, with one notable exception. Primarily responsible to Rome, these local governors cared little for the Jews or the Christians. They apparently were only concerned with keeping the peace, however harsh it might have been and with maintaining the steady flow of tax money into Roman coffers. Assigned to this border province of the empire, these petty bureaucrats who governed there were never among the best of Roman officials and often were among the worst. The following table sets forth these rulers and their periods of authority in light of the best data presently available.

Roman Procurators Over Jerusalem

Pontius Pilate	A.D. 26-36
Marcellus	A.D. 36
Marullus	A.D. 37-41
Agrippa I (King)	A.D. 41-44
Cuspius Fadus	A.D. 44-46
Tiberius Alexander	A.D. 46-48
Ventidus Cumanus	A.D. 48-52
Felix	A.D. 52-60
Festus	A.D. 60-62
Albinus	A.D. 62-64
Florus	A.D. 64-66
(First Jewish Revolt)	A.D. 66-74

Furthermore, for our purposes, two of the dates in the above table stand out as being of special significance. The date of the death of King Herod Agrippa I in A.D. 44 is as firm as any date within this era. This has to be assumed as a fixed point for our reconstruction. In addition, the date of the transfer of authority from Felix to Festus in A.D. 60 is almost as firmly fixed. This also shall be assumed for our purposes as being a firmly fixed point within this chronological reconstruction.

We also have two other dates which we must use in our chronological reconstruction. The first of these dates is the time of the rule of Gallio at Corinth. Paul appeared before this man, and that gives us an important point of reference (Acts 18:12). According to an inscription at Delphi which has a slight ambiguity in it, Gallio served as proconsul over Achaia, which included Corinth, for a year. This has to have been either A.D. 51-52 or A.D. 52-53 with the term of service beginning in midyear in either instance. The final date which has to be considered as a point of reference for this study is the year Jesus was crucified, which was A.D. 32 according to our earlier chronological reconstruction.

This is the basic chronological data from which we must work as we attempt to establish the detailed chronology of the era of the early churches. In addition to this basic data, we also need to remind ourselves that throughout the ancient Near East during this era, records were not kept in the way which they are today. No absolute calendar even existed which was followed by every nation. Rome counted years from the founding of their city. Other nations reckoned the years of their history from a variety of beginning points.

In addition to the confusion which these factors generate, there was not even any agreement among nations as to when a year began. Rome apparently counted the New Year from a time near what we call January 1. The Jews generally, but not universally, accepted Passover as the beginning of the year. Furthermore, many people accepted the autumnal equinox as the beginning of the year. In attempting to deal with our absolute chronology, we have to try to determine which system was used by each specific author and how it may relate to those used by others who recorded the same event. Such a process is a long way from being an exact science at this time.

The Pivotal Date: Gallio in Corinth

To me, the most important date in establishing a chronology of Paul and his missionary journeys is that of the rule of Gallio as proconsul over Achaia. He and Paul actually confronted one another. Luke tells us: "But when Gallio was proconsul of Achaia, the Jews made a united attack upon Paul and brought him before the tribunal. . . . But Gallio paid no attention to this" (Acts 18:12,17).

According to an inscription at Delphi, Gallio was serving as proconsul of Achaia at the time of the twenty-sixth acclamation of Claudius as *imperator*. This would have occurred within the year of A.D. 52. Since Gallio's term began in midyear, he would have ruled either from mid-51 to mid-52 or from mid-52 to mid-53. Thus Paul could have been before Gallio's judgment seat any time within that twenty-four-month period. However, the fact that the

Jews left Paul alone after this for the "many days longer" (Acts 18:18) that he remained there probably indicates that they had sought to have him condemned at a time in Gallio's reign when he still had some period of service left to him. Gallio's continued presence in Corinth made further attacks upon Paul untenable.

It appears to me that the best assumption at this point is Gallio ruled from A.D. 52 to 53. Further, I am also assuming that Paul was brought to him after the midpoint of Gallio's rule, probably in the spring of that year. We must recognize that if the other data does not fit, then we shall have to alter this choice. Thus our first semifixed point of chronology for the life of Paul and spread of Christianity is *spring, A.D. 53.*

The Felix-Festus Interchange

As the table indicates, Felix was replaced as procurator in Judea in A.D. 60. Again, this transition probably occurred at about mid-year. The date of this event becomes important for us because Paul was being imprisoned in Caesarea at that time. Further, he was brought before each of these men for a hearing of the charges against him. Luke again recorded these events.

> After some days Felix came . . . and he sent for Paul and heard him speak upon faith in Christ Jesus. But when two years had elapsed, Felix was succeeded by Porcius Festus; and desiring to do the Jews a favor, Felix left Paul in prison.
> Now when Festus had come into his province, . . . he went down to Caesarea; and the next day he took his seat on the tribunal and ordered Paul to be brought (Acts 24:24,27; 25:1,6).

Luke's testimony clearly reveals that Paul faced both of these Roman governors. At this point, we have a second date in Paul's life and ministry nailed down. The fact that Paul was in prison in Caesarea in A.D. 60 is even more certain than the date when he was brought before Gallio in Corinth.

Furthermore, according to Luke's evidence, Paul had been held in Caesarea by Felix for at least two years (Acts 24:27). This means that his arrest should probably be placed in A.D. 58. In addition, at a hearing before Festus, Paul appealed for a hearing before Caesar. This was granted, and they departed for Rome sometime later, near the time of the Day of Atonement ("the feast") in A.D. 60.

Herod and Paul

A third possible date which we can establish for the life and ministry of Paul is found in the relationship between the lives of Herod and Paul. The major importance of this date relates not merely to Paul but to the early history of the entire Christian community.

King Herod Agrippa I died in the late spring of A.D. 44. But how does Paul relate to this? Again, Luke gives us our clue, reporting that

> the church in Jerusalem, . . . sent Barnabas to Antioch. So Barnabas went to Tarsus to look for Saul; and when he had found him, he brought him to Antioch. For *a whole year* they met with the church . . . .
>
> About that time Herod the king laid violent hands upon some who belonged to the church. . . . On an appointed day Herod put on his royal robes, took his seat upon the throne, and made an oration to them. . . . an angel of the Lord smote him, . . . and he was eaten by worms and died (Acts 11:22,25-26 to 12:1,21,23; italics mine).

It appears then that we can conclude that Paul and Barnabas had begun their ministry in Antioch in A.D. 43. A year later, they had carried relief to Jerusalem during the great famine (11:26-30). While they were there, Herod died, apparently only shortly after the Feast of Passover or Unleavened Bread (12:3,20-23). Immediately after the death of Herod Agrippa, Paul and Barnabas returned to Antioch from Jerusalem, taking John Mark with them (v. 25). This almost certainly occurred in the summer of A.D. 44. These related dates give us a third fixed point in the life of Paul and the early church.

The Jerusalem Council

Another major point for cross-referencing the chronology of Paul's life and ministry is the great Jerusalem Council (15:1-35). If we can establish a date for that, several other events will fall into place. This church council followed the first missionary journey which in turn followed the death of Agrippa I. On the other hand, it preceded the second missionary journey. On that venture Paul was hauled before Gallio at Corinth. The first missionary journey had to follow Paul's time in Jerusalem in the spring of A.D. 44. The second just as obviously included the spring of A.D. 53 (possibly minus a year).

Beginning with the confrontation before Gallio in Corinth in A.D. 53, we can now work backward in an attempt to arrive at a date for the Jerusalem Council. Paul had been in Corinth eighteen months when he was brought before Gallio (18:11). Since we have assumed that this date was the spring of A.D. 53, then he must have arrived in Corinth about the midyear or later in A.D. 51.

Before Paul came to Corinth, he had preached in Philippi, Thessalonica, Beroea, and Athens (16:12-40; 17:1-34). He had originally arrived in Philippi by sailing there from Troas (16:11-12). He was far too experienced a traveler to ever make such a sea journey in the winter, even if he could have paid a ship's owner enough to make him risk such a voyage. In addition, the narratives of his ministry in all four of the Macedonian cities prior to Corinth appear to have been quite rushed and fraught with danger and opposition. Thus it seems that Paul made his journey across the sea to Philippi in the late fall of A.D. 50 or early spring of A.D. 51. It appears more likely to have been A.D. 51.

Prior to the sea voyage from Troas, Paul and his companions had begun this second missionary journey by traveling overland from Antioch. He had traveled north and then west on a journey where he strengthened the churches which he and Barnabas had started on the first missionary journey (15:40 to 16:10). This would have been a long trip over some fairly severe mountain terrain. This entire trip should have taken several months at the very best.

Paul would have been quite familiar with the geography of this region as it was near his home in Tarsus. He would have known that some of the worst mountains of the region are located immediately to the north of Antioch. With that kind of knowledge, it is reasonable to assume that he would never have started through them in the winter. It seems likely, then, that Paul would have begun this journey at least as early as mid-summer, A.D. 49. This would have allowed him about fifteen to eighteen months to get to Troas, which appears to be a reasonable length of time for what he accomplished along the way.

However, before Paul departed from Antioch on the second missionary journey, he and Barnabas had been there for some time (15:30-35). Immediately before this, they had been in Jerusalem for the great council dealing with the issue of Gentile converts and what could be expected and demanded of them (15:1-29). If our reconstruction of the first part of the second missionary journey is at all correct, the great Jerusalem Council would probably have been held in A.D. 48, most likely in the late summer or early fall of that year.

Beginning with Paul's return to Antioch in the summer of A.D. 44, we can also work forward in an alternate attempt to arrive at a date for the Jerusalem Council. We have no way of knowing how long after the arrival of Paul, Barnabas, and John Mark in Antioch that the first missionary journey began. There is a distinct "feel" to the text that some considerable amount of time passed between their arrival in Antioch from Jerusalem and the beginning of the missionary enterprise. Again, as travel in that region either by sea or land was unwise in the winter, let us assume that the first missionary journey began in the spring of A.D. 45. This would have been about a year after their return from Jerusalem. It could have been later. It is unlikely that it would have been any earlier.

If Paul and Barnabas departed for Cyprus in the spring of A.D. 45, they would have preached there at least during the summer and fall (13:4-12). This is a likely period since they had been there long enough to attract the interest and attention of the proconsul. We should carefully note that they were not dealt with as rabble rousers but as people with something important to say. For them to have gained the kind of reputation which attracted the attention of a Roman official, it is likely that they had been there for several months. That being so, we are brought at least to the late fall of that year.

When the mission on Cyprus ended, the missionaries from Antioch again set sail, this time going northward toward Perga in Pamphylia (13:13). However, this trip would not have been made in winter either. Thus it is most likely that the overseas trip to the mainland at least took place no earlier than the spring of A.D. 46.

The mission of Paul and Barnabas to the northeastern corner of the Mediterranean world led them to Pisidia, Iconium, Lystra, and Derbe. Then they turned back, visiting the converts of the first part of their mission and strengthening the churches which they had established (13:14-51 to 14:1-26).

Following that mission, Paul and Barnabas sailed back to Antioch. There they reported on the success of their endeavors and "remained no little time with the disciples" (14:28). Again, we can only guess at intervals of time, using our best knowledge of the time needed to accomplish the things which they did and factoring into this the times when such travel would not have been tenable. From this standpoint, it appears that the earliest time when they could have returned to Antioch was the spring of A.D. 47, but the fall of that year is far more likely. This, however, would then put the visit of Paul and Barnabas to Jerusalem for the great council in the spring/summer of A.D. 48. This is precisely the date at which we arrived when we approached from the other direction. This at least appears to establish the probability that we are on the right track in our chronological reconstruction of this part of the ministry of Paul and the early church.

Early Christian Dates

It is far more difficult to try to arrive at specific dates for the earlier period of Christianity. However, we must make the attempt. In his epistle to the churches in the region of Galatia, Paul asserted that he made his first visit to Jerusalem three years after his conversion (Gal. 1:18). He then reported another visit to Jerusalem "after fourteen years" (Gal. 2:1).

If the second visit to which Paul referred is the same one as the Jerusalem Council, we have already established that as being A.D. 48. Fourteen years before that would have been A.D. 34. This would apparently establish the time of the first visit with his conversion thus being in A.D. 31. However, this is impossible because Jesus was apparently not crucified until A.D. 32.

Four solutions have been suggested as ways of solving this dilemma. Let us consider each of them.

(1) Some interpreters assume that the data is wrong. However, Paul's statements do not even suggest the possibility of his figures either being rounded or estimated. To the contrary, they are presented as absolute facts.

(2) Others suggest that the second visit listed in Galatians and the Jerusalem conference are not the same visit. If this is true, it means that Paul left out the Jerusalem Council in his list in Galatians. We do know that he did not mention his relief visit to Jerusalem in the epistle. This is clearly possible

but doesn't seem likely in the developing narrative of the epistle. Further, it isn't easy to find a place in Luke's record in Acts in which to fit an additional unrecorded visit to Jerusalem.

(3) Yet another suggested solution which has been proposed is that the second visit Paul mentioned in Galatians was not fourteen years after the first visit but was being dated from his conversion, just as the first visit was. This is a real possibility. It would place Paul's conversion in A.D. 34 and his first visit in A.D. 37. The chronology fits very well. However, the grammar of Galatians makes it appear that that was not likely to have been what Paul intended. We must not be guilty of accepting a solution merely because it is convenient.

(4) One system of dating used in the ancient Near East counted any part of a calendar year as a whole year. If Paul had used such a system, three years could be only slightly more than one twelve-month period, and fourteen years could be less than thirteen calendar years. This could then place his first visit to Jerusalem as early as A.D. 36, and his conversion would then probably have been about A.D. 34. To me, this is the more likely solution, given the data presently at hand.

Beginning with Pentecost in A.D. 32, the Christians began to proclaim their good news, seeking to win converts to their new faith. It appears then that the early churches had about two years for their initial development. Near the end of this time, in A.D. 34, the persecution would have been intensified under the leadership of Paul. Following his conversion, the churches apparently had several more years of gradual, but generally peaceful expansion. Paul would have visited Jerusalem in A.D. 36 and shortly thereafter departed for Tarsus.

The next datable event is the martyrdom of James and the arrest of Peter (Acts 12:1-23). This clearly occurred just before and during the Feast of Passover or Unleavened Bread, apparently in A.D. 44.

Summary

In order to facilitate the student's use of the dates which we have established for the chronology of the early church, the following table presents the conclusions which we have reached to this point.

Significant Dates for Early Christianity

Date	*Event*
Mar./Apr. 32	Crucifixion
June 32	Pentecost
34	Paul converted
36	Paul's first visit to Jerusalem
43	Paul and Barnabas in Antioch
44	Relief visit to Jerusalem, James martyred, Peter arrested, Herod dies
48	Jerusalem Council
Spring 53	Paul before Gallio
58	Paul arrested in Jerusalem
June/July 60	Paul before Festus
Autumn 60	Paul sails to Rome

With these dates now before us, we are ready to proceed with our study of this era. As the table reveals, we do not have a very good chronological outline of the early days in the spread of the gospel of Christ, but we at least have this much on which to build.

19
The Background

$\mathbf{A}$s was also true of the earlier historical periods which we have studied, the primary area of the world with which we are concerned in this part of our study is Palestine. However, in this era, our interests have now at least been extended to the north as far as Antioch and Tarsus, both located on the northeastern coasts of the Mediterranean. These two cities were located in the Roman provinces of Syria and Cilicia respectively. Also, our geographical interests have been extended toward the northeast from Galilee to include Damascus, a major city of the Decapolis. That notwithstanding, however, our primary concern is still with the regions of Judea, Samaria, and Galilee, even as it was in our study of the period of the life and ministry of Jesus.

As before, we are concerned with the history of this geographical region as it impinged upon and influenced, either directly or indirectly, the lives and ministries of the early Christians and the churches which they founded. Again, although precise historical boundaries are somewhat difficult to identify, the general period of our concern in this chapter begins with the end of the earthly ministry of Jesus. This is usually associated with His crucifixion, resurrection, and ascension, which we have dated as occurring in A.D. 32.

Further, I have designated the end of this era as being the beginning of Paul's first missionary journey. This could hardly have occurred any earlier than the spring of A.D. 45, the year following the return of Paul and Barnabas from their relief visit to Jerusalem (Acts 11:27-30). Thus, for our purposes here, the formative period of early Christianity appears to be confined to the period from mid-A.D. 32 to late A.D. 44 or early A.D. 45.

Developments in Rome

Tiberius (A.D. 14-37)

As a part of the Roman empire throughout this period, the primary historical influence upon the region of our concern continued to be Rome itself. Jesus was crucified, and His disciples began their ministry near the end of the reign of Tiberius Caesar. Unlike the emperors before and after him, Tiberius had a major concern for the conditions under which the people of the empire lived. This imperial concern was extended even to the conquered people who lived on the extremities of the empire and thus included the Jews in Palestine, as well as those settled throughout the territories of Rome. These are generally classified as the *Diaspora,* a term which is derived from a Greek word which means the dispersed ones.

Tiberius' concerns for the welfare of his people led him to seek a reduction in the burdens which Rome placed upon them, particularly the heavy taxation. However, even though the reduction of taxation would have clearly pleased the Jews of Palestine, at the same time any foreign taxation was considered to be unthinkable. The very orthodox believed the payment of foreign taxes was idolatrous. Thus Tiberius' policies did not relieve the basic stresses which existed between the Pharisees or Zealots and their Roman overlords.

As we noted earlier, Tiberius had ordered the execution of his chief administrator, Sejanus, in A.D. 31. This had been based largely upon his belief in Sejanus' treachery. However, it had also been significantly influenced by the anti-Semitic policies of the administrator.

Tiberius' act thus reveals both a fear of treachery as well as a sympathy for the Jewish people themselves. While the latter should have brought comfort to the Jewish inhabitants of his territories, the former would have brought suspicion upon anyone who might have been suspected of any form of treachery. This would certainly have included the Zealots. It would probably also have included the Pharisees, Sanhedrin, and entire priesthood. These larger groups would also have included the scribes and Sadducees. In addition, the people of the entire region of Galilee were quite hostile toward Rome. Thus that whole region would most likely have been viewed with great suspicion by Tiberius and his governors.

One final feature of Tiberius' reign which would have affected the inhabitants of Palestine beneficially also grew out of the emperor's desire to alleviate the burdens of his people. In order to provide both stability and consistency in the government and for the people of the provinces, Tiberius made the appointments of both civil and military authorities for extended periods of time. This was in stark contrast to the policies of either his predecessors or successors. For the early Christians, however, this particular imperial policy meant that during the first part of their time without the physical presence of Jesus, they were not disturbed by changing winds of government. To the contrary, they were able to operate within a relatively stable social environment, at least for that era.

Caligula (A.D. 37-41)

All of this changed with the death of Tiberius and the accession of Caligula to the imperial throne. The grandson of Germanicus, one of Rome's leading generals, Caligula was Tiberius' nephew. At one time he had been Tiberius' rival but had later become his heir. Actually named Caius, he had grown up in a military camp where he had earned the nickname of Caligula, "Little Boots."

Orphaned at the age of seven by the death of his father, who had probably been assassinated by poison, Caligula had been reared by his mother. However, she was arrested and imprisoned when he was seventeen. Following this, he lived for a time with each of two elderly matriarchs. Even if he had brought with him no congenital problems, as some historians suspect, these experiences were enough to leave him with a warped personality as well as distorted and highly suspicious thought-processes.

Whatever problems he may have brought with him to the throne, they were exacerbated by a serious illness in A.D. 38, shortly after his accession. At least from that point he clearly had a serious mental illness. Following his illness, he made the most ridiculous administrative decisions. These extended from having his horse made a Roman senator to having himself designated as a god. In addition, he apparently reversed the policies of Tiberius against anti-Semitism. If he were not actually anti-Semitic, he at least allowed anti-Semitism to arise and flourish in several places within the empire.

These acts of Caligula clearly bore upon the situation which the early Christians faced in Palestine. His irrational and capricious administrative decisions meant that the political situation suddenly became most unstable. Further, Caligula's order for a statue of himself to be placed in the temple of Jerusalem meant that an immediate spirit of rebellion flashed through the land. Although Caligula's death prevented that order from being carried out, if it had been, there would almost certainly have been a revolution. The fear of such meant that political unrest would have been the rule of the day during those few years.

Claudius (A.D. 41-54)

Caligula was assassinated by the soldiers of his own Praetorian Guard in A.D. 41. Prior to that time, the Roman senate had always named the emperor. However, the rebellious army showed its growing power by naming Claudius as the new emperor. Although the senate's approval was still officially necessary, it was merely a rubber stamp upon an already accomplished fact. However, both the assassination and the manner of naming the new emperor revealed a major instability in Roman governmental affairs as well as the growing power of the military. All of this would clearly have affected the kind of administration which the Jews and Christians in Palestine would have experienced. Uncertainty of administrative policies as well as a growing military influence would have borne heavily upon the people of the region.

However, this early uncertainty gave way to a surprising stability. Claudius, as the uncle of Caligula, had at least some legitimate claim upon the throne. He had been picked by the army as a weak and ineffectual person whom the generals could easily control. The senators who reluctantly approved him feared precisely that outcome. Perhaps no one was as opposed to Claudius becoming emperor as he was himself.

To everyone's surprise, Claudius became an able administrator and a strong ruler. Having been a petty but experienced bureaucrat, he turned to others of like qualities for his major appointments. He alienated the nobility of Rome by gathering in his administration the leading freed slaves of the empire. These freedmen had generally won their freedom by having been good administrators for the noble families. As such, they had learned the practical art of politics: how to get things done. From this background, these freedmen brought their experience to the new task of government with enthusiasm and effectiveness. In addition, the new emperor also revealed himself to be an able military strategist.

From the standpoint of the early Christians, Claudius' reign turned out to be most beneficial. He restored political stability to their immediate region and eased the rising threat of rebellion which was present in the brief reign of Caligula. Further, his policies and abilities brought a new era of peace and quiet to the entire Mediterranean world. This meant that in those early days of facing growing hostility from the Jews, the first Christians at least did not have to fear the imperial government. With the exception of the last year or two of Caligula's reign, the entire era was one in which the early Christians had little to worry about from Rome or its policies.

Developments in Palestine

Obviously, political developments in Palestine were of more immediate concern to the early Christians. They lived there. They were carrying out their early ministries there. The real issues of life and faith were being faced there on a daily basis.

Pilate in Judea and Samaria (A.D. 26-36)

As Roman procurator of Judea and Samaria, Pontius Pilate is the one who ultimately condemned Jesus to death. For that act and because his name is therefore recited regularly by multiplied millions of Christians as a part of the Apostles' Creed—"suffered under Pontius Pilate"—he is the one official whom we all know. At least, we know his name.

Little is known of Pilate or his rule following Jesus' crucifixion. A petty bureaucrat as well as a protégé of Sejanus, Pilate clearly feared being accused of anti-Semitism or being thought to be more loyal to Sejanus than to Tiberius. Pilate went to any extreme to keep the peace in the region, but this brought about his downfall.

According to Josephus, during the latter days of Pilate's administration, a Samaritan prophet gathered a large group of people on the slopes of Mount Gerizim. At that time, he had promised to reveal the hiding place of sacred temple vessels which had supposedly been deposited there in 586 B.C. at the time of the Babylonian conquest of Jerusalem. Pilate, however, informed by his spies of the gathering, suspected a revolt. He therefore sent his troops who attacked the unarmed crowd, slaughtering many people. This was reported to the Roman legate of Syria. His act was viewed as anti-Semitic as well as foolish, and Pilate was ordered to Rome to give an account to Tiberius. However Tiberius died before Pilate arrived. Although numerous legends exist as to Pilate's ultimate fate, the only thing known for certain is that Pilate disappeared from the records of history at that time. A tradition which indicates that he was banished to Gaul may be correct.

As far as the Christians were concerned, Pilate's record appears to reveal that he was motivated in those later years of his administration by an overwhelming fear of alienating the Jewish leadership in Jerusalem. This led him to authorize Jesus' crucifixion. This means that at the least he would have tried to stay uninvolved with their opposition to and persecution of the early Christians, regarding such acts as internal matters with which they could deal with impunity.

Herod Antipas in Galilee and Perea (4 B.C. to A.D. 39)

Obviously, the major part of the rule of Herod Antipas occurred before the time with which we are presently concerned. Herod was described by Jesus as "that fox" (Luke 13:32). This was an apparent reference to a sly, sneaky character. He was also shown to be somewhat controlled and manipulated by Herodias, his wife, at the time of the execution of John the Baptist (Matt. 14:6-11). This image is further emphasized by the fact that she led Herod to appeal to Caligula to make him king of the region over which he governed. However, this request backfired, and Herod was banished by the Roman emperor into the region of Gaul.

Herod Antipas showed himself to be sly, weak, and ineffectual as a ruler. During his rule, he apparently left the Galilean Christians alone and relatively free from any kind of governmental interference.

Philip in Northern Transjordan (4 B.C. to A.D. 34)

Of all the sons of Herod the Great, Philip alone was a good ruler, governing his people with understanding and justice. He was a loyal supporter of Rome and her policies. Furthermore, as the region over which he ruled had not originally been a part of the promised land, it was primarily inhabited by Gentiles rather than by Jews. Therefore, when the Jewish leaders of Jerusalem began to persecute the early Christians, they were able to flee into this region where they could find relative safety and security, at least at the first. This was probably one reason why the first Christian refugees apparently headed for Damascus, one of the major cities under Philip's control. His death was genuinely mourned by the citizens of the territory. This probably would have included some of those first Christians who had moved into the region seeking a more secure environment in which to live and minister.

Vitellius in Syria

Throughout the period of history with which we are now concerned, all of the regions of Palestine with which we are concerned were a part of the larger Roman province of Syria. This province was under the direct military control of Vitellius, who served as legate there. It was he who removed Pilate from his position as procurator, sending him to Rome to face Tiberius. Vitellius also removed Caiaphas from the high priesthood at about that time. He may also have suspected that Pilate and Caiaphas were too much involved with one another's policies and taken that opportunity of totally cleaning Judea's administrative house. Vitellius may have also suspected that the Jewish hatred of the Samaritans could have motivated Caiaphas to encourage Pilate in his brutal attack on the Samaritans.

When Vitellius removed Pilate, he appointed Marcellus as procurator until the Roman emperor had time to make an official imperial appointment. The Roman legate's acts apparently met with mixed reactions from the Jewish people of Judea. They would have rejoiced at the removal of Pilate and probably been very upset at the high-handed removal of their high priest.

In order to deal with the situation more effectively, Vitellius made a hurried trip to Jerusalem at Passover in A.D. 36. At that time, he sought to win the favor and approval of the Jewish leaders. This he accomplished by eliminating the Roman taxes on fruit. He also released the official garments of the high priest from Roman control, allowing the new high priest to wear them at that great festival.

Shortly after the accession of Caligula, Vitellius was replaced as legate of Syria by Publius Petronius (ca. A.D. 38). During Vitellius' time of authority, he had sought to be an effective ruler for Rome. His policies had essentially offered a time of peace for the Jews and Christians, at least insofar as Roman authority went.

Agrippa I (A.D. 37-44)

Following the death of Philip (A.D. 34), the northern Transjordan region over which he had ruled was returned to the direct control of the Syrian legate. However, upon the succession of Caligula as emperor of Rome, he appointed Agrippa I as king of that region. Agrippa was a grandson of Herod the Great and had been educated in Rome. There he had received the best of Roman education but had also been the companion and friend of many Roman nobles, not the least of which was Caligula.

Agrippa had been very intemperate in his youth, a characteristic which stayed with him until his death. At one time he had been banished from Rome by Tiberius. Unable to get along with a number of rulers and family members, he had moved his site of banishment on several occasions. He was allowed to return to Rome in A.D. 36. However, his rashness quickly got him in trouble again. He was overheard saying that he wished that Caligula were emperor. When this was reported to Tiberius, a man who suspected treachery on every hand, Agrippa was imprisoned and faced an imminent death.

However, Tiberius' death and Caligula's accession totally reversed Agrippa's fortunes. Caligula ordered Agrippa's release and appointed him king over Philip's territories, adding much of Syria to it. In addition, he had the iron chains taken off of Agrippa and awarded him a chain of gold of equal weight. The Roman senate was so fearful of Caligula that they not only confirmed Agrippa's appointment as king, but they gave him the senatorial title of prefect as well. Further, when Herod Antipas was banished by Caligula from his position as tetrarch of Galilee and Perea, that region was given to Agrippa, and he became king there as well (A.D. 40-44).

Though not directly ruling over large numbers of Jewish people at the beginning, he did receive authority over them when he took over Galilee and Perea. However, he had sought to be a friend of the Jews from the beginning of his reign. When anti-Semitic riots broke out within the empire, he interceded for the Jews and got the riots ended. Further, when Caligula sought to have his image placed in the Jerusalem temple, Agrippa journeyed to Rome where he was temporarily able to bring about a change of official policy.

Because of his intercessory journey to Rome, Agrippa was there when Caligula was assassinated in A.D. 41. Along with the Praetorian Guard, he played some part in getting Claudius named as the new emperor. In return for this, Claudius added to Agrippa's territories the region of Judea and Samaria, appointing him king there as well. This temporarily ended the line of Roman procurators there. Thus by A.D. 41 Agrippa ruled over as large a territory as had been ruled over by his grandfather, Herod the Great.

With the blossoming of his fortunes to this extent, Agrippa changed his name to Herod Agrippa. This was a legitimate change, since he was actually a part of the Herodian family, but it may also reveal a growing megalomania on his part. Upon his return to Palestine, he immediately went to Jerusalem to establish a royal residence there. When he sought further to strengthen his position by building a fortification wall on the north of the city, as well as by forming a coalition of minor kings in the region, Rome stepped in. They forced him to cease his fortifications and disband his coalition.

King Herod Agrippa did win the support of the Jewish leaders by a number of dramatic acts. He took the chain of gold originally given to him by Caligula and hung it in the temple over the entrance to the treasury. He also made a major thank offering to the temple and paid for the sacrifices of a number of Nazirites. Such acts were considered to be great demonstrations of piety. The New Testament tells of his attempts to please the Jews by ordering the execution of James and the arrest of Simon Peter (Acts 12:1-19). He also refused to allow his daughter to marry a Gentile until he was circumcised and converted to Judaism. He was perceived as being so orthodox that the Pharisees gave him the title of "Brother."

King Herod Agrippa's piety was most likely quite superficial and hypocritical, a matter of expediency only. His early life was wholly opposite. Further, outside of Jewish territory his acts bore no such resemblance to Jewish orthodoxy. In his non-Jewish regions, he was a major supporter of Hellenism.

The sudden death of King Herod Agrippa brought his reign to an unexpected end (vv. 20-23). It also occurred at the time when the churches were about to break forth in their great missionary advance to the heart of the empire. During his reign, the Christians clearly faced opposition and persecution. However, this appears to have been a deliberate political policy on his part rather than heartfelt opposition to their message or mission.

Other Significant Developments

Perhaps the only other significant development of this era was the outbreak of anti-Semitism in the empire. As we have noted, such attitudes were in direct opposition to the policies of Tiberius. However, this was not the case with Caligula. We have no way of knowing why this was so. What we do know was that major riots broke out in Alexandria and were apparently allowed to go unchecked on the authority of Caligula. The property and persons of the Jews were attacked and destroyed at this time. These riots were apparently brought to an end by the direct intercession of Herod Agrippa.

This anti-Semitism must have created a great deal of uncertainty on the part of Judaism in their attitude toward the Roman empire. While many of the Jewish people and some of the Jewish leaders had been in opposition to Rome all along, the official position of the Sanhedrin had been one of collaboration. The outbreak of anti-Semitism had to bring that entire policy into question. Further, as this seems to have occurred at a time when Christianity was beginning to prosper, as well as to reach out to Gentiles, it most likely merely added fuel to official Judaism's hostility toward Christianity. At least, it did nothing to ease the growing tensions between the two groups. Further, these radical changes in official policy should have shown both the Jews and Christians that relying upon government support for either religious group was problematic at best. New rulers bring new policies. Rapidly changing policies bring insecurity. Religious authority can never rest upon political power.

With this background, then, we are now ready to consider the early days of Christianity. This was the political and social stage upon which Christians acted out the next scene in the great drama of redemption.

20
The Early Days: Prosperity and Crisis

A very astute student of personality and history who had known Jesus of Nazareth might possibly have predicted that His life could have influenced the course of history. Even from merely a human perspective, the life of Jesus was outstanding enough to attract some notice. His life quickly and persistently drew the attention of both friends and enemies. Furthermore, the nature of His martyrdom also might at least have made His name a footnote on the pages of history.

However, no one, not even with the leap of the wildest imagination, would ever have suspected that the first followers of Jesus could have influenced the future of the world. Those whose names we know are remarkably unpromising people. Four of them, Simon Peter, Andrew, James, and John, were fishermen from Galilee, definitely not the kind of people who might be expected to change the course of history. Matthew, on the other hand, was a traitorous little quisling official who was despised by his own people as well as by those whom he served.

Yet the unbelievable thing happened. This group of frightened, cowed, unpromising disciples transformed the world of Judaism, the eastern Mediterranean world, the Roman world, and ultimately the whole world with the message which they proclaimed and the lives which they lived. They believed that they had "good news" to share with all people. They shared it in such a fashion that others believed it. It is our task to examine their ministry and proclamation in the light of the historical forces which were at work in their world. There was a divine side to their achievements, but for our purposes here we are concerned with the human side. Those first disciples were creatures of their time, even as we are creatures of ours. Let us examine their successes and failures against the background of the world in which they lived, served, and died.

A Time of Fear

From a human perspective the story of Jesus should have ended with His death and burial, but it did not. His burial was followed by the unbelievable: His resurrection and, after a few weeks, His ascension (Acts 1:9). At this point, the question in the minds of the apostles and the question asked by thoughtful contemporary historians must be the same: Now what? What were the disciples supposed (or expected) to do next?

In examining the nature of those immediate followers of Jesus, several features clamor for our attention. The first of these is how few they really were. Luke tells us that their number was only about 120 (v. 15). We have no way of knowing how large a group the disciples of Jesus may have been at their most numerous. We do know, however, that at one time there were at least four thousand and at another time this number had swelled to five thousand (Matt. 14:21; 15:38). In both instances these numbers only included men, so the accompanying women and children would probably have more than doubled this number. We also know that during the latter part of Jesus' ministry the numbers began to fall away so rapidly that Jesus questioned whether or not all of them might leave Him (John 6:66-67). At the last, when Jesus was arrested in Gethsemane, "they all forsook him, and fled" (Mark 14:50).

Common grief and shared sorrow brought some of them together again following the crucifixion. The shared experience of the resurrection drew some of the others back into the circle. Paul later records that the resurrected Jesus "appeared to more than five hundred" of the disciples (1 Cor. 15:6). Whether this occurred in Galilee or whether some of these had afterwards left Jerusalem, thus diminishing their number, we do not know. All we do know is that less than two months after Jesus' death the congregation in Jerusalem stood at about 120 persons. This would certainly not have seemed to be very impressive to those who remembered the great throngs of Galilee or the crowds greeting Jesus when He had entered Jerusalem only two months earlier. It would have been bad enough to see the numbers decline slowly, but to experience such a rapid falling away had to have been utterly discouraging. From a human perspective, the memory of the resurrection would have faded quickly in the light of the harsh reality of the rapid disappearance of companions. The discouragement had to be quite real for the disciples who were left in Jerusalem.

In addition, the disciples who remained in Jerusalem were almost certainly afraid. Their fear had come crashing down upon them when Jesus was arrested in the garden. He had been seized and crucified; why should not the same thing happen to them?

Peter's immediate fear had been so great that he had denied even knowing Jesus on that cataclysmic night. Of all the followers of Jesus, only John and Mary are mentioned as being close enough to be identified at the scene of the crucifixion itself. Others were probably present, but they must have remained hidden among the crowd of bystanders.

At first glance, we might suppose that the resurrection would have alleviated their fear. It may have done so to some extent, but two aspects of fear remained for them. First, they suddenly had even more reason to fear the Jewish and Roman authorities. With Jesus dead and on the way to being forgotten, the officials might ultimately have left the disciples alone. However, with Jesus' tomb empty and tales of His resurrection circulating, fresh attention was being called to His message and followers. This attention meant that the official danger to the apostles had become a rapidly increasing reality. Their fear of both the Sanhedrin and of Pilate had to be increasing. It would not fade and go away.

The disciples' fear of the authorities had been with them in varying degrees since early in Jesus' ministry. A new dimension had been added to their fear following His resurrection. People are generally frightened by change. This is intensified when the change is radical and not understood. When Jesus was raised from the dead, the world of the disciples was turned upside down. Resurrection was beyond comprehension. They had *no* frame of reference with which to understand what had happened to their Lord, their world, or them personally. Fear of the unknown was suddenly thrust upon them.

This fear may have begun to fade after the first few days. After all, Jesus was once again with them to comfort and guide, but then another incomprehensible event took place! He ascended! Some forty days after He had returned to them through resurrection, He left them by His ascension (Acts 1:3,9). Fear, a nameless terror, must have gripped them. Not only did they have to face the growing hostility of the Jewish leaders, but they had to face it alone. Jesus was gone again. Though His second going was not as catastrophic, it was far more inexplicable.

They again gathered in fear, at least some of them, in the upper room in Jerusalem. There they waited; they were waiting for something Jesus had promised but which they did not understand—the coming of God's Holy Spirit (v. 8). They prayed (v. 14). They waited. They certainly talked about Jesus and His teachings, but most of all they waited.

The time spent in waiting led to a deep sense of purposelessness. They, like most of us, could not abide inactivity. We want to be busy, and so did they. With nothing to do, they decided to do something, so they replaced Judas. (We know that God Himself later apparently replaced Judas with Paul, but they ran before Him). Once again, the big fisherman from Galilee took the lead. The criteria which was established for the new apostle was that he must have been a witness of the entire ministry of Jesus from His baptism to His ascension (vv. 21-22). So they selected Matthias with the intent that he should become one of the twelve apostles (v. 26). However, one thing went wrong. He is never heard of again. No question can be raised as to this man's goodness, but he appears to have been their man for the job, not God's. Not being able to live with their fears while they waited on God, they decided to run God's kingdom their way, and that had led nowhere. So the feeble, frightened, fearful Christians of Jerusalem gathered in the upper room and impatiently waited upon God.

The local officials of Judaism and Rome waited also. They, too, had certainly feared the outcome of the immediate reports of the resurrection, but as the days passed into weeks, the Sanhedrin and Pilate must certainly have concluded that there was nothing to fear. Thus they decided that there was no need to act. And clearly, no word of those local happenings in Jerusalem made its way to the principal capital of Roman Syria, much less to the imperial capital in Rome.

Pentecost

The Jewish festival of Pentecost got its name, as we noted earlier, from the Latin word for *fifty*, since it occurs fifty days after the ceremony of the barley sheaf during the Feast of the Passover or Unleavened Bread. It celebrated the beginning of the grain harvest but was given no other historical basis in the Old Testament. To understand as fully as possible the significance of this particular feast for the first Christian community, three specific points need to be considered.

First, we need to be aware of the chronology involved at this point. The day of Pentecost should have occurred that year on the fifty-first day after Jesus' crucifixion. If the forty days which Luke says intervened between the resurrection and ascension is to be taken literally, then there were nine days by our reckoning between Jesus' ascension and the coming of the Holy Spirit. On the other hand, "forty" is frequently used in the Bible as a large number which has been rounded. In that case, we do not know precisely how long this intervening period was. However, in either instance, the period spent in waiting by the disciples was clearly long enough for time to begin to drag. Enough days intervened for them to begin to have anxieties, if not real doubts, about what Jesus had intended for them. The temptation had to have been quite real for them to give up and go home to Galilee. Some of them may have already done so.

Second, Jerusalem at any time was a center both of commerce and religion. Jews from all over the world came there at special times of religious celebration. Thus at any time, we might have found business people of many nationalities on the streets of Jerusalem. During the pilgrimage festivals, however, the city would have been even more cosmopolitan. Jews from throughout the Diaspora would have been present to celebrate.

Third, from the standpoint of any reasonably orthodox Jew, the Day of Pentecost was peculiarly appropriate for the coming of the Spirit and beginning of the proclamation of the gospel. Pentecost celebrated the beginning of the grain harvest. How appropriate it was for the beginning of the harvest of souls for the new kingdom of God.

As usual when we approach the description of very sacred events, we are left strangely unable to give a detailed depiction. Such experiences are so unique and personal as to defy any ultimate description. What appeared to the disciples was something "like" fire (Acts 2:3). What they heard was similar to the sound of a wind (v. 2). The point Luke was making is that what they experienced defied description. Yet it had to be described. The symbols of fire and wind are familiar throughout the Bible as being present when God appeared. (Theologians call these appearances "theophanies.) Luke's point was quite clearly made. The disciples had no doubt that God had come to them in a real and unique way. What they experienced was both recognizable and not subject to debate on their part.

As a result of the coming of God's Spirit upon them, the frightened and cowed disciples were suddenly emboldened to go forth from their hiding place and tell what God had done in Christ Jesus. Even more significantly, they were empowered with the ability to speak other languages. At a time when the city was filled with people speaking a multitude of languages, the disciples were able to communicate with them. Further, they were able to do this at a time when what they communicated would be carried to the ends of the earth by those who heard.

The reaction of the people in Jerusalem to this sudden outbreak on the part of the disciples was exactly what we might have suspected. Some thought that the disciples were drunk. Peter, once again the spokesman for the group, put that rumor to rest (vv. 13-16).

Other bystanders listened, and hearing the disciples' words, they believed! The end result of that day's activities was that the number of believers increased by about three thousand on that one day.

The results of Pentecost for the church of Jerusalem are fairly well known. The converts, both new and old, began to pool their resources to meet the needs of those to whom the church ministered (vv. 44-45). Further, they joined together in study of the teachings of those who had been closest to Jesus throughout His ministry. Finally, they maintained their relationship to the temple and their old faith, while adding additional worship and fellowship experiences to their lives (vv. 42,46-47). As a consequence, the church continued to grow beyond that initial outbreak on Pentecost.

On the other hand, the results of Pentecost for the Jewish leaders had to be just as striking. It must have seemed to them as if the world had caved in. They thought they had put an end to the entire "Jesus business" when they crucified Him. That came apart when the reports of His resurrection began to circulate. The Sanhedrin had clearly expected the early Christians to try to get everyone to believe in the resurrection, so they put out the tale that Jesus' followers had stolen His body (Matt. 28:11-15). However, when the Christians had done nothing to spread their resurrection faith abroad, the Jewish leaders stopped worrying. The disciples were still frightened, and apparently no further action toward them had been planned.

Furthermore, the attention of the high priest and his followers had been directed from the "Jesus business" toward the great Day of Pentecost, a high and holy day for them. When it arrived their world had come tumbling down. The movement which they thought they were rid of was back on the scene with a vengeance. Pilate, like any good governor, was most certainly aware of the sudden unrest in the center of his territory. He could afford to watch and wait for a time, but the Sanhedrin did not have that luxury. They had to act. They could not ignore what was heresy to them. From their perspective, the Christians had to be dealt with and dealt with quickly.

First Confrontations

The wrath of the Sanhedrin was aroused by the daring of the apostles. This led them to strike at the Christians with speed. Direct confrontation had been inevitable from the first words spoken by Peter on the Day of Pentecost. It was not slow in coming.

The healing of a lame beggar outside the temple became the immediate trigger of a confrontation with official Judaism (Acts 3:1 9). Not only was this an act of mercy, to a people long familiar with the symbolic acts of the prophets it was a deliberate challenge. Under Old Testament law, no one who was physically deformed could enter the sacred place of worship (Lev. 21:17-20). This man had been healed of his deformity and thus could enter the temple with Peter and John (Acts 3:8). The meaning was clear: The old way had shut people out from God, and the new way brought them in through God's act of mercy.

Peter and John took advantage of the amazement of the bystanders to proclaim the good news of God's grace. The news of the miraculous event and the disciples' message was quickly reported to the Sanhedrin and brought an even quicker response. It is significant that the initial reaction came from the priests and Sadducees, not from the Pharisees (4:1). The Christians' proclamation of the resurrection was already beginning to divide the opposition.

As a consequence of their action, Peter and John were imprisoned. However, in spite of the open opposition of the Sanhedrin, people still accepted the new faith (v. 4).

At the trial of the two apostles, Peter was no longer the fearful denier he had been at Jesus' arrest. Instead, he spoke in a manner which deliberately confronted the Sanhedrin. Two features are quite significant here. First, the Jewish leaders who were the intellectual elite of Judaism were amazed at the boldness and ability of the unlearned and ignorant men (v. 13). They were aware that whatever it was which gave them this ability, it was somehow related to the fact that "they had been with Jesus" (v. 13). (This does not put a premium on being unlearned and ignorant. Others, such as Barnabas, were apparently not so characterized. A later disciple, Paul, was one of the intellectual giants of that or any other age. The focus was not upon their ignorance but upon their obvious relation to Jesus.)

The second major feature of this initial confrontation is the fact that the miracle could not be denied (v. 14). The lame man was well known and old enough for his own testimony to be considered quite trustworthy (v. 22). Coupled with an obvious division in the court, this ultimately led to nothing more than the disciples being threatened (vv. 18,21). This was the beginning but not the end of the confrontation between the Jewish leaders and Christian community of Jerusalem.

While the open and official opposition of the Sanhedrin to the church of Jerusalem did not deter the Christians' continued witness, it apparently did keep some people in Jerusalem from uniting with them (5:13; an alternate but less likely edition of the text may mean that the ambivalence of the Sanhedrin kept anyone from interfering with the church for a while). On the other hand, new converts did continue to be added (v. 14). Further, their notoriety attracted more and more attention in Jerusalem (vv. 15-16).

The situation, at least from the perspective of the high priest, was getting more and more out of hand. Once again some of the apostles were seized and thrust into prison (vv. 17-18). Following a miraculous escape, they were again brought into open court for a trial (vv. 19,25-26). This time the division within the Sanhedrin in their attitude toward this movement became much more open. Peter, however, was neither awed nor cowed by his confrontation with the high priest and the Sanhedrin (vv. 27-32). The apostles' blunt and confrontive response to their accusers merely fueled the anger already directed at them. Some of the Sanhedrin wanted to execute the Christians immediately (v. 33). However, Gamaliel, one of the leading Pharisees (also Paul's teacher, cf. Acts 22:3), urged that they bide their time in dealing with the Christians (5:34-39). By calling the attention of the Sanhedrin to earlier experiences with Theudas and Judas, two false messiahs whose movements had finally come to nothing, Gamaliel insisted the high court did not need to defend God's kingdom. God was quite able to take care of it for Himself.

For the moment, at least, Gamaliel's advice carried the day. Thwarted by the cooling of the court's anger, the high priest had the disciples beaten to demonstrate their weakness before the court and then released them following a renewed warning to keep silent about their newfound faith (v. 40).

Rather than being discouraged, however, the disciples rejoiced that they had suffered for Jesus' sake. They remained as bold as ever. As Luke says: "And every day in the temple and at home they did not cease teaching and preaching Jesus as the Christ" (v. 42). However, the gathering storm was about to unleash its full fury upon them.

During his recording of these confrontations, Luke applied the term *church* to the Jerusalem disciples for the first time (v. 11). The use of this particular term carried special meanings for both Jew and Gentile. To the Jew, it described the "congregation" of Israel. This referred to the entire people of the covenant who had been set apart as the people of God. To the Gentile or more particularly to the Greeks, the term referred to the free men who made up the citizens of a city. Both of these usages bring significant meaning to its application to those Christians of Jerusalem. They were free and equal citizens of the community who had been gathered by God into His new covenant and set apart as His holy people. We must remind ourselves that Luke nowhere says that this was when the disciples began to be called a church. Yet we must at least consider this possibility, since it is the time when in his record he began to use the term.

The black thunderheads which had been gathering over the heads of the Jerusalem church suddenly unleashed all of their fury upon the disciples. The scene was brightened by the flash of lightning of the ministry of Stephen, one of those selected ministers to the Grecian widows of the Jerusalem church (6:1,5). His witness to some of the Greek Jews in Jerusalem led them to plot against him in order to get rid of him (v. 11). However, the Sanhedrin had already been further antagonized by the fact that now even some of the priests themselves had become converts (v. 7).

When Stephen was brought to trial, the same tactics used against Jesus were tried. False witnesses sought to accuse him of blasphemy (vv. 13-14). When confronted by the high priest, Stephen gave a simple recitation of Old Testament evidence of the continual rebellious disobedience of the Hebrew people, finally lumping the Sanhedrin with their ancestors, as being of the same ungodly nature (7:51-53). This aroused their anger, but it was not until Stephen insisted that Jesus was presently in the seat of divine power with God that they lost all self-control. Such a statement ascribing divinity to Jesus was patently blasphemous to them (vv. 56-57).

Although the Sanhedrin could not legally execute anyone, like a mob they sentenced Stephen, carried him forth from the temple and city, and stoned him (v. 58). Among those standing by, watching in approval, was a young man named Saul (7:58; 8:1). With the lightning flash of Stephen's stoning, the storm broke over the head of the church in Jerusalem. The Sanhedrin's patience was at an end.

Attempts at Ministry

During the time that the early Christians were experiencing both the initial outpouring of God's Spirit and the Sanhedrin's hostility, they did not allow the vehemence of the latter to distract them from the purpose of the former. The church from its earliest days became involved in ministry. It begs the question to insist that Jesus had showed them how to minister to human need. At least until Pentecost, until the outpouring of God's empowering Spirit upon them, they revealed little evidence of compassionate concern or ministry in any form. Afterwards, the situation began to change.

We have already noted that the ministry of the apostles was a major source of the Sanhedrin's opposition to them. The early Christians clearly had no desire to separate themselves from Judaism, the faith of their fathers. They simply added new (Christian) forms of worship to their old ones (2:42; 3:1). On one such occasion they healed a lame man (3:6-7). The apostles' sense of ministry to human need was quite keen. To them such opportunities offered just one more means of sharing God's love and blessing.

Those who made up the church of Jerusalem are said to have been "of one heart and soul" and to have held all their possessions in common (4:32). The point of this was clearly that each member's needs might be met (v. 34). We must not misunderstand this. No one was apparently compelled to turn over possessions to the church, but the fellowship was of such a nature that they felt that individual possessions were best used for the common good.

No one was condemned for not giving possessions to the church. Ananias and Sapphira were condemned for claiming to have done more than they actually did (5:3-4). Barnabas, on the other hand, was praised for sharing the whole price of the sale of a field with the entire congregation (4:36-37).

The church from its earliest days recognized that it had a responsibility to share God's blessings in a manner which enabled them as a whole to meet one another's needs. They quickly realized that they still lived in a real world with human needs which ought to be met. Adequate financial resources were clearly a necessary part of this.

Being empowered by God's Spirit, however, did not destroy the human nature of the early Christians. (Nor does it destroy ours, either.) Problems grew out of the generosity of its members. Some, like Ananias and Sapphira, envied the praise which others received, so they sought to gain similar praise. This became their goal rather than ministry to human need. On the other hand, others became suspicious that they were not getting their fair share of the church's benefits. The basis for this conflict had its foundation in the old Hellenist-Hebrew controversy. Both groups were Jews, but the Hellenists were not as "orthodox" as the "mainline" Hebrews. In general, Hellenists believed that they were trying to adapt to a new world while they suspected that the Hebrews were trying to hold onto days long gone. The Hebrews, on the other hand, accused the Hellenists of compromising their faith on the altar of being up-to-date, while they perceived themselves as being "defenders of the faith."

The generations-old controversy broke out in the new churches. The Hellenists suspected that their needy widows were not getting a fair share of the charity from the church (6:1). In an act of amazing wisdom, the church selected seven men to take care of the matter, making sure that the distribution of the church's blessings was done fairly. All seven had Greek names, indicating that they were themselves of a Hellenistic background (v. 5). All but one were almost certainly Jews of the Diaspora. Nicolaus was "a proselyte of Antioch." This means that he was a Greek by birth who had become a converted Jew. With these distributing the resources, no one would have been able to accuse them of neglecting the Hellenist widows. The church's ministry was being handled in a wise and businesslike manner.

In addition to their ministry to their own number, the church, like Jesus before them, continued to meet human need all around them. They healed the lame and ministered in a loving manner to an unloving world (5:12,15-16). The end result of this was that people in need began to seek out the Christians. The point is the early Christians showed their love for people wherever they went. They were truly "ministers."

Thus ministry became a significant part of the early church's program, but without question, the greatest part of its program was its evangelism—its enlarging mission.

An Enlarging Witness

According to Luke's record, Jesus' final words to the disciples were words of commission. "You shall receive power when the Holy Spirit has come upon you; and you shall be my witnesses in Jerusalem and in all Judea and Samaria and to the end of the earth" (Acts 1:8). Three features stand out in this record. First, Jesus' words were not a command but a description. When the disciples were empowered by the Holy Spirit, they would normally and automatically become witnesses to Jesus. Second, the enlarging sphere of their witness was also described. Beginning where they were, the apostles and their fellow Christians were to take the gospel to the ends of the earth. Luke followed this story as it led from Jerusalem to Rome, but it obviously led in other directions as well. Further, although the disciples did not immediately recognize the fact, their mission of witness was to *all* people. No one was left out of the widening circles.

Third, Jesus' description of the church's mission came in response to a theological question (1:6). This kind of inquiry had become typical of the Judaism of the day. In turn, however, such questions led to a sterile faith which turned on the minutest matters of orthodoxy with little or no concern for the human predicament. Jesus was plainly describing the primary mission of the Christian community to be one of witness rather than one of becoming *bogged down* in the details of mere intellectual curiosity. Further, the Christians did not have to know everything before they could describe what they did know.

When the Spirit of God descended upon the Christian community at Pentecost, Jesus' earlier description of them began to come to pass. They were both empowered and gifted to begin the accomplishment of their task of witness. We have only the words of Simon Peter in Acts, but the entire community was involved in their sharing of the good news of Jesus.

Although we do not know what each of them said, the places in Acts where we do have records of the Christians' message all have a generally common outline. (1) The life of Jesus is described with emphasis upon His suffering and death. (2) His resurrection and exaltation as God's Son is set forth. (3) It is pointed out that this was all in direct fulfillment of Old Testament prophecies. (4) The hearers are finally exhorted to repent of their sins and to accept Jesus as Lord, bringing the forgiveness of sins into their experience. We may safely assume that this was the primary thrust of their ongoing witness.

The disciples began to bear this witness as soon as God's Spirit came to them. They spoke their message in public in Jerusalem to people from all over the world (2:5-11; 3:12-26). When put on trial before the Sanhedrin, the disciples bore witness to Jesus rather than defending themselves (4:8-12; 5:29-32).

Further, when the church in Jerusalem suffered division over its ministry to the widows, the apostles sought for a way to meet the need so that they could give a primary emphasis to their witness (6:3-4). Yet even here we discover that other Christians in addition to the apostles gave their witness when an opportunity was provided (7:2-56).

Unfortunately, these early Christians seemed to continue to focus their attention upon Jerusalem. They witnessed to people there who were from other parts of the world. We can probably safely assume that at least some of them carried the gospel with them as they returned home. On the other hand, this spreading of the gospel by osmosis does not at all seem to be the kind of thing which

Jesus had in mind when He commissioned them. In fact, we almost seem to have a tower of Babel all over again (cf. Gen. 11:1-9).

Another impetus to go to the ends of the earth appeared to be necessary. The Christians appeared to have been faithful in bearing witness where they were and to those with whom they came in contact. On the other hand, they apparently failed to go to the ends of the earth with either a deliberate plan or an active purpose. Their witness was enlarging, but it was slow, far too slow.

21
Days of Expansion and Persecution

During the first two years of the ministry and witness of the early Christians, growth had come. Luke is quite precise about that in his record in Acts. The Christian community had begun, apparently, with their number somewhere in the vicinity of about 120 persons (Acts 1:15). These were the ones who had remained in Jerusalem following Jesus' death and resurrection.

Pentecost, with its miraculous outpouring of God's Holy Spirit, had seen the number of the Jerusalem Christians increased by about three thousand converts (2:41). A continued witness on the part of the disciples over the next few months brought their number up to about five thousand *men* (4:4). This method of counting people was typical of the culture of the day. Women and children were generally considered as little more than property by most of the Mediterranean world. Men alone were considered to be of importance. Only they counted. This number of men might mean that the actual number of Christians, including women and children, was anywhere from two to four times larger than this basic figure.

Beyond this point, all we know is that "the disciples were increasing in number" (6:1). Whatever this may imply, clearly it was enough growth to terrify the Sanhedrin. Yet, the witness of the church still appears basically to have been focused on Jerusalem. This focus needed to be enlarged for them to fulfill the command of Jesus. Their vision had to be lifted beyond their immediate homeland.

At the same time, however, even though Luke tells us nothing about it, some Christian churches were obviously established in Samaria and Galilee. Paul's conversion brought a time of peace to all of these congregations (9:31). We can understand groups of believers settling in these places. We can also probably assume that converts in Jerusalem from other lands at the time of Pentecost had also carried their faith home with them.

Thus it is certainly false to limit Christianity's spread to Jerusalem and Judea alone in the first two years following Jesus' death. It is probably false even to limit it to Palestine. However, there is no question that those first apostles still had their attention focused there. For them to become what Jesus intended, *people on a mission to the ends of the earth,* something more had to be done. This was not long in occurring.

Saul, the Persecutor

The person who served as the human catalyst in providing an impetus for the spread of the gospel was a bitter enemy of the Christian cause, the young Saul. We do not know much about his background, but we can piece together a few details through which we can begin to understand him.

Saul's birthplace was Tarsus, a major city of the Roman province of Cilicia (21:39; 22:3). Although being born in this decidedly Greek city, Saul was also a Jew of the tribe of Benjamin (Rom. 11:1). Saul's Jewish heritage was even further enhanced by the fact that he was a Pharisee and the son of a Pharisee (Acts 23:6). His very name proclaimed his heritage because it came from his nation's first king. Further, Saul was trained as a rabbi, studying under the tutelage of Gamaliel of Jerusalem (22:3).

The heritage and training of Saul prepared him for the tasks he was later called upon to perform. He was a master of the sacred Scriptures of Judaism, our Old Testament. He thought and taught like a rabbi, and although brought up far from Jerusalem, was a master of the ancient Hebrew and the contemporary Aramaic languages of the Jewish people. At the same time, his home city of Tarsus provided him with a larger world view than the more provincial Palestinian Jews would have possessed.

In addition to these matters, Saul had inherited Roman citizenship from his father (16:37-38; 22:24-28). Such citizenship was a prized possession. We have no way of knowing how Saul's father obtained this, but it was most likely a result of rendering some significant service to the empire. For whatever cause, it is quite clear that Saul prized this citizenship and the rights which came with it.

Numerous suggestions have been given to explain the later change of Saul's name to Paul. The change occurred as his Christian ministry reached out beyond the Jews to the Gentiles, apparently so as not to alienate those whom he sought to reach. It is possible that Saul simply chose a Greek name which was similar, thus arbitrarily selecting "Paul" as a replacement for "Saul." On the other hand, it was not uncommon in that era for children with such a mixed heritage to have a double name representing both cultures. Thus he may have been named Saul-Paul from the very beginning, simply emphasizing the latter name as the Gentile mission developed.

A great debate rages over whether or not Saul was ever married. No wife is ever mentioned, but if the expression at the stoning of Stephen that "Saul was consenting to his death" (8:1) means that he was a member of the Sanhedrin, then he would have had to had a wife. Some interpreters believe this to be so and hold that his marriage had been unhappy, having been terminated either by divorce or his wife's death. These interpreters assume that much of Saul's later "negative" attitude toward women grew out of his bitter personal experience. On the other hand, Luke's expression may only mean that Saul approved of the judgment of the Sanhedrin in the execution of Stephen. In this case, the interpreters conclude that Saul was a bachelor for all of his life. We have no definitive evidence.

Saul was a "tentmaker" (18:3). Those who studied to be rabbis were required to have a trade by which to support themselves. This trade apparently was later used by Saul to supply his financial needs for much of his Gentile mission.

Out of this background came Saul the persecutor, a man thoroughly "zealous of the traditions" of his fathers (Gal. 1:14). We do not know when he was first confronted by this new faith of the Christians. As a student of Gamaliel, Saul probably heard of the Christians before the crucifixion of Jesus and may have been a witness to it. He would almost certainly have heard of the resurrection as soon as it began to be reported in Jerusalem. As far as we know, his first *direct* contact with the Christians most likely occurred when the leaders of the synagogue of the Cilicians were confronted by Stephen (Acts 6:9). At the very least, Saul approved of the condemnation and stoning of the bold disciple (8:1). While Saul apparently did not actually stone Stephen, he kept the robes and cloaks of those who did (7:58).

For Saul, the end result of his whole experience with the Christians in general and with Stephen in particular led to the conclusion that this new movement was heretical in the worst degree. A general persecution of the Christians broke out under the auspices of the Sanhedrin, and Saul became its leader (8:1,3-4). Some further executions occurred, apparently with Roman approval, and Saul bore witness against them before the Sanhedrin. Saul also apparently tortured Christians until they blasphemed against Jesus (26:10-11). Other Christians were certainly imprisoned and were most likely beaten for their so-called heresy. So zealous and oppressive was the persecution under Saul that many of the disciples who had earlier faced the Sanhedrin with boldness now fled from Jerusalem (8:1b). The amazing thing, however, is that even though they fled in fear through Judea and Samaria, they told their story as they went. Instead of stopping the spread of the Christian faith, the persecution merely caused it to spread abroad more rapidly (8:4-6).

We have no way of accurately reconstructing the chronology of this era. However, the events as Luke recorded them appear to have moved quite rapidly. It was not long before the number of Christians in Jerusalem had been reduced to the extent that the effort of persecution was not bearing sufficient fruit. Apparently very few Christian communities or churches seem to have sprung up close by.

However, a major center of Christianity appears to have arisen in Damascus, about 150 miles north of Jerusalem. This site may have been chosen by the Christians as being relatively secure, since it was in the territory governed by Philip. It may also have been chosen due to the location of the large settlement of Essenes (apparently related to the people of Qumran). However, some of these reasons would have changed with the death of Philip in A.D. 34. For about three years (A.D. 34-37) Damascus fell under the direct government of Roman Syria.

Probably due to the transition in government and the now relatively large distance between Damascus and those Romans ruling it, Saul and the priests of Jerusalem took an opportunity to extend their persecution of the Christians all the way to that city (9:1-2). Although Saul was converted along the way (we shall return to that subject later), the persecutions did not wholly cease. They were simply interrupted for a while (9:23,29,31). In their immediate surprise, disappointment, and wrath following the conversion of Saul, the fury of the leaders of Judaism was now wholly directed toward him. He was viewed by them as a traitor.

For about a decade the Sanhedrin apparently allowed the churches to live in peace. However, they were clearly unhappy with that situation. It may have been that their energies were more immediately involved with the threats brought to their nation and faith by the rule of Caligula in Rome (A.D. 37-41). Further, the outbreak of anti-Semitic riots in Alexandria during this period was an equal threat to their position within the empire. For whatever reason, however, with the conversion of Saul the Sanhedrin's persecution of the church was temporarily abated.

Saul, the Convert

No better term exists by which to describe the event or experience which transformed Saul the persecutor into Saul the Christian spokesman than conversion. However, Saul never used that term to describe his transformation. He described what happened to him as a "heavenly vision" and as "revelation" (Acts 26:19; Gal. 1:12). Transformation there was, and the end result was that Saul was converted from being Christianity's most bitter enemy into becoming its most ardent supporter.

As Saul journeyed to Damascus for the purpose of arresting and harassing the Christians there, he had a transforming experience (vision, revelation) with Jesus Christ. Several features of that experience need to be examined and pondered. (1) Saul clearly considered his experience to have been unique. With all of his later missionary zeal and evangelistic fervor, the apostle never seems to have believed that his experience should be duplicated in the lives of others. (2) We have no way of knowing what impact the witness of Stephen and others had upon him. As the leading persecutor of the Christians, he probably knew more about Jesus and His followers than anyone outside the faith and many within it. When Jesus appeared to him on the way to Damascus, Saul's mind had already been prepared by those whom he had oppressed. (3) Saul's conversion was not from a life of great moral evil. As a leader of the

Pharisees, he had lived a life which was basically good and blameless (Phil. 3:6). Yet he was quite aware that obedience to the law did not lead to being at peace with God (Rom. 8:10). (4) Neither was Saul's transformation the abandonment of one religion for another. He never considered himself to have abandoned Judaism. Near the end of his life he was in the temple observing Jewish rites when he was arrested and imprisoned (Acts 21:26-27).

The ultimate point appears to be this: along the way from Jerusalem to Damascus, Saul saw Jesus (9:5). The end result was his conversion and baptism. All the zeal and energy which had been devoted to stamping out Christianity was suddenly rechanneled into propagating that same faith. The early churches' greatest enemy suddenly had become their greatest proponent. Saul the oppressor now became Saul the witness. He was truly a new man in Christ.

It is difficult to work out the chronology of the first years of Saul's Christian experience, as we noted in chapter 19. Apparently he went into the Arabian desert following that experience for an extended time of prayer and meditation (Gal. 1:17-18). He needed time to assess the nature of his faith and to assimilate his new experience. When he did begin to preach in Damascus, his preaching aroused such hostility that he eventually had to flee for his life (Acts 9:23).

Luke implies that the opposition to Saul in Damascus came from the Jews alienated by his supposed "treachery" (9:22). Saul's own later account notes that the governor of Damascus, responsible to King Aretas, the Nabatean ruler of the ancient Edomite territory, was trying to apprehend him (2 Cor. 11:32). This probably indicates that the Jewish leaders had successfully involved the civil government in opposition to Saul. The unrest which he was causing in the city was clearly disturbing the peace. So Saul fled not only to escape personal but official enemies as well.

Upon his flight, Saul chose to go to Jerusalem. This was the most dangerous place in all the world for him, because that was where the Sanhedrin and priests were who felt so utterly betrayed by Saul. At the same time, that was also where the apostles were. Saul wanted to meet with them and desperately be accepted by them. Further, although he made much of the fact that his faith was his own, he did apparently want to be sure that he was in the same stream of thought with the other apostles (Acts 9:26-27; Gal. 1:18).

Saul probably arrived in Jerusalem in mid to late summer of A.D. 36. As any one would have suspected, when "he attempted to join the disciples . . . they were all afraid of him, for they did not believe that he was a disciple" (9:26). The Jerusalem disciples had every reason to fear him. They also had every reason to be suspicious of him, but big-hearted Barnabas reached out to Saul in love and brought him into the church, urging that they give him a chance (v. 27). This loving act of Barnabas involved great risk, but it grew out of his great love for Jesus and His church. He was not only willing but eager to minister to one who had been his enemy.

Thus Saul was accepted into the church of Jerusalem. From that base he witnessed in Jerusalem, proclaiming Jesus as Lord (vv. 28-29). Because he had earlier led the opposition, it is easy to imagine that his message in Jerusalem caught the attention of all who heard. Further, it is also easy to understand that this was a situation which neither the high priest nor Sanhedrin could allow to continue. The fact that the "Hellenists" were those with whom Saul had his most direct confrontation would indicate that even those among whom he might have found the most sympathy were alienated by him. So once again a plot was made against his life. He fled from Jerusalem, heading home to Tarsus (v. 30).

Expanding Circles of Witness

The Jewish officials were clearly perturbed by Saul's conversion or "treachery" as they would have called it. For the period of time after he began to preach in Damascus until his final flight from Judea, all of their energies had apparently been devoted to destroying him or at least eliminating his witness where his earlier activities were known. When he fled from Jerusalem they obviously felt (wrongly) that they had won. Their energies had been depleted in the attacks on him, and numerous other pressing concerns demanded their attention. Insofar as the Christians were concerned, "the church throughout all Judea and Galilee and Samaria had peace and was built up" (v. 31). In the time of the persecution by Saul, they had carried the gospel as they fled in fear. Now they carried it outward in a time of peace as they followed the leadership of God's Holy Spirit.

Prior to the conversion of Saul, another one of the seven Hellenistic Christians who had been selected to serve in ministering to the Christian widows had broadened the Christians' witness. Philip had carried the good news of Jesus both to Samaritans and the servant of Queen Candace of Ethiopia (8:5,27-28). The Samaritans, though despised, were at least half-Jews. The Ethiopians were Semites and thus related to the Jews, though even more distantly. The fact that the Ethiopian was a eunuch, however, meant that he was excluded from worshiping in the temple proper. However, he had been on a pilgrimage to the Holy City. With Philip's witness, people who had been shut out of the old faith were brought in to the new, but after Saul's conversion, an even more rapid expansion began.

We first note that Peter made a journey from Jerusalem to Joppa, the seaport of Jerusalem. On the way he passed through Lydda (the ancient Lod) (9:32,36). In both places he visited with disciples who were already in place. These were apparently the result of the witness of other, nameless Christians who had borne witness there.

So far as we know or have any reason to know, the Christians in both of the places were also Jews. Thus they still would have been of the same racial and religious background as the first disciples. In fact, following the destruction of Jerusalem in A.D. 70, Lydda became a major center of rabbinic training. This probably indicates that it was already a center of Judaism in the time we are considering. Once again we see the church growing, but it was growing out of the same old Jewish soil. That, however, was about to change in the decade of peace.

While in Joppa, Simon Peter was sent for by a Roman centurion from Caesarea. He is described as being of the "Italian Cohort," a cohort made up of free men from Italy. The fact that his family was living with him in Caesarea most likely indicates that he had retired from active military service and had settled in Caesarea, the official Roman capital of the province of Judea. He is described as being a "devout man who feared God with all his household, gave alms liberally to the people, and prayed constantly to God" (10:2). These terms used to describe him are frequently used to refer to those Gentiles who had generally accepted the Jewish faith without actually having been circumcised and become Jews. They usually worshiped at the synagogue.

Peter made one of his typical impetuous acts when he preached the gospel to this Gentile, even though he may have been active in the synagogue of Caesarea. Following their conversion, Peter baptized Cornelius and his family (vv. 44-48). This is the first recorded instance of Gentiles becoming Christians, although we must remember that this man was most likely already aware of the Hebrew Scriptures and sympathetic to the Hebrew faith.

The radical redirection of the Christian mission to include Gentiles startled the church of Jerusalem, and Peter was called upon to explain his actions. Beginning with the story of his vision and concluding with obvious evidence of Cornelius' conversion, the big fisherman reported the entire experience to his fellows (11:1-18). Although it appears that not all the Jerusalem Christians were pleased with what had happened, they at least accepted the fact and "glorified God." Some, however, seem simply to have been "silenced." The note of joyous acceptance is missing.

The next step in the enlarging mission of the church went even beyond a Gentile who was a worshiper of the God of Israel. As the Christians had fled from Jerusalem and continued to spread even further afield, they had established churches among Jewish converts in places as widely scattered as Phoenicia, Cyprus, and Antioch (11:19). However, in Antioch, for the first time of which we have any record, Christians witnessed to Greeks who had no previous relations with Judaism, and some believed! (vv. 20-21). Thus a church began with *little or no Jewish* roots. This so startled the Jerusalem church that Barnabas was sent to investigate (v. 22). Big-hearted Barnabas, however, did more than go to find facts. He entered into their ministry. He quickly recognized that both he and the church needed a kind of leadership which he could not provide. On his own authority, without checking with the Jerusalem church, Barnabas went to Tarsus and brought Saul back with him (vv. 23-26).

Together Barnabas and Saul ministered in Antioch for "a whole year" (v. 26). This was apparently from early A.D. 43 to early A.D. 44. The important feature of their joint ministry there was the results. Teaching the new converts the claims of Christ, they led them to live so that they began to be called "Christian" by their enemies. This is the first time that this name was applied to believers. Their enemies recognized by the lives of these believers that they were followers of the Christ Saul and Barnabas preached.

In the widening circle of Christian mission, however, a bold new frontier had been crossed. The church was no longer Jewish only but now had become both Jewish and Gentile.

The Persecution Renewed and Intensified

The Jewish priests and the Sanhedrin must have felt as if they were on a roller coaster during this era. They had felt on top of affairs when Jesus was crucified. With the reports of His resurrection, they surely felt that they had plunged into an abyss. However, when weeks passed with no overt proclamation of this by His disciples, they must have begun again to feel secure. Then came Pentecost and they were back in the depths again. However, with the stoning of Stephen followed by the deliberate policy of intense persecution led by Saul, the disciples in Jerusalem began to scatter, and victory seemed within the grasp of the Jewish leaders. Then new groups of those pesky followers of Jesus started up as they settled like sparks throughout the region. Emotions would have reached a new high as Saul departed for Damascus, followed by another low at the report of his treachery. Their attacks on him in Damascus which led to his escape and flight would have had both its high and low. Then he showed up in Jerusalem, leading to an even deeper depression for the Jewish leadership.

The other Christians, from the standpoint of the Sanhedrin, could be ignored for the moment. Saul could not. He had to be dealt with. They had discovered that arguing with Saul led nowhere. Further, trying to get others to "take care" of him had led nowhere either. So a deliberate policy was apparently adopted "to kill him" (9:29). The hatred of the Sanhedrin and their persecution of the cause of Christ was renewed and intensified, but this time it was all directed toward one person—Saul of Tarsus.

In the final days of Jesus' life on the night of His betrayal and arrest, we discovered that at least one of the disciples was a friend of servants in the palace of the high priest (John 18:15-16). It is not unlikely that either through that connection or by way of some of the priests who had been converted that word of this new policy toward Saul was brought to the disciples in Jerusalem (Acts 6:7; 9:30). In any case, when the disciples learned of the death sentence against Saul, they helped him to escape. Following his departure, the persecution of the Christians was relaxed for a while, as we have noted, but the hatred, suspicion, and fear of the Jewish leaders was still present. Though not openly hostile, their determination to exterminate Christianity merely simmered, waiting for the proper moment to overflow the land.

That moment arrived when Agrippa I was named king of Judea and Samaria in A.D. 41. He had already sought on several occasions to show himself to be a friend of the Jews. (A summary of these activities can be found in chapter 19.)[1] As the new Roman ruler over the Jewish people, he set out on a deliberate policy of further trying to win the support and loyalty of the Jewish leaders. This gave them the opportunity for which they had been longing and gave Herod Agrippa the occasion for which he was seeking. They had a need, and he had the power to meet it. The Christians were to be the victims of the plot.

Legally, the Sanhedrin still could not execute anyone, but as Rome's representative Herod Agrippa could do so. At least, he could execute anyone but a Roman citizen. That exception apparently did not include any of the followers of Jesus in Jerusalem.

A major famine struck Judea in A.D. 43-44. It was so severe that the church in Antioch sent Barnabas and Saul to carry financial aid to the suffering Christians in Jerusalem (11:30). However, we must note that the Jews of Judea were also suffering.

Herod chose that time to act. Since he could not relieve the consequences of the famine, he could at least do something to bring pleasure to and win further support from the Jewish leaders. Thus in the spring of A.D. 44, seeking to win further Jewish approval and having been made aware of the Sanhedrin's vehement hatred of the Christians, "Herod the king laid violent hands upon some who belonged to the church" (12:1). James, the brother of John and son of Zebedee, was seized and executed (v. 2).

When Herod discovered just how much this pleased the Jewish leaders, he immediately arrested Simon Peter (v. 3). However, due to the forthcoming celebration of the Passover, Peter's execution was delayed until the festival was over (vv. 3-4). The apostolic leader's miraculous escape from prison had to have been a shock both to Herod Agrippa and the Sanhedrin.

During the early days of the church in Jerusalem, Peter had been the obvious leader. However, somewhere along the way James, the brother of Jesus, had become the presiding official of the Jerusalem church. Peter felt it essential that word of his escape from prison be relayed to James (v. 17).

Following his escape, Simon Peter went immediately to the house of Mary, the mother of John Mark (v. 12). However, knowing that this would be the first place the soldiers of Herod would search for him, Peter then went elsewhere to spend the night. He may even have followed the earlier example of Jesus and spent the night at the home of Mary, Martha, and Lazarus in Bethany. On the other hand, one tradition suggests that he ultimately fled all the way to Antioch.

When Herod discovered Peter's escape, he had the guards executed (vv. 18-19). Then, like a disappointed, pouting child, Herod departed from Jerusalem to the official residence in Caesarea. By that act he was separating himself from the whole affair. Shortly thereafter, possibly in the late spring or early summer, Herod was stricken and died (v. 23).

The escape of Simon Peter, accompanied by the departure and death of Herod, brought that era of renewed persecution to an end. This does not mean that the hatred ended, only that the official policy of systematic oppression was apparently terminated. Contrary to either the desire or the plans of the Sanhedrin, their policy of confrontation and persecution had ultimately been ineffective. In fact because of and in spite of the official persecution, the churches continued to grow and thrive. Although the church in Jerusalem had been seriously and significantly weakened, that was not the whole story, or even the major one. Contrary to all expectations, Christianity was spreading as the Christians continued to witness. Luke's assessment of the end of this period is both simple and straight forward: "the word of God grew and multiplied" (v. 24).

Note

1. A more detailed report can be found in chapter 8 of my book, *A History of the Bible Lands in the Interbiblical Period* (Nashville: Broadman Press, 1989).

22
Summary

One historical period generally passes into another with no noticeable boundary. This is almost always true for those who live through such transition. It is almost as true for the students of history who look backwards down the corridors of time. Such was certainly the case when the period which we have been considering came to an end. A historian of the Roman empire seeking for a point of transition near to this time would most likely have found it in A.D. 41 at the time of the death of Caligula and accession of Claudius. A historian of Judea or Palestine might have found the point of transition to be the death of Herod Agrippa I in A.D. 44. This could have served for us but for political rather than religious reasons.

This period of the organization, stabilization, and self-realization of the early churches seems to me, from the standpoint of a historian of the New Testament era, to have come to a point of major transition when "Barnabas and Saul returned from Jerusalem" to Antioch in the late spring or early summer of A.D. 44 (Acts 12:25). Up to this point in the witness, ministry, and mission of the churches, outreach had been more or less accidental on the part of the Christians, but it had been done and had been done successfully. However, from the human perspective, evangelism had more or less occurred when the Spirit moved in a special way and when special opportunities presented themselves. After this time a new, deliberate program of missionary activity was undertaken by the church in Antioch and led by Barnabas and Saul.

Furthermore, up to this time, the center of Christian activity had been Jerusalem. After A.D. 44, Antioch became the major center of Christian leadership. Jerusalem continued to be important until the city was destroyed in A.D. 70, but its significance steadily waned up to that point.

Given that A.D. 44 is the point of termination for the early period of the church, what had been accomplished in the twelve years since Jesus' death? First and perhaps most important of all, they had survived. Facing harsh persecution and intense opposition from the leaders of Judaism; facing hostile argument from the best educated people on the eastern Mediterranean; facing threats, imprisonment, and even death; facing all these things the Christian cause had survived. The worst which could have been done to them had not exterminated them.

Second, not only had the first Christians survived, they had in many ways thrived. Their numbers had enlarged. Further, among their converts had been numerous leaders of the opposition, and this included at least one of their most significant opponents, Saul. Even though many Christians had fled from Jerusalem, they had started new churches where they went.

Third, with no deliberate mission strategy, the Christians now included very diverse segments of the world's population. Among the Jewish Christians were the very orthodox and the Hellenists. They also included Sadducees, Pharisees, priests, and those who had belonged to no party of Judaism. In addition, the Christians now included in their number Jews, Samaritans, Greeks, Romans, and at least one government official from Ethiopia. Churches were in existence as far afield as Damascus and Antioch. It is possible and even likely that they had spread further than this.

From the standpoint of evangelism we might conclude that everything was looking good for the disciples' continued march outwards, but this was not so. Problems were on the horizon, problems of a more serious nature than persecution by opponents. Envy, jealousy, and suspicion had already created internal problems in the churches. This revealed that the Christians still had their old human nature. Further, long-term differences between races were still present. This was to show up again in later controversies as to whether or not Gentiles had to become Jews in order to be Christians.

In addition, the conflict between "orthodox" Jews and the Hellenists was just below the surface in many of the early churches. This type of conflict has shown up again and again over the centuries in the disagreements between those who seldom wish to consider anything new and those who think that only that which is "new" has any value.

Perhaps the biggest weakness to be found in the early churches in A.D. 44 was in the lack of a sense of mission. They had obviously been evangelistic, but their evangelism had generally been one of opportunism, merely taking advantage of the opportunities as they were present. What was lacking was a deliberate plan and program of mission. They needed a strategy to carry the gospel to the ends of the earth. They were ready to go. They had the power from God's Spirit to go. All they lacked was a plan and the commitment to carry it out. That was not long in coming. As it came, we move into the next era of church history.

Part 5
Witnesses to the End of the Earth

Some might say that the mission and ministry of the New Testament church took on a radical new dimension with the conversion of Saul of Tarsus on the highway to Damascus (Acts 9:1-9). Others might suggest that this radical change took place with his arrival at Antioch of Syria, when Barnabas brought him in to assist in ministering to that congregation (11:25-26). Legitimate and weighty arguments can be given to support either of those positions.

However, it appears to me that the real alteration in the nature of the mission of the New Testament church took place when the church at Antioch, acting under the leadership of the Spirit of God, sent Barnabas, Saul, and John Mark on what has come to be known as the first missionary journey (13:2-5). It may legitimately be argued that this was not so much a new direction for the church as it was a new perception on their part of what their ultimate direction had been all along. A debate at this point is not the issue. Insofar as the early disciples were concerned, from this point on the church began to act with a deliberate missionary strategy. They now consciously sought to carry the gospel to other cities, lands, and people.

As we seek to examine this period and the way the churches carried out their mission in it, we need to be quite aware of two major, interrelated facts. First, the Book of Acts follows the specific ministry of the apostle Paul. Other apostles and disciples apparently are included in the narrative only as they shared in and related to Paul's mission. Second, as we shall see later, this does not mean that other disciples and churches were not involved in the expansionist strategy and labors of the early churches.

As we have noted on numerous occasions, no historian can record *everything* which happened at any time. Thus we cannot assume that the other apostles or disciples were not involved in the expansionist mission and ministry of the church in this era. In fact, as we shall consider later, there is abundant evidence both inside and outside of the New Testament to the contrary.

On the other hand, the New Testament narrative, as recorded from this point, by Luke, does follow the labors and adventures of Paul. Thus, by the nature of the case, we should expect that when we examine all of the available evidence we would have far more information relating to his ministry than to that of any other individual or group. That is precisely the case which we find as we read the biblical narratives.

This emphasis upon the ministry of Paul is further underscored when we discover that a significant part of the rest of the New Testament is identified as being the writings of Paul. Admittedly, we do have writings from others, but the author of Hebrews is unidentified and the so-called General Epistles make up only a small part of the New Testament. If we did not have additional evidence, we might conclude that the early church had very few persons who were involved in its expansion. However, that simply was not the case.

Much like the expanding ripples in a pond after a stone is tossed in, the churches seem at about this point in history to have begun a rapid expanse in all directions. God's Holy Spirit for His own purposes recorded in Acts the missions of Paul, but the historian of the era must seek for the larger picture. We who study this history must be aware of the larger historical context of the spread of those who went forth sharing the good news of Jesus Christ.

23
Chronological Considerations

As we noted in chapter 18, the chronological issues related to the history of the earliest years of Christianity and those more directly connected to the time of Paul and beyond are impossible to separate. In order for us to deal with the former, we had to begin with data specifically related to Paul. That allowed us to identify dates in the era and then to correlate these with the earlier period. We have now concluded our study of that early period and are ready to move on beyond.

We must again begin by facing those issues which are directly involved with the period of the great missionary expansion carried out by those early churches. This is the era when the gospel of Jesus Christ was carried all the way from a small province on the eastern end of the Mediterranean world to the center of the Roman Empire and beyond.

Basic Data

The foundational information with which we must begin this study is essentially the same as that used in chapter 18. Therefore, it will be helpful to go back to that chapter and review it before proceeding further with this study. However, a summary of the data which specifically applies here, along with a summary of the conclusions at which we arrived in that chapter are included in the tables which follow. This will at least keep the essential information conveniently available for study and reference. Beginning with these dates, we are now ready to attempt to identify other dates of significance for the later history of the New Testament era.

Roman Emperors and Judean Procurators

Emperors	*Procurators*
Tiberius (14-37)	Pontius Pilate (26-36)
	Marcellus (36)
Caligula (37-41)	Marullus (37-41)
Claudius (41-54)	Herod Agrippa I, King (41-44)
	Cuspius Fadus (44-46)
	Alexander (46-48)
	Cumanus (48-52)
Nero (54-68)	Felix (52-60)
	Porcius Festus (60-62)
	Albinus (62-64)
[Rome burns (64)]	Florus (64-66)
	[First Jewish Revolt (66-74)]
Galba (68-69)	
Otho (69)	
Vitellius (69)	
Vespasian (69-79)	[Jerusalem falls (70)]
Titus (79-81)	
Domitian (81-96)	[Persecution of Christians (96)]
Nerva (96-98)	
Trajan (98-117)	
Hadrian (117-138)	

Early Christian Dates

Date	*Event*
32	Crucifixion
June 32	Pentecost
34	Paul's conversion
36	Paul's first visit to Jerusalem
43	Paul and Barnabas in Antioch
44	Relief visit to Jerusalem, James martyred, Peter arrested, Herod dies
48	Jerusalem conference
Spring 53	Paul before Gallio
58	Paul's arrest in Jerusalem
June/July 60	Paul before Festus
Autumn 60	Paul departs for Rome

The Missionary Journeys

As we noted earlier, Paul and Barnabas, taking John Mark with them, apparently returned to Antioch from Jerusalem shortly after the death of Herod Agrippa (Acts 12:25). This would most likely have been in the summer of A.D. 44. We do not know how long they stayed there before beginning the first missionary journey. However, it appears that a considerable amount of time had passed. Sea journeys would have been unlikely during the winter. Thus it appears probable that the missionaries from Antioch would have made the voyage to Cyprus at the earliest in the spring of A.D. 45.

When Paul and Barnabas returned to Antioch from that journey, they reported on their adventures of starting new churches. "They remained no little time with the disciples" (14:28). Following this, they were sent by the church at Antioch to the great Jerusalem conference (15:2-3). As this seems to have occurred in A.D. 48, it appears likely that they returned from their missionary enterprise in A.D. 47. This would also fit in well with what they accomplished on that trip.

Following the Jerusalem Council, Paul and Barnabas returned to Antioch. They remained there for a while. Ultimately, Paul set forth on his second missionary journey, accompanied by Silas (vv 30,35-40). As winter travel in the highlands of Pisidia and Galatia would have been next to impossible, their departure to those regions could not have taken place prior to the spring of A.D. 49. However, it could have been later, more likely in midsummer. It was on this journey that Paul was brought before Gallio in Corinth (18:1,12). We have temporarily concluded that this may have occurred in A.D. 53. Again, this timing would have allowed an adequate length of time for them to have accomplished all that is recorded in Luke's account in Acts.

After being freed by Gallio, Paul remained in Corinth "many days longer" (v. 18). Then he returned to Antioch by way of Ephesus and Caesarea (vv. 19-22). This journey appears to have been made in some haste, apparently trying to end the sea voyages before the winter storms set in. Therefore it is most likely that Paul was back in Antioch by late fall in A.D. 53, bringing his second missionary journey to a conclusion.

Paul remained in Antioch for "some time" before he set forth into the region of Galatia and Phrygia to visit the disciples there (v. 23). Even if Paul had been unaware before, by now he had enough experience in traveling through this region that he did not try to begin such a trip during the winter months. Thus we can conclude that this third missionary journey could not have begun earlier than the spring of A.D. 54. Given the number of places which Paul had to visit, he probably would not have arrived in Ephesus until late summer of that year (19:1). He remained in Ephesus longer than any other place which he had visited in his travels, staying for about three years (19:8,10; 20:17,31). Depending upon the system of dating reflected in Paul's words, this could have been anywhere from one-and-a-half to slightly more than three years. Since Paul was speaking to people from Ephesus, a major Roman city, it seems likely that he would have been using their system of chronology, putting his departure from Ephesus in A.D. 57. Thus I conclude that he probably left Ephesus in the summer of A.D. 57, finally going on to Corinth.

When Paul arrived on the Macedonian peninsula, he journeyed southward, ultimately arriving in Achaia, where he probably made his headquarters in Corinth. We are told that he had planned on sailing from there but, because of threats on his life, chose to go overland to the north instead (20:1-3). To have thought about sailing, he would not have departed earlier than February. Thus I put his departure from Corinth in February, A.D. 58. This would have left enough time for him to have made the journey which intervened between Ephesus and Corinth. This would also mean that he had probably arrived in Corinth about November, A.D. 57.

From Corinth, Paul went to Philippi from which he sailed immediately after the Feast of Unleavened Bread (Passover). Making several stops along the way, Paul would probably have arrived in Jerusalem in the summer of A.D. 58.

Paul was arrested in Jerusalem shortly thereafter (21:27). After an initial hearing followed a serious threat on his life, Paul was transferred to the Roman prison in Caesarea (23:23-35). This would most likely have occurred in the late summer or early autumn of A.D. 58. Paul was held in prison there by Felix until he was recalled in A.D. 60. Luke further records that Paul was held by Felix for a period of two years prior to the ruler's recall by Rome

(24:27). This brings all of our dates into line, offering apparent confirmation of the validity of our assumptions and reasoning.

Paul certainly set sail for Rome and his appeal to Caesar in the late summer of A.D. 60. This was a slow voyage in a coaster. Finally, however, they started on the major trek across the Mediterranean from Fair Havens after the fast day, the Day of Atonement (27:9). This would have been early October of A.D. 60. Fourteen days later they were shipwrecked on Malta, where they spent the winter (27:27 to 28:1).

Following their three-month stay on Malta, Paul and his companions set sail for Rome on an Alexandrian ship in late winter of A.D. 61 (28:11). Alexandria furnished most of Rome's grain, particularly that used early in the year. In all probability, then, this ship would have been carrying grain to Rome. Since this ship had the Twin Brothers (Castor and Pollux) as its figurehead, it probably would have set sail at the end of January. There was a festival to those pagan gods celebrated about that time. Such an occasion would probably have been seen as a good omen by the ship's captain.

The first ships to arrive in Rome after the winter would have made the most profit and each captain would have been trying to sail as soon after the winter as he possibly could. Any good omen to justify sailing earlier would have been grasped. After a rather uneventful trip, the ship, along with Paul, came to Puteoli, the seaport for Rome (v. 13). From there, Paul and his companions would have finally proceeded overland to Rome. There Paul was kept under house arrest (v. 16). This would most likely have still been fairly early in the spring of A.D. 61.

For at least two years Paul remained under house arrest in Rome (v. 30). We do not know what happened to him after this. He almost certainly had his hearing before Caesar. Then he would have either been freed or condemned, but the chronological data of Acts ends at this point. The New Testament record simply fades away here, at least insofar as any chronological detail is concerned.

The Remainder of the Century

The missionary expansion of the early church did not stop with Paul's arrival in Rome. The Christians continued to carry the gospel toward the ends of the earth. Numerous traditions have to be considered here, though none have sufficient validity to give us any additional chronological detail.

In addition, most of the New Testament was written in the years which followed Paul's arrival in Rome. Obviously, Paul's Letters all come either from his missionary journeys or from his Roman imprisonment. On the other hand, it appears that most of the rest of the New Testament comes after this. However, although scholars can deduce evidence as to the dates of the writing of the various books, these are still uncertain enough to be left out of our chronological reconstruction of the era at this point. Thus, for our purposes in this chapter, we must now bring our reconstruction to an end.

Summary

In order to facilitate the use of the conclusions at which we have arrived in this part of our study, the following table brings together a helpful summary.

Chronology of Paul and Beyond

Date	*Event*
Summer 44	Paul returned to Antioch
Spring 45	First missionary journey begun
Summer 47	First missionary journey ended
48	Jerusalem Council
Summer 49	Second missionary journey begun
Spring 53	Paul before Gallio
Late fall 53	Second missionary journey ended
Spring 54	Third missionary journey begun
Late summer 54	Paul's arrival in Ephesus
Summer 57	Paul's departure from Ephesus
November 57	Paul's arrival in Corinth
February 58	Paul's departure from Corinth
Late April 58	Paul's departure from Philippi
Late summer 58	Paul's arrival in Jerusalem, third missionary journey ended, Paul arrested
Summer 60	Paul before Festus
Late summer 60	Paul sailed for Rome
Late October 60	Shipwrecked on Malta
Late January 61	Paul sailed for Italy
Early spring 61	Paul arrived in Rome
63	Paul's imprisonment ended

24
The Background

When we approach the era of the first planned missionary expansion of the early church, we find a major change in the focus of our study of the world of the New Testament. For the first time, the geographical focus of our attention becomes significantly larger than the area of Palestine. For at least the first part of this era, Jerusalem and the church there does continue to wield a major influence over the early Christian communities. However, that influence was waning and apparently ceased to exist at all following the siege and conquest of Jerusalem by the Romans in A.D. 70.

Throughout the history of the Mediterranean world in this era, the dominant political influence continued to be the Roman Empire. Certainly, insofar as the missionary expansion of the churches was concerned, no other historical force was comparable to the impact which affairs in Rome had upon the endeavors of the Christians. From a human standpoint, both the direction and effectiveness of the early Christian witness appear to have been influenced and molded by imperial politics.

We have seen throughout our study the importance of trying to understand the historical stage upon which each act of the divine drama of redemption was played out. In order to accomplish this here, we need once again to survey the major historical features of the era. Our major focus will be upon Rome and its politics and imperial policies. However, at least for the earlier parts of the era, we shall continue to have a significant interest in the cradle of Christianity: Jerusalem and its environs.

Developments in Rome

Claudius (A.D. 41-54)

Following the assassination of Caligula in A.D. 41, Claudius became emperor of Rome, beginning his reign shortly before the period with which we are immediately concerned. He was thrust upon the throne by the Praetorian Guard as an object of ridicule whom they believed they could control. Even though the senate confirmed him as emperor, no one including Claudius himself believed that he could in any way be a success.

Unprepared for the imperial administration, Claudius gathered around himself capable administrators to direct his government. These were generally freedmen, former slaves who had been given freedom because they had earned it as faithful and effective stewards, military aides, and estate managers for their former owners. They were proven and successful administrators who gave Rome a cadre of practical and experienced bureaucrats.

With an effective administration at home, Claudius was able to devote some attention to military matters abroad. Again, surprising everybody including himself, he added several provinces to the empire with perhaps the most notable being Britain. An unlikely candidate for greatness, Claudius rose to the occasion which confronted him and must be reckoned as one of Rome's most able leaders. From the standpoint of Christians within the empire, Claudius brought stability to their world and eased the threat of rebellion which the reign of Caligula had brought.

Claudius' reign, however, was not without difficulties, the greatest of which came from within his own family. His problems there sowed the bitter seed which produced a tragic harvest for the empire in general and Christians in particular. His death in A.D. 54 was probably not mourned by Christians within the empire but certainly should have been, since dark days for them were to follow.

Nero (A.D. 54-68)

A great-nephew of Claudius, Nero succeeded him upon the imperial throne. Nero was the son of Claudius' fourth wife, Agrippina, who in turn was a daughter of the great Germanicus. Agrippina had persuaded Claudius to adopt Nero and name him heir to the throne in A.D. 50. She had so much power over her husband that he had done this even though he had a natural son who could have succeeded him.

Although Nero succeeded to the throne without conflict, the possibility of future difficulties was always present as long as Claudius' natural son lived. He died in A.D. 55, more likely as the result of poisoning than by natural causes. This left Nero with a clear and unthreatened claim to the throne.

At least at the beginning of his reign, Nero showed himself to be a fairly able administrator, carrying on with the same kind of bureaucracy that Claudius had. However, three qualities showed up in Nero's personality which were his ultimate downfall and for which he is most remembered. First, he had a highly developed ego which significantly influenced everything he did throughout his reign. Second, he considered himself to be an artist in many fields of human endeavor. Coupled with his ego, this led to a major emphasis upon the self-indulgence of the senses. Third, also related to his ego, Nero would brook no opposition of any sort, either real or imagined. The end result of this was a streak of violence toward all who opposed or might oppose him. It is actually for this trait that he is most remembered.

Nero began to plan and promote all sort of contests, extending all the way from musical competitions to athletic games. In these, Nero always competed and always won. Further, to avoid any supposition that he was dominated by anyone, he had both his mother and wife executed.

The lavish nature of his games and entertainments plunged Nero's administration into severe debt. In addition, during his administration, he was forced to engage in a number of external wars for the defense of his empire. To pay for both the games and wars, he began to accuse the leading nobles of Rome of treason. His accusation was sufficient to bring about their condemnation and execution, upon which he confiscated their property and wealth. However, even with this he was left in difficult financial straits.

As an artist, Nero wished to rebuild the entire city of Rome to suit his tastes. In A.D. 64, a major part of the city was destroyed by a fire which lasted for several days. Contemporary tradition indicates that he rejoiced during the conflagration, playing a lyre and reciting poetry describing the beauty of the new city which he would build. This gave rise to the proverb of Nero's fiddling while Rome burned. Unsurprisingly, bitter hostility of the people of Rome who survived the fire was aroused. In an attempt to divert their anger from himself, Nero blamed the Christians for the fire. This in turn led to a brief but bitter persecution. This may even have been the occasion for the executions of both Peter and Paul.

A failed plot to assassinate Nero drove him from the city in A.D.

65. He made a tour to Corinth, engaging in further contests along the way. His violence became ever more pronounced, as he executed both those who either did too well or too poorly. In the meantime, unrest increased in Rome. During Nero's administration, his policies had cost him friends and strengthened the resolve of enemies. Although he returned to Rome in A.D. 67 in an attempt to regain control of the situation, he was unsuccessful. When the Praetorian Guard again arose, Nero fled for his life. In despair, he committed suicide in A.D. 68. Nero is remembered as a selfish, sadistic, and despotic tyrant rather than as the artistic genius he wished to be.

Galba to Vespasian (A.D. 68-79)

Nero's policies had left a power vacuum in Rome with no clear claimant to the imperial authority. The first two years following his death were chaotic for the wider empire as well as for the city of Rome. Immediately following Nero's suicide, the Praetorian Guard named Galba emperor (A.D. 68-69). In Spain at the time, Galba immediately set forth for Rome, arriving in the fall of A.D. 68. However, he proved to be an unusually inept administrator. His every act alienated someone and seemed to win him no support at all.

As a consequence of the empire-wide unrest, Vitellius who was commanding the legions in the Germanic regions was acclaimed emperor by his troops in January A.D. 69. This gave Rome two emperors at the same time. In the meantime, Otho, who was commanding the Praetorian Guard, assassinated Galba and was also proclaimed emperor. Although the name of one was different, Rome still had two emperors.

The rival armies of Otho and Vitellius met in battle in April A.D. 69. When the troops of Otho were defeated, he committed suicide rather than face humiliation and execution. However, Rome's situation was hardly improved by this. Upon receiving the report of the victory of his armies, Vitellius raced from Germany and marched into Rome. Arriving in July A.D. 69, his first act was the utter humiliation of those troops who had supported Otho.

However, a new factor became involved in Rome's crisis of leadership in the person of Titus Flavius Sabinus Vespasianus, more commonly known as Vespasian. He had been leading Rome's forces sent to quell the Jewish revolt in Palestine. He had initially supported both Galba and then Otho, but the death of both of them left him with his own ambitions. He marched toward Rome and along the way was engaged in several battles with the troops of Vitellius. The end result of these conflicts was that Vitellius was assassinated, and Vespasian was proclaimed emperor upon his arrival in Rome. This meant that Rome had been ruled by four different emperors during A.D. 69, a year which has come to be known to historians as "the year of the four emperors." Such chaos in leadership gave birth to a corresponding chaos throughout most of the empire. Neither Rome nor any other major empire had ever experienced such a year of crisis and conflict.

Upon assuming the imperial power, Vespasian faced three major but related crises. First, the army was in utter disarray. However, Vespasian was first and foremost a military man of great skill. He was respected by military commanders throughout the imperial forces. He quickly won both their allegiance, trust, and admiration. The disarray of the military was quickly overcome and was no further problem for the remainder of his reign.

Second, the government was impoverished. Although it was never a popular move, Vespasian recognized that he must raise taxes to meet the empire's immediate and critical needs. When the treasury was replenished, he had the resources to improve the functions of his government, and the end result was one of grudging approval by both the nobility and commoners of Rome.

Third, related to the first two but worthy of separate mention, the administrative bureaucracy was disorganized and utterly incapable of governing an empire. Here, Vespasian was at his weakest. He had no preparation for ruling an empire. On the other hand, he had achieved success in the military because he was a hard worker, had a great deal of common sense, and had never been handicapped by any sort of pampering. He was rough, honest, and fair, ultimately achieving remarkable success as an administrator. Rome prospered under his leadership, and he was truly mourned throughout the empire when he died in A.D. 79.

Titus Onwards (A.D. 79-   )

Titus, who had been associated with his father as a military commander in Judea and an administrator in Rome, had a brief but very popular reign as emperor (A.D. 79-81). He was succeeded upon the throne by his brother Domitian (A.D. 81-96).

Unlike either his brother or father, Domitian was beset both by a deep sense of inadequacy and a corresponding fear of all opposition. In seeking both to avoid opposition and undergird his authority, Domitian proclaimed himself to be divine, taking the title *Dominus et Deus noster* (Our Lord and God). Further demonstrating his fear of any who asked questions, in both A.D. 89 and 95 he ordered the exile of all philosophers from Rome. In addition, as his relation with the Roman senate deteriorated, he began a sporadic but increasing persecution of the senators and nobility. This gave rise to the legend that he was Nero come back to life *(Nero redivivus)*.

Both Jews and Christians suffered under the administration of Domitian, some even accepting the concept that he was a revived Nero. Although the temple of Jerusalem had been destroyed for more than twenty years, he levied a temple tax on all Jews and engaged in anti-Semitic attacks upon them. Further, he also ordered widely scattered but intense persecutions of Christians within the empire near the end of his reign.

For all practical purposes the New Testament era seems to have closed during or shortly after the reign of Domitian. However, events in Rome for the next few decades did influence the early churches and the world in which they ministered.

Domitian was succeeded briefly by Nerva (A.D. 96-98), a scion of the ancient nobility of Rome. His administration, though brief, did seek to restore Rome's economy and relations within the empire. Even though he did not fully succeed in this, he did manage to have Trajan named as his successor. Trajan ruled until his death in A.D. 117, bringing a successful conclusion to many of the goals of reconciliation and restoration. He in turn was succeeded on the imperial throne by his nephew, Hadrian (A.D. 117-138).

Ruler of the Roman province of Syria when he was named emperor, Hadrian made several extensive tours of the empire, visiting Africa, Egypt, Judea, Syria, Greece, Asia Minor, and Britain. By such on-site administration, Hadrian managed to solidify both his military and political control of the empire. He was a patron of the arts but was violent toward any opposition. Near the end of his reign, the second Jewish Revolt under Bar Kochba took place (A.D. 132-135). Hadrian crushed it with extreme violence. He also brought his reign to an end with a series of executions of those in positions of leadership of whom he suspected disloyalty or treason.

Developments in Palestine

Herod Agrippa (A.D. 37-44)

At the same that these affairs at the center of the empire were developing, events at the periphery were also moving in directions which were to be of significance to the early Christians who were committed to carrying their good news to the ends of the earth. In Palestine, perhaps the most significant development was the career of Herod Agrippa I.

The grandson of Herod the Great, Agrippa was four years old when his father Aristobulus had been executed in 7 B.C. He had at that time been sent to Rome where he had received the education of a Roman nobleman and was the companion of the sons of some of Rome's leading citizens. One among these was Caius, also known as Caligula.

Agrippa, however, despite his opportunities and perhaps because of them, grew up as a spoiled youth to become an utterly intemperate man. He went so far into debt that he was essentially banished to Idumea in A.D. 23. Due to the intercession of his sister Herodias, at that time the wife of Herod Antipas, he was allowed to move to Tiberius where he was given a luxurious home and a pension, although he was still not allowed to return to Rome. These experiences allowed him to get to know and understand his Jewish background and the deep emotions of the Jewish people toward their religion and conquerors.

By A.D. 36, however, Agrippa had a major disagreement with Antipas who was both his brother-in-law and uncle. Banished from the territory over which Antipas ruled, Agrippa was finally allowed by Emperor Tiberius to return to his beloved Rome. It wasn't long, however, before he was deeper in debt. Further, he was overheard to say that he wished his friend Caius were emperor. Agrippa was immediately imprisoned and faced imminent execution.

However, at that point Agrippa's fortunes changed for the better. Tiberius died before Agrippa was executed, and Caligula (Caius) ascended the imperial throne in A.D. 37. He immediately released his friend Agrippa from prison and appointed him king over the territory which had been ruled by Philip, adding much of Syria to it. As an additional reward for Agrippa's having wished that Caligula were emperor, Caligula had a chain of gold that was equal in weight to his iron prison fetters given to his friend. Under pressure from the new emperor, the Roman senate confirmed Agrippa's appointment, naming him a Roman prefect as well. Further, following the banishment of Herod Antipas the previous year, Agrippa was also named king of Galilee and Perea in A.D. 40.

Since he was of the Herodian family, Agrippa adopted the name during this time of Herod Agrippa. Throughout his reign, he sought to be a friend of the Jews. It was his intercession for the Jews of Alexandria which brought them deliverance from the anti-Semitic oppression which they were enduring. Further, when Caligula decided to have his statue placed in the temple of Jerusalem, Agrippa journeyed to Rome to try to dissuade him. He succeeded in this temporarily.

It was this journey of intercession for the Jews which placed Agrippa in Rome in January of A.D. 41 when Caligula was assassinated. Although the details are unclear, he apparently wielded some influence in the affairs which led to the enthronement of Claudius. This led to his being rewarded by having his earlier appointments confirmed and being named as king of Judea and Samaria as well. As a consequence, by mid-A.D. 41, Herod Agrippa ruled over a territory equal to or greater than that ruled by his grandfather, Herod the Great. Although his authority was severely restricted by Rome in matters of international diplomacy and military matters, he still exercised a great deal of autonomy in regard to the internal affairs of his lands.

Agrippa quickly won the support of many of his Jewish subjects through numerous acts of piety. He hung the chain of gold given to him by Caligula over the entrance of the temple treasury, paid the vows of a number of Nazirites, and offered a major thank offering. The New Testament described the extremes to which he went in this pursuit by noting the execution of James and arrest of Simon Peter (Acts 12:1-19). The success of Agrippa's policies can be measured by the fact that the Pharisees actually gave him the title of "Brother."

Little doubt exists that Agrippa's acts toward the Jews were more rooted in political expediency than in actual piety. Nothing in his early life gives any basis for such piety, and his acts outside of Palestine generally show him to have been insincere at the least and most likely quite hypocritical. Outside of Judea, his coins bore his image in contrast to those minted in the Jewish territories.

Further, in general, most of his policies outside of Judea were quite Hellenistic.

Upon Agrippa's sudden death (v. 23), Claudius abandoned the Herodian line and reinstituted the appointment of procurators to govern the region. The province was also returned to the administrative responsibility of Syria.

The Procurators (A.D. 44-66)

With the reinstitution of the procurators, political conditions in Palestine began to deteriorate. Almost without exception these Roman rulers were inept and utterly insensitive to the feelings of the people whom they governed. In addition, the Jewish leaders faced this new imposition of foreign rulers with resistance. Even though they would never have accepted them with enthusiasm, we might have suspected that they would have been realists enough to have acknowledged the utter inevitability of their situation. They simply had no other choice. From the moment of this change in administration, both the actions of Rome and those of the Jewish leaders made the ultimate rebellion of the province of Judea inevitable.

Cuspius Fadus served as procurator from A.D. 44-46. He alienated the Jews by insisting that he had the authority to maintain custody of the high priestly robes and appoint the high priest. This struck right to the heart of Jewish religious sensibilities. He also reacted violently and without mercy at the threat of a would-be messiah named Theudas, parading his head in Jerusalem as an object lesson to other rebels. Instead of discouraging further rebellion, the brutality of Fadus actually seems to have encouraged it.

Fadus' decision in regard to the high priesthood was overruled by Rome, with that power being vested temporarily in a brother of Herod Agrippa who was king of Chalcis. Following his death in A.D. 49, he was succeeded both as king of Chalcis and as guardian of the high priesthood by Agrippa's own son, later known as Agrippa II.

The next procurator of Judea was Tiberius Alexander (A.D. 46-48), a Jew from one of the leading families of Alexandria and nephew of the philosopher Philo. Upon becoming a Roman administrator, he had renounced his Jewish faith. This act must have seriously alienated the Jewish leaders in Jerusalem. During his term he was forced to deal with a rebellion of James and Simon, sons of the Galilean Zealot, Judas. Alexander, an "apostate," had these two "loyal" Jews executed by crucifixion, an act which further alienated the local populace. A severe famine during his governorship and his inability to bring significant relief to his citizens created even more problems.

Conditions in Judea became still more disastrous under the rule of Ventidus Cumanus (A.D. 48-52) who succeeded Alexander. Shortly after his accession, he and his troops were in Jerusalem at Passover. When a soldier made an insulting (obscene?) gesture, the Jewish pilgrims rioted. The Roman soldiers, at Cumanus' orders, sought to restore the peace with swords. The confrontation was so violent that twenty to thirty thousand people were killed.

Sometime thereafter, a Roman was beaten and robbed near Jerusalem. As punishment, Roman troops were loosed on the nearby villages in a rampage of pillaging. During this, a soldier publicly tore up a copy of the Torah. Within a very brief period after this, Cumanus accepted a bribe from the Samaritans not to punish the Samaritan murderers of some Galilean pilgrims. In reaction, some Zealots invaded Samaria, murdering everyone they could find, including women, children, and the very aged. Cumanus retaliated by a brutal attack on the Zealots.

The situation was so out of hand that Quadatus, the governor of Syria sent Cumanus, some of the Jewish leaders, and some of the Samaritans to Rome to be tried by Claudius. Agrippa II, who happened to be in Rome at the time interceded for the Jews who were freed. The Samaritans were executed, and Cumanus was banished for having accepted the bribe. He was succeeded by Antonius Felix (A.D. 52-60). His appointment was suggested by the high priest of Jerusalem, but his rule turned out to be even more disastrous than the prior ones.

Felix was a freedman who had been the slave of Claudius' mother. He was brutal and governed by an insatiable lust. He was married three times, even taking one of his wives, Drusilla, from her husband by force. He took what he wished, did what he pleased, and cared little for the law and less for public opinion.

Felix's utter disdain for his Jewish subjects and their sensibilities coupled with his mismanagement of government affairs caused the party of the Zealots to experience both a growth in membership and public support for their causes. At this point, the Zealots confined their attacks to political opponents. However, as the attacks from Felix increased in severity, a subgroup of Zealots emerged who turned into assassins. They mingled with large crowds and would quietly stab Roman officials and collaborators with daggers known as *sica*. Thus this group came to be known as the *sicarii*. As a result, assassinations in Jerusalem became so common that no Roman or Roman sympathizer was safe on the streets. At the same time, some of these *sicarii* were employed by Felix to assassinate Jonathan, the Jewish high priest.

In addition to the political unrest of the Zealots, religious unrest added to the discomfiture of the land. Some religious fanatics sought to overthrow the Roman rule and were dealt with in Felix's usual brutal fashion. Further, the Jewish priesthood itself fell into disarray with rival factions actually stealing tithes and food from one another, leaving others to starve to death in utter callousness. It was during this time that Paul was imprisoned in Jerusalem and brought to trial before Felix (23:24).

Sometime near the end of this period, riots broke out in Caesarea with both the Jews and Gentiles claiming precedence of citizenship. When Felix responded with his usual brutality, the riots grew in violence. Felix arrested their leaders and sent them to Rome. However, Nero recalled him because of his inability to control the situation. In his place, Nero appointed Porcius Festus as procurator of Judea (A.D. 60-62). However, after being bribed, Nero also ruled that the Gentiles in Caesarea had priority of citizenship. This gave Festus an impossible situation to face as he sought to govern the Jewish people.

As a consequence, the activities of the *sicarii* increased in Jerusalem. In addition, false messiahs sprang up throughout the land. Festus reacted with brutality and violence, yet as fast as one uprising was quelled, another seemed to arise. In addition, a dispute arose between the Jerusalem priesthood and Agrippa II at this time. Agrippa had added a tower to his home which was tall enough to overlook the temple area. The priests in turn built a wall which prevented Agrippa from looking down into the temple precincts. Agrippa then appealed to Festus, who ordered the wall demolished. The priests appealed to Nero who allowed the wall to remain. All of this added to the intensity of the unrest among the people.

At this point, Festus died unexpectedly. In the three months before his successor arrived, the high priest sought to take over the government and settle several old scores with numerous executions. Seeking to end the anarchy, Agrippa II, who had the power of appointing high priests, stepped in, removed the reigning high priest, and appointed a new one. However, this only increased the problems as the followers of the two rival claimants to the high priesthood engaged in street fighting in the streets of Jerusalem.

Albinus was appointed to succeed Festus and ruled from A.D. 62-64. Apparently motivated only by greed, he faced the anarchy in Jerusalem and Judea as an opportunity. He accepted bribes from both claimants to the high priesthood as well as from the *sicarii* and then let them all fight it out. Whenever he did arrest anyone, the prisoner was allowed to buy his way to freedom. The situation in Jerusalem was now wholly out of control.

In one last attempt to bring order out of this chaos, Gessius Florus (A.D. 64-66) was sent to replace Albinus. His only qualification for his post seems to have been the fact that his wife was a friend of Nero's wife. Unfortunately for Judea and Jerusalem, he was even more greedy than his predecessor. Under his rule cities and villages were plundered to increase his own personal wealth. Further, any thief was allowed to practice his trade as long as the governor got a share of the take. Affairs in Jerusalem were at white heat. War had clearly become inevitable.

The First Jewish Revolt (A.D. 66-74)

The simmering hatred between the Jews and the Romans flashed into open rebellion in A.D. 66 due to confrontations in Caesarea and Jerusalem. Nero's decision about citizenship relegated the Jews in Caesarea to a second-class status. As a further insult, the Gentiles there sacrificed a bird in front of the synagogue. This not only made it unclean, it also implied that the Jews were no better than lepers because such a sacrifice was a normal part of ritual for the treatment of a leper. The Jews appealed to the procurator, Florus, bribing him to render a judgment in their favor. He took the bribe but ignored their cause.

Shortly thereafter, Florus went to Jerusalem and plundered the temple treasury. In mockery of his "poverty," the Jews took up an offering for him. This act so incensed the procurator that he ordered his troops into the city to loot and kill. At this point, the Jews took up arms and penned one cohort in the fortress of Antonia while driving the rest of the Roman soldiers back to Caesarea.

Agrippa II sought to persuade the Jews to restore the peace and this held, at least for the time when a representative of the legate of Syria was there investigating the situation.

However, for both Jews and Romans the point of no return had been passed. The Sanhedrin soon ruled that no sacrifices would be accepted from aliens. This brought an end to the daily sacrifices for the emperor, an insult to the entire imperial government. At this point Zealot troops attacked the Roman soldiers garrisoned at Masada. After a wholesale execution of the foreign troops, the Jews occupied the fortress. Turning their attention to Jerusalem, the Zealots marched into the holy city where they burned the palaces of all Romans and Roman collaborators, including those of Agrippa II and the high priest. All such persons were either driven from the city or forced to take refuge in the Antonia. At long last, Jerusalem was wholly free of Rome's occupying forces.

The conflict immediately flashed throughout the region. Jews were slaughtered in Gentile cities, and Gentiles were treated with equal violence in Jewish cities. In a vain attempt to restore peace, the troops of Cestus Gallus, the governor of Syria, marched into the land. However they were quickly driven away from Jerusalem and given a shattering defeat at Beth-horon.

Quickly realizing that their only hope lay in an organized army rather than the riotous rabble of the Zealots, the Sanhedrin elected Flavius Josephus as commander of all Jewish forces in Galilee. This was the region of strategic importance because any Roman attack had to come from that direction. The defense of this region under any conditions would have been quite difficult. The Zealots did not trust Josephus and made an abortive attempt on his life. Further, the cities of Galilee generally supported the Romans rather than the Jews of Jerusalem. However, the rural people of Galilee were more nationalistic and did support Josephus and his aims.

Since Cestus Gallus had committed suicide following his ignominious defeat, Nero sent Vespasian with two legions to restore order in the inflamed province. He was also to be joined by a third legion from Egypt under the command of his son, Titus. This army experienced a number of minor victories in A.D. 66 and 67 and finally captured Josephus' Galilean fortress at Jotapata after a siege of forty-seven days. Although the Jewish leaders vowed to commit suicide before their capture, Josephus was taken alive and is suspected of having betrayed both his fortress and companions. Brought before Vespasian, Josephus predicted that the Roman would soon become emperor which so pleased him that Josephus was freed and became the Roman's protege.

By the end of that year, all of Galilee was in Roman hands. Within the next year Perea, Idumea, and part of Judea had also fallen. However, during this time John of Gischala, a Zealot leader, escaped to Jerusalem. There he faced several other Jewish leaders but by A.D. 68 was firmly in control. However, he was also facing the growing threat of the Romans as Vespasian and his legions marched on the city of Jerusalem.

At that point, Nero committed suicide, throwing the empire into tumult. While Vespasian waited to see what would happen in Rome, two major rivals of John sought to wrest control of the city from him, a process which significantly weakened the defensive posture of the city. It was at this point that Vespasian was named emperor and left for Rome, turning his troops over to his son Titus.

By A.D. 70, the Jews were so sure that God was going to intervene to save their city that throngs of pilgrims gathered to celebrate the Passover. However, the strife between the rival political and military leaders was so strong that their forces actually burned the food supplies of one another, creating major supply problems. This was further intensified by the presence of the massive numbers of pilgrims.

At that time the troops under Titus invaded Jerusalem. The battle was fought street by street in one of the more brutal and vicious conflicts of human history. So desperate did the situation become that cannibalism was actually practiced by the defenders of the city. The temple finally fell, and its walls were pulled down. Although the main revolt was over, three fortresses held out. Two fell shortly thereafter, but Masada was a different matter. It had been occupied by the Zealots since A.D. 66 and was strongly defended. It held out before the Roman troops until A.D. 74. When it was finally taken, only two women and five children survived.

Judea was made into a senatorial province, and peace was restored. The occupying authority was harsh, and the peace was brutal. The people who survived the conflict paid an ongoing price that was beyond comprehension or computation.

Palestine to Bar Kochba (A.D. 74-135)

For all practical purposes, the destruction of Jerusalem and its temple ended the direct influence of Palestine over the early churches. However, one major development occurred which did exert an indirect but significant influence over the early churches which we at least need to consider briefly. Following the first Jewish revolt, no mention can be found in any contemporary document of either Zealots or Sadducees. The Pharisees and scribes were the only two parties to survive. The survivors of these were among the rabbis who began to spring up in great numbers after this time. The title is found either as *rab,* "teacher," or *rabbi,* "my teacher."

The rabbis sought to help the faith of Israel survive. They did this in combining the tradition of scribe and Pharisee by teaching the Scriptures of the Old Testament and applying those teachings to life. Several centers or schools of rabbis developed in the region with one of the major ones being at Jabneh (Jamnia), somewhat south of Jaffa. One of the major contributions of this school was the attempt to establish a canon of authoritative books for the Hebrew Bible.

Further, with the utter destruction of the temple, the synagogue movement got a big push. These synagogues ultimately furnished the popular platform for the teaching of the rabbis.

Much less is known of the so-called second Jewish revolt, under the leadership of Bar Kochba, than is known of the first one. In A.D. 132, however, revolt once again broke out in Palestine. Its exact limits are unknown, but it apparently included almost all of Judea. The revolt enjoyed several initial victories, probably due to surprise and the smallness of the Roman garrisons there at the time. Due to the initial successes, larger numbers of Jews thronged to join in the conflict.

The end was never in doubt, though fought with such bitterness and fanaticism that it took longer in coming than anyone might have imagined. The Romans listed 50 fortresses and 985 fortified villages which had to be taken one at a time. The three-year conflict is said to have left a death toll of 850,000 people. While ultimately victorious, the Romans themselves must have endured significant defeats. Throughout this period, Hadrian's reports to the Roman senate consistently left out the traditional phrase: "All is well with me and my legions."

The end was both bitter and bloody. So many Jews were carried captive to Rome that it was said that in Rome's slave markets the price of a Hebrew slave was only slightly more than that of a horse. Finally, Jerusalem was turned into a Gentile city, Aelia Capitolina, and Jews were forbidden to enter on penalty of death.

The end of Jerusalem as the city of the Jews left them with only a backward look to what had been. For the Christians, though the death of Jerusalem had to sadden those who knew their heritage, it did not drive them into despair or even major grief. They were not looking back but were looking forward to a "city . . . whose builder and maker is God" (Heb. 11:10).

25
Paul's Early Ministry

From the historian's perspective, at least four features stand out in studying the first formative years of Christian history. First, the early Christians possessed a deep sense of commitment to the belief that Jesus of Nazareth had been raised from the dead. They showed great courage as they proclaimed this belief. Perhaps most amazing of all, those early disciples believed that this same Jesus was both Lord and Christ. Not only was He believed to be the Messiah of Israel, He was believed to be the Son of God Himself.

Threatened, persecuted, punished, and pursued because of their faith, those first disciples still managed to share the gospel with those persons with whom they came in contact. The worst that the Sanhedrin could threaten or do was not sufficient to keep them from proclaiming this amazing belief. Even the martyrdom of some of their number did not keep others from holding to and sharing it.

Second and equally amazing, some people who heard the message of those first disciples believed that what they proclaimed was true. Among the first new converts to the faith were priests and Pharisees as well as some people of wealth and power. The obvious intellectual and social limitations of many of the first Christians did not keep others of differing levels of society from accepting the faith which they proclaimed.

Third, it was flight to avoid persecution rather than a missionary strategy which initially caused the Christian communities to be spread as far from Jerusalem as they were in those early years. These Christians believed they had a commission from their Lord to carry the gospel to the ends of the earth. However, they were apparently in no rush to obey. It was actually the fear of persecution which sent them abroad, not their commitment to a missionary imperative.

Fourth, in spite of the fact that the early churches apparently had neither a missionary strategy nor a deep commitment to carry the gospel to the ends of the earth, opportunities were seized by them to witness. Their success in taking advantage of such opportunities increased both the geographic region over which the churches were scattered as well as the numbers of people in those regions who were believers. The gospel had been carried by both new and old believers to the far reaches of the empire. The churches had also broken away, at least partially, from their original Jewish cradle because among the new believers were some Gentiles.

The Church at Antioch

For the first years of Christian history, the church at Jerusalem had been the acknowledged center of the Christian community. The original apostles still seemed to make it their base of operations, even though it was from that center that the Sanhedrin's persecution took shape and gathered impetus. However a church of significance had sprung up at Antioch in the Roman province of Syria. It was of sufficient strength and importance that the congregation there had been able to send monetary relief to the church at Jerusalem when a major famine struck (Acts 11:29-30).

We may conclude that it was typical of the church in Antioch to be generous with those in need. We may also conclude that it was characteristic of them that they would have chosen to send this relief by the hands of Saul and Barnabas. Barnabas had obviously been a leader of the church in Jerusalem and would have been quite welcome when he returned there. Saul, on the other hand, had been that church's leading persecutor and had been accepted as a part of their congregation with great reluctance. These two men who would have been viewed so differently in Jerusalem were viewed as equals in ministry and trustworthiness by the church in Antioch.

During the time of the relief visit by Barnabas and Saul, Herod died (12:23-25). Shortly thereafter, these two ambassadors returned to their ministry in Antioch. Their scriptural connection with this event in secular history gives us a point in time by which we can date their ministry.

The church at Antioch where Barnabas and Saul labored had apparently been started by Christians who had originally fled the persecution of Christians in Jerusalem led by Saul. It is quite significant that the people there who had fled had accepted his ministry, apparently without question. This says something of their openness and willingness to believe that God can change anyone.

Further, the church at Antioch had willingly crossed the boundaries of race, taking in Gentile converts without question. This openness led to some problems for the church in Jerusalem, but it clearly had posed no difficulties for these gospel adventurers in Antioch. The names of the leaders of that church show something of its cosmopolitan nature (13:1). Simeon, called "Niger," was most likely a black man from Africa. Manaen is described as "a member of the court of Herod the tetrarch." There is some evidence that Manaen was actually a half-brother of Herod, a very unlikely prospect for Christianity. Add Barnabas and Saul to this, and the church is seen as having leaders who represent a very diverse congregation.

With this kind of variety among its leaders, it is not surprising that the church at Antioch was open to heeding the missionary imperative of their Lord. God placed the world in their hearts and set apart two of them to take the initial steps in going. With no apparent jealousy or rancor among those who were not selected, the daring Christians at Antioch accepted the idea that if the world was going to be reached for Christ, they had to make a deliberate effort to do it. Accidental missions could no longer be an acceptable program. At least for the Christians in Antioch and the representatives they sent forth, missions now became intentional. They had become a church on mission.

The First Missionary Journey

The first missionary team on record was made up of Barnabas and Saul. Further, in addition to Barnabas and Saul, the team was completed by the presence of John Mark, a cousin of Barnabas who had come to Antioch with them when they returned from their errand of mercy to Jerusalem (13:5; Col. 4:11). Since Barnabas' name is listed first, we may conclude that he was apparently the leader.

According to our earlier conclusions, Barnabas and Saul probably made the trip from Antioch to Seleucia in the early spring of A.D. 45.

Seleucia was the nearest seaport to Antioch, and they intended to sail to Cyprus from there (13:4). The overland journey between these two cities was about sixteen miles, approximately a half-day's walk. The sea journey from Seleucia to Salamis would have been about 125 miles, but had to be made against the prevailing winds. Such a trip normally took several days of very difficult sailing.

The choice of Cyprus as the site for the first intentional missionary endeavor was probably due to the fact that this was the home country of Barnabas (4:36). As leader of the team, he had apparently made the choice.

The Mission to Cyprus

Little is really known about the missionary enterprise of Barnabas and Saul on Cyprus (13:4-12). They landed at Salamis, the port on the eastern end of the island. Their initial approach to their task was one which Paul followed all the rest of his career: first making contact with the Jewish synagogues. This was probably adopted for several different reasons. Both Barnabas and Saul were Jews, and these people were related to them, thus giving them an immediate point of contact. Further, since they were Jews, they also had a deep concern that their people hear the good news of Jesus. In addition, the Christian movement had sprung from its Jewish heritage in the Old Testament Scriptures. Thus there was always a point of contact from which the Christians could begin a ministry. They had a common faith and shared a common hope.

We have no way of knowing how long Barnabas and Saul stayed at Salamis or of evaluating their ministry there. They apparently had no spectacular results, since no reference is made either to any successes or failures.

From Salamis they journeyed to Paphos, the center of the Roman government of the island and thus the residence of Sergius Paulus, the Roman proconsul. Along the way, they passed through several villages which would have included Old Paphos itself. Old Paphos was the center of the licentious worship of Aphrodite. The missionaries may have been tempted to stop there, but they pressed on to the capital. This also set a pattern for much of Paul's future ministry. He seems always to have sought out the strategic centers for his major efforts. These places may either have been centers of government and influence or population. He always seems to have chosen the places where he could have the greatest influence.

Four things stand out from the missionary efforts in Paphos. First, they had a major confrontation with a Jewish false prophet who sought to interfere with their ministry and prevent the Roman governor from becoming involved with Barnabas and Saul. Saul is clearly the spokesman for the team. Viewed from a Roman standpoint, this may have indicated that Barnabas was the more important person with Saul being his spokesman or representative.

Second, Saul's name shifts in the narrative to Paul. As a Roman citizen, he had certainly been given a Roman name at birth, which was most likely Paulus. As a Jew, however, he also would have had a Jewish name. This was probably Saul. This shift in Luke's use of his name may indicate that a definite shift had taken place in the direction of his ministry. He had clearly accepted the responsibility of being the missionary to the Gentiles. His Jewish name might henceforth be a handicap.

Third, Sergius Paulus, a significant Roman official, apparently became a believer. Luke consistently shows through the Book of Acts that the Romans did not have any inherent opposition to the Christian faith. To the contrary, they are regularly seen as being tolerant of it, if not actually becoming believers.

Fourth, during the stay in Paphos, Paul clearly became the leader of the team. Up to this point, the narrative has always spoken of Barnabas and Saul, in that order. After this, we are told of "Paul and his company" (13:13). Paul's drive and abilities were such that he naturally gravitated to the position of leader. On the other hand, it is to Barnabas' everlasting credit that he could step back into Paul's shadow with no hint of jealousy or misgiving.

The Mission to Asia Minor

We have no way of knowing how long Paul and Barnabas stayed on Cyprus. However, almost certainly it was in the late summer of A.D. 45 or spring of A.D. 46 that the team set sail from Cyprus to the coast of Asia Minor, landing at Perga. For reasons which are set forth below, I conclude that the journey to Perga was more likely made in the spring of A.D. 46.

Paul was too familiar with the geography and climate of this region to have made this journey in the winter. The brutal winter storms of the western Mediterranean made sailing untenable. Further, inland from this whole coast were towering mountains, some of which rose to heights of more than nine thousand feet. The winter snows made travel through those regions at such times utterly impossible. Thus Paul would have arrived on the coast early enough to get through them before the winter snows or late enough for the snows to have melted before he sought to travel.

When the missionaries arrived at Perga, "John [Mark] left them and returned to Jerusalem" (v. 13). For John Mark to return immediately implies that they arrived in the spring of A.D. 46. He would not have been able to make this trip during the winter.

The reason (or reasons) behind John Mark's decision to abandon his companions and return home is (are) unknown. No question exists that Paul considered John Mark's action to be similar to that of a soldier who deserted his post. Years later, when Paul and Barnabas got ready to make their second missionary journey, Paul refused to allow John Mark to come along (15:36-38).

Since John Mark returned to Jerusalem rather than to Antioch, some have suggested that he was simply homesick. Others have suggested that as he was Barnabas' cousin, he could not stand the idea that Paul had become the leader. Still others have suggested that John Mark had been willing to be the aide to his cousin but refused to fill the same role for Paul. Admittedly, a person with Paul's single-mindedness would have been hard to work with. Some have also suggested that both Paul and John Mark got sick when they arrived at Perga and that John Mark turned homeward while Paul pressed on.

Another explanation for John Mark's turning homeward may be closer to the truth and may better explain the facts as we know them. It could be that John Mark and Paul had a major difference of opinion as to the best way to carry on their work. John Mark may have felt that the young Christians and new churches needed something more left behind by the missionaries than the fading memories of their messages. He may have decided that these young churches needed something written to help them solidify their faith and grow in it. Paul, on the other hand, may have felt that he was too busy starting churches to be bothered with writing for them.

If this is the case, John Mark may have turned homeward to

write something for the new churches so that they would have some record of what Jesus did and taught. A significant number of contemporary scholars believe that Mark's was the first Gospel written. This gospel might have been the result of his departure. On the other hand, when Paul continued his ministry over the years and revisited churches which he had started, he began to discover that they had gotten into all sorts of problems. Finally he began writing his letters (epistles) to them to deal with these problems.

It may well be that Paul's many writings, all of which were produced after his first missionary journey, came as a result of a later change in strategy which was based upon his personal experience. This would then explain why it was that Paul later worked closely with John Mark, even calling him a fellow worker (Philem. 24; Col. 4:10). It would also explain the fact that when the end was near, John Mark was a companion whom he wanted to have close by, requesting, "Get Mark and bring him with you; for he is very useful in serving me" (2 Tim. 4:11).

Although Paul had landed at the seaport of Perga in the province of Pamphylia, he apparently had no desire to stay there. Instead, he quickly moved northward, crossing the mountains which towered before him in order to get to the major Roman military road which ran east-west through the southern part of Asia Minor. We must remember that Paul was a native of Tarsus which was on this road two to three hundred miles to the east. This exposure there to troops, pilgrims, and caravans would have caused him to know of the cities which lay along the route.

The journey of Paul and Barnabas intersected that Roman road at Antioch of Pisidia (Acts 13:14-50). The student should be warned not to confuse this city with the other of the same name but in a different province where the church was which had sent these missionaries forth. We should note that Rome constructed her roads to enable troops and trade goods to move rapidly throughout the empire. That same system of roads made it easy for the Christian missionaries to carry the gospel from Jerusalem to Rome.

Antioch had originally been established during the Seleucid empire to be a fortress to keep the region secure. Rome had turned it into a colony. At such a place large numbers of retired soldiers were given lands and allowed to settle there. Such a place served as a center of Roman society and helped keep the far reaches of the empire loyal to Rome. Paul, as a Roman citizen, liked to carry his gospel to centers of Roman civilization.

Once again, Paul began his ministry by going to the synagogue. As a visitor, he was invited to speak and did so forcefully in a typically rabbinic fashion. However, his message had such a strange ending that throngs came back to hear him a week later. This so aroused the jealousy of the leaders of the synagogue that they began to argue with Paul, even attacking him personally. Turning his back upon the Jews who had rejected his message, he began to reach the Gentiles with the good news of Jesus (vv. 44-48).

The end result of Paul's ministry in Antioch was twofold. First, the city served as a center from which the gospel was carried into the region. By accident, Paul had discovered that urban centers, when evangelized, influence the entire region which surrounds them. Second, the Jewish leaders who had been given a first chance at the gospel became so bitter at Paul's success that they drove Paul and Barnabas from the city (vv. 49-50).

The two missionaries turned eastward from Antioch and journeyed to Iconium. There they met with results similar to what they had experienced at Antioch (13:51 to 14:5). However, Paul and Barnabas faced opposition both from Jews and Gentile leaders. Yet, at the same time, they had converts from both groups. At Iconium, their opponents even made plans to stone them. However, when Paul and Barnabas learned of it, they fled from the city. Having so narrowly escaped death, they moved on eastward along the Roman highway. Their strategy continued unchanged, so they moved steadily from city to city, using each of the cities as bases from which to reach the surrounding countryside (14:6).

Their first major stop along the way was Lystra, which was also a Roman colony like Antioch. At Lystra Paul performed a miracle of healing. Immediately, the superstitious inhabitants assumed that Paul and Barnabas were gods come down to earth. Probably due to the fact that they did not understand the local dialect, Paul and Barnabas did not at first realize what was happening. It was only when the priest of Zeus prepared to offer sacrifice to them that they comprehended the citizens' misconceptions. Even then, as he rejected the worship of the people, Paul sought to use their own superstition as an opportunity of bearing witness to his faith (vv. 8-18).

At that point, those who had opposed Paul and Barnabas at

Antioch and Iconium arrived at Lystra for the purpose of stirring up the citizens' anger. So successful were they that Paul was stoned, dragged out of the city, and left for dead (v. 19). Paul was not dead, though he was certainly seriously injured. When he revived, he went back into Lystra to rest overnight. The next day he and Barnabas once again set forth on their missionary journey, moving on to Derbe (v. 20).

The journey to Derbe must have been difficult because of Paul's physical condition following his stoning. Nothing is known of their mission there. However, Paul and Barnabas must have stayed for some time, meeting with a measure of success because we are told that they "made many disciples" there (v. 21).

At this point, they decided to head back home. This may have been due to Paul's physical condition and need for rest and recuperation. They decided not to journey on along the Roman highway in the same direction they were going, even though it led first to Paul's home in Tarsus and then down to their home church at Antioch of Syria. Instead, they turned back along the way from which they had come.

Paul and Barnabas did this in spite of the opposition which they had faced there and the obvious dangers which would have been in store for them on their return. This was apparently done to strengthen the congregations which they had established and encourage them to faithfulness and courage. Those people had to face opponents every day. Paul at least wanted them to see that he had the courage to do what he was asking them to do.

In addition, Paul was well aware that in order to survive and grow, any human institution needed an organization. As he visited those first congregations he had established, he "appointed elders" who were to furnish leadership in his absence (v. 23). When their ministry to those new congregations was completed, Paul and Barnabas turned southward through the mountains, going back to Perga. Again, this journey had to have been made in the summer and was probably in A.D. 47.

This time, when Paul and Barnabas came to Perga, they were not under the same pressure of time which they faced a year earlier and stopped to preach (v. 25). Although it is not mentioned, it appears probable that they established a church there. However, since the fall season for sailing was about to end, they soon moved further down the coast to Attalia from which they were more likely to catch a ship bound for Syrian Antioch. It is likely that they arrived home in the fall of A.D. 47.

When the missionary adventurers returned home to Antioch, they were received with joy. The entire congregation welcomed the weary travelers home. Paul and Barnabas spent "no little time" with the disciples at Antioch, sharing the good news of how God had blessed their missionary enterprise (vv. 26-28). This would apparently indicate that Paul and Barnabas spent the winter of A.D. 47/48 resting and recuperating in Antioch, sharing the story of their successes and defeats in proclaiming the gospel in Asia Minor.

The Jerusalem Council

From the standpoint of ministry and mission, the most significant feature of the missionary journey of Paul and Barnabas was the journey itself. As far as we know, this was the first time when a church had adopted and carried out a specific plan to carry the gospel to the lost world. On the other hand, from the standpoint of theology or doctrine, perhaps the most significant feature of that missionary journey was the fact that churches which were specifically and primarily Gentile had been established.

As the news of the success of that first missionary journey made its way to Jerusalem, many of the Jewish Christians there were deeply disturbed by it. The reason for this problem was that those who felt themselves still constrained by the traditions of their past wished others to be so bound as well. Many among them believed that no one could be a Christian who had not first become a Jew, the outward symbol of which was circumcision (15:1).

Representatives of those Jewish Christians who were so upset made their way to Antioch and began to trouble the church there. "Dissension and debate" broke out over this issue, with Paul and Barnabas taking the lead on the part of the freedom of the Gentile Christians (v. 2). The end result of this disagreement was that the church in Antioch sent a delegation to Jerusalem to discuss the entire matter with the apostles. The news of the success of the Gentile mission was received with joy in Phoenicia and Samaria (v. 3). Both groups represented people who had historically been treated as outcasts by the Jews. They might have rejoiced over anything which discomfited their hereditary enemies.

According to our calculations, the Jerusalem Council was probably held in the summer of A.D. 48. The initial debate over the issue was hot and heavy (vv. 6-21). However, even Simon Peter spoke out on the side of the freedom of the Gentiles from having to become subservient to the Jewish Torah.

The end result of the Jerusalem Council was a victory for the side of those who believed that Gentiles should not have to become Jews. Thus the church of Jesus Christ was forever freed from those who would have kept it merely a sect of Judaism. At the same time, in the interests of Christian brotherhood, the council did urge the Gentile Christians not to use their freedom as a means of troubling Jewish Christians. They were urged to avoid those acts of freedom which would have been especially troubling to their Jewish brothers (vv. 22-29). With the exception of unchastity, Paul seldom referred to the other items listed here in any of his sermons or letters. On the other hand, he did refer to the principle of not offending one's brother (1 Cor. 8:1-13).

One of the more fascinating sidelights of the council at Jerusalem was the fact that apparently it was James, the brother of Jesus, who presided over it (Acts 15:13-21). As far as we know, he was not even a believer at the time of Jesus' death. However, even if he were, it is surprising and significant that the official leader was not one of the original apostles. Truly, they were leaving the administration of the business of the church in the hands of others.

Following the Jerusalem Council, Paul and Barnabas returned to Antioch along with the delegation sent to give a report to the church in Antioch (vv. 30-31). The church rejoiced at the decision, and the delegation returned home. However, Paul and Barnabas stayed in Antioch and continued their ministry there (v. 35). This was most likely during the winter of A.D. 48/49. When the spring thaws came and travel once again became possible in the mountains of Asia Minor, the hearts and minds of Paul and Barnabas turned again toward their mission field.

The Second Missionary Journey

Contention and Separation

Sometime during this interval, John Mark had rejoined Paul and Barnabas in Antioch. This probably occurred when they returned there after the Jerusalem conference. During the months following their return to Antioch, Paul and Barnabas both had felt the tug of their missionary commitment and leading of God's

Spirit as they began to think of new opportunities and tasks. When the spring of A.D. 49 arrived, the warming of the weather warmed their hearts as well.

When Paul and Barnabas began to make specific plans for a renewed missionary effort, they had a major disagreement (vv. 36-39a). Barnabas, the loving and forgiving one, wanted to take John Mark with them again. Paul, however, who seems to have placed singleness of purpose above all things, would not consider taking him along since he had let them down once.

The sad end of this dispute was that these two great men of the faith parted company, each going his own way for justifiable reasons. From a human standpoint, Paul seems to have forgotten that it was Barnabas' love which had made it possible for him to even get in the church of Jerusalem (9:27). Furthermore, it was also Barnabas who had brought Paul into the ministry and mission of the church at Antioch as well (11:22-26). As heartbreaking as the disagreement was, the separation of Barnabas and Paul meant that there were now two teams on the road carrying the gospel to the ends of the earth.

As might have been expected, Barnabas and Mark returned to Cyprus, Barnabas' homeland. Their intent was apparently to revisit the churches which they had established on their first visit. On the other hand, Paul took another companion, Silas, and went back to the churches in Asia Minor which he and Barnabas had started there (15:40-41).

The Mission in Asia Minor

When Paul and Silas set out, they decided not to go by way of sea but to journey overland, following a major north-south highway which joined the east-west one north of the Amanus Mountains. They crossed these mountains through a narrow pass known as the Syrian Gates. Beyond this they came to Issus, where Alexander the Great had defeated the Persians centuries before.

Turning eastward from the junction of the highways, Paul passed through the region of his homeland, Tarsus. From there, they moved upward through another mountain pass known as the Cilician Gates. The snow in this pass does not normally melt until early June, giving us a basis for assuming that this journey could not have been earlier than the summer of A.D. 49.

The missionaries then came to Derbe and Lystra, two of the

cities where Paul and Barnabas had established churches on their first journey. At Lystra, Paul found Timothy, a convert from that first visit, and invited him to join their team. Since Timothy had a Greek father, he had never been circumcised into Judaism. However, lest he become a stumbling block to their mission, Paul had the young man circumcised (16:1-3). Paul, who had fought so vigorously to keep Gentiles from having to be circumcised, was just as vigorous in insisting that Timothy go through that rite of initiation. An uncircumcised Jew on his team would have offended other Jews. Paul never used his freedom either to offend or insult.

Luke gives no record of Paul's visiting either Iconium or Antioch. However, since we are told that Timothy had a good reputation among the people at Iconium, we can assume that the missionaries did stop there. Further, it is unlikely that Paul would have failed to visit Antioch, the location of the first church he established in Asia Minor.

After visits to those congregations, Paul faced a dilemma. He wanted to go to Asia (the Roman province); the capital of which was Ephesus. In some way, he was aware that God's Spirit was forbidding that at the moment (v. 6). Southward were the mountains and beyond that the small ports of Perga and Attalia. From there the natural thing would have been to go home or to Cyprus. He did not wish to do this yet. Behind him were the cities he had just visited. The only other direction open to him was northward into the region of Phrygia and Galatia (literally, "Galatian country"). This probably refers to parts of Phrygia inhabited by Galatians, rather than to the province of Galatia itself.

It may even have been an illness which turned Paul away from Asia to Galatia. He later reminded the Galatians how sick he was when he first arrived there (Gal. 4:13-15). Farther to the north opened the Roman province of Bithynia. Once again, Paul discovered his way was blocked by God's Holy Spirit (Acts 16:7). This, too, may have been communicated to him through a health problem. The only way left open to him was due west toward the seaport city of Troas (v. 8). Yet when he arrived there, his way was blocked again, this time by the Aegean Sea. Across that sea stood the shores of Europe. He must have been quite frustrated at this point.

At least two things happened at Troas which were of significance for the future of Paul and Christianity. First of all, one night he had a vision or dream of "a man of Macedonia" pleading with him to come there (v. 9). The second significant feature of Paul's visit to Troas shows up in Luke's narrative of what followed the vision. He says simply, "When he had seen the vision, immediately *we* sought to go on into Macedonia" (v. 10, italics mine). Luke, the beloved physician, apparently had joined Paul and his party at Troas. That may have been due to Paul's physical condition. For whatever reason, however, the man who is responsible for the Books of Luke and Acts seems to have become a part of the Christian mission while Paul was at Troas. As a physician, he may even have been the reason Paul was there in the first place.

The Mission in Macedonia: Philippi

Paul and his party crossed the Aegean by ship and landed at the port of Neapolis. This had to be done either prior to the onset of the late autumn and winter storms or after their end in late winter or early spring. Thus this voyage could have occurred in the late summer or early fall of A.D. 49. However, that would have left very little time before the journey for all which Paul and Silas had done since they had left Antioch. Thus it appears more likely that the journey across the Aegean would have occurred in the spring of A.D. 50.

Neapolis was at one end of the Via Egnatia, a major Roman road which crossed the Macedonian peninsula. Paul always seems to have traveled Rome's great highways, apparently believing that they led to major centers of population. They did. He followed the Via Egnatia to Philippi, "the leading city of the district of Macedonia, and a Roman colony" (v. 12). If our chronology is correct, Paul's approach to Philippi was probably very cautious, due to recent events in the heart of the empire.

In A.D. 49, there had been significant unrest among the Jews in Rome under Emperor Claudius. Further, riots had occurred because of unrest among the Jews regarding one "Chrestus." This may be a variant spelling of *Christus* (the Latin word for *Christ*) and refer to unrest because of the witness of Christians there. In any case, many Jews had been expelled from Rome at that time. Because of this unrest within the empire toward Jews, Paul could not have been sure what kind of reception he would receive in this imperial colony.

Apparently there was no synagogue at Philippi where Paul might begin his ministry as he customarily did. Therefore, knowing Jewish customs of the time, he sought a Sabbath meeting place where abundant water was available for the ritual washing of the hands which was required (vv. 13-15). There Paul found a group of Jewish women who gathered each Sabbath for worship and study. Presenting his message to them, he made his first European converts. Among them was a woman named Lydia who opened her home to Paul and his party.

With the passage of time, Paul became better known in the city. One day he was accosted by a slave girl who was being exploited by her owners as a fortune teller. Paul healed her of demon possession but was set upon by her owners. He and Silas were arrested, beaten, and imprisoned (vv. 16-24). As outsiders who were obviously Jews, they apparently became the victims of the prejudice of the Roman magistrates. What they endured was so like a mob that Paul had no opportunity to declare his Roman citizenship.

During the night an earthquake freed Paul and Silas, but they remained where they were. However, since the doors were opened, the jailer assumed that his charges had fled. In despair, the jailer started to commit suicide but was restrained by Paul. Amazed that men would have remained there when they could have left, he questioned Paul and became a Christian, along with his whole household (vv. 25-34).

The next day, the Roman magistrates decided to release their prisoners and then discovered what they should have found out earlier; Paul and Silas were Roman citizens. This frightened the officials because they had acted illegally against Roman citizens. Men had been removed from office for far less. Following a public apology, Paul and Silas were released. However, they were asked to leave the city. The magistrates probably feared some sort of riot like those which had broken out in Rome. Paul and Silas apparently only remained in the city long enough to say good-bye to their friends and then set forth again. They traveled with bloody backs and a great deal of pain. The reason for their haste was probably their own fear of a riot that might destroy the young church (vv. 35-40).

The Mission in Macedonia: Thessalonica and Beroea

Having departed from Philippi, Paul, Silas, and Timothy still followed the Via Egnatia as it led on through Amphipolis and Apollonia (17:1). No mention is made of any missionary activity in either of these significant Greek cities. This may have been due to their own weakness and the need for a time of recuperation. It may have been due to Paul's desire to press on toward his next major goal, Thessalonica, the capital of the province. Thessalonica was the largest city of Macedonia and had been given autonomy of government by the Romans. Although the Roman governor of the province lived there, the city was actually governed by six politarchs and was far more a Greek city than a Roman one.

In Thessalonica Paul's ministry was supported on at least two occasions by offerings sent by the church at Philippi (Phil. 4:16). Once again Paul began his ministry by preaching at the local synagogue, continuing there for at least three Sabbaths (Acts 17:2-4). Paul and his companions had immediate success, reaching some of the leaders of the Jews, some of the God-fearing Greeks, and a number of leading women of the community.

However, the success of the missionaries aroused the jealousy and anger within others within the community. In an attempt to seize Paul and his companions, they attacked the house of Jason who had given hospitality to the missionaries. Failing to find Paul, Jason and some of the brethren were carried before the politarchs of the city. The charge leveled against Paul, his companions, and the entire Christian community was that they had "'turned the world upside down'" (v. 6). To this was added a charge of sedition or even treason in that they proclaimed "'another king, Jesus'" (v. 7).

The former charge upset the peace of the Jewish community, but it was the latter which disturbed the civic authorities. Provincial governments had been removed by Rome for far less. Thus the rulers took steps to assure that no such proclamation was made in their city (vv. 8-9). Fearing not only for their safety but for their very lives, Paul and Silas (and apparently Timothy as well) were slipped out of the city under the cover of darkness and sent on their way.

For the first time in Paul's major missionary travels, he turned aside from the Roman highways which up to that time had provided him with the avenues for the spread of the gospel. Instead of going on westward on the Via Egnatia, he turned southward to Beroea. This may have been done due to the fear of his opponents in Thessalonica sending messengers on ahead to stir up trouble. The next city to the west was Pella, the old capital of Philip of Macedon. That alone should have attracted him. Instead, however, he went to Beroea. This was a city of some significance, being the capital of the third district of Macedon.

Luke describes the Jews of Beroea as being "more noble than those in Thessalonica" (v. 11). This could refer only to the fact that they were more gracious in receiving Paul and his message. On the other hand, it may also indicate that they had immigrated there far earlier than the others and had become more important in their community and better adapted to it.

Paul and his gospel message were well received by the Jewish leaders of Beroea. In addition, some of the very prominent Greeks of the city responded as well (vv. 12-13). However, news traveled fast, and it was not long before Paul's Jewish opponents in Thessalonica heard of his successes in Beroea. It is at least possible and probably likely that they had been trying to find out where he had gone. Having located him, representatives were sent to arouse the community against Paul.

Once again, Paul had to flee for his life (vv. 14-15). The fact that Silas and Timothy remained behind in Beroea shows that at least at this point the opposition was aimed primarily at Paul rather than at the Christian community as a whole. This was probably due to the fact that he was both the spokesman and leader of the mission team.

Paul fled by sea, indicating both his haste to get away and a fear of being followed had he departed by road. Since this was most likely in the winter of A.D. 50/51, it would have been a dangerous voyage if he had been crossing the Aegean. However, as his destination was Athens, this major crossing was not necessary. Most of the voyage would have been made in the narrow inside passage between the islands and mainland. This would have meant that the ship would have been sheltered from the storms of winter. Paul was escorted by friends from Beroea as far as Athens, the center of intellectual achievement of ancient Greece. Seeing him safely there, they returned home along with Timothy, carrying a message to Silas that he and Timothy should join Paul at Athens (1 Thess. 3:1-2).

The Mission in Macedonia: Athens

Formerly a city of greatness, the Athens in which Paul arrived was merely a shadow of its earlier accomplishments. At that time it was still a center for education, but its students and teachers were more fascinated by the fine points of argument than with actual learning. They were more concerned with winning a debate than with discovering real meaning to life.

In Athens, Paul quickly began to preach his good news of Jesus, once again starting at the Jewish synagogue. However, he also proclaimed his message in the marketplace (Acts 17:16-17). His new "philosophy" fascinated the philosophers there who were constantly seeking for something new to think about. They had heard Paul speak of Jesus and "the resurrection" (*anastasis,* the Greek word meaning resurrection) (vv. 18-21). Given their pagan and idolatrous background, they assumed these to be the names of a god and goddess.

Eager to hear more, the philosophers escorted Paul to the Areopagus in the center of town where learned discourses were held. There Paul shared with them his faith, beginning with their own superstitions, a strategy which has since been used by missionaries over the centuries (vv. 22-31). When Paul spoke to those "intellectuals" about resurrection, their skepticism led many of them to turn him away with a polite dismissal. His mission there was not wholly a failure because some followed him, accepting his message and his Lord (vv. 32-34). Realizing that the cynicism of the Athenians had closed their minds to his message, Paul moved on to Corinth, probably in the spring or early summer of A.D. 51.

The Mission in Macedonia: Corinth

Of all the cities Paul had visited in his journeys to that point, he had been in none like Corinth. It was both an old city as well as a new one. Ancient Corinth, a center of art and architecture, had been destroyed by the Romans in 146 B.C. However, recognizing its strategic location, Julius Caesar had ordered the city rebuilt and turned into a Roman colony.

What made its location so important was the fact that the journey by sea around Achaia was extremely dangerous. The isthmus of Corinth was narrow and low enough to allow freight to be off-loaded and carried across by cart while the ships themselves were pulled across on rollers. This made Corinth into a major seaport and center of commerce. Because of this, the population of the city was quite cosmopolitan. Numerous temples were built to gods from all over the world. The city also became a center of sexual immorality and licentiousness. In fact, the reputation of the city was so bad that one of the worst insults which could be leveled at a person was to be said to "act like a Corinthian."

To that international city of wickedness, Paul came to tell about Jesus. According to his own words, he approached the people of that city with great anxiety and fear (1 Cor. 2:3). In Corinth, he began to engage in his trade as a tentmaker (Acts 18:1-4). In doing so, he met Priscilla and Aquila who were of the same trade and who had been driven from Rome under the persecution of Claudius in the summer of A.D. 50. They were Jews who were also apparently Christians. They welcomed Paul into their home. From that base, he began to preach each Sabbath in the local synagogue—his usual practice.

As usual, Paul found his message basically rejected by his own people. Having been joined at about that time in his ministry by Silas and Timothy, Paul then moved the site of his preaching services to a house next door to the synagogue (vv. 6-11). From this new location, he experienced amazing success in winning converts to Christianity. However, by having such success on their very doorstep, Paul further aroused the hostility of the Jewish people. This was only exacerbated by the fact that the president of the synagogue became a Christian.

The self-professed "wisdom" of the Athenians had stood in the way of their faith. In stark contrast, the absolute moral poverty of the Corinthians apparently led them to be more open in hearing and responding to Paul's preaching.

Paul stayed in Corinth eighteen months, longer than he had stayed in any of the previous sites of his missionary endeavors. However, the hostility of the Jews continued to build until they at last brought Paul before the Roman proconsul, Gallio. (This was apparently sometime during the winter of A.D. 52/53.) His opponents charged him with illegal worship. We do not know all that was entailed by this charge, but Judaism had been designated by Rome as a *religio licta*, a "legal religion." The Jews were apparently seeking to separate Christianity from this umbrella of protection. However, the Roman ruler refused to get involved in this dispute (vv. 12-17). He carried his noninvolvement too far because he even refused to intervene when the Jewish leaders beat the synagogue president for having become a Christian.

We have no way of knowing how much longer Paul stayed in Corinth after this experience. Luke tells us that he "stayed many days longer" (v. 18). However, since he planned to sail away when he left, this probably put his departure in late spring of A.D. 53. He left behind a church which he had nurtured more than any church he had started. It also turned out to be the church which was to give him the greatest trouble of any church which he started.

The Journey Homeward

With the ease of sailing in the summer, Paul set forth to return to Antioch. Accompanied by his new friends Priscilla and Aquila, he sailed from Cenchrea, the seaport of Corinth, and crossed the Aegean to Ephesus. At long last, he had arrived at the capital of Asia to which he had aspired earlier.

In Ephesus he sought out the synagogue and shared his faith in Jesus with his fellow Jews. Amazingly, he did not seem at first to experience much (any?) opposition there (vv. 18-22). He must have been torn between his desire to remain there and his need to return home before the winter storms set in. However, he apparently arrived at a compromise. Leaving Priscilla and Aquila to carry on his mission, he again set sail for Palestine. He arrived at the port of Casearea, visited the Jerusalem church briefly, and then went on to Antioch. This seems to have occurred about A.D. 53 in the late fall.

26
Paul's Later Ministry

From the standpoint of the New Testament historian, at first glance there is little reason to have a break between our study of the first two missionary journeys of Paul and his third one. The primary reason which is usually suggested is merely to get the material into more manageable blocks.

On the other hand, if the chronology which we have suggested for these journeys is at all correct, then the secular historian immediately finds a significant basis for treating the study of the background history of this part of the New Testament era in two parts. As we noted earlier, Claudius died in A.D. 54 and was succeeded upon the throne of the empire by Nero.

The total difference between these two rulers and their influence upon the empire gives a radically different background for understanding the earlier missionary journeys of Paul from his journeys during the reign of Nero. It is this significantly different feature which leads us to treat these two periods of Paul's missionary travels in different sections. Claudius' reign furnished an era of peace and stability to the empire. In general, it also furnished this to the Christians, with the major exception of the riots in Rome. To the contrary, however, the reign of Nero gave anything but peace and stability to either the empire or Christian communities. Therefore we have chosen to deal with these two periods separately.

The Third Missionary Journey
Mission to Asia

Paul had once again returned to the comfort of the fellowship of his home church in Antioch following his second missionary journey. We have no way of knowing how long he stayed there before starting on the third journey, since Luke simply says that "after spending some time there he departed" (Acts 18:23). If our calculations and estimations are anywhere near correct, he had probably arrived at Antioch in the late fall of A.D. 53.

Since his intent at the beginning of the third missionary journey was once again to return to the churches he had started in Asia Minor, Paul clearly could not do this before the spring of A.D. 54. A sea journey would have been impossible before then, due to the winter storms. An overland journey would have had to be even somewhat later to allow time for the snow to melt in the mountain passes. Although we do not know for certain, it would appear that his journey was overland, and therefore I conclude that this journey from Antioch northward and westward began in the early summer of A.D. 54.

In specifying the provinces which Paul visited in the first part of this trip, Luke only mentioned Galatia and Phrygia. However, a look at any good map reveals that he had to pass through the other provinces of this region in order to get to these. Apparently he passed through them fairly rapidly, while spending a bit more time in these latter two regions. This would be logical in that the churches in these two provinces were newer. Paul probably felt more anxious about them.

While Paul was making these visits, another missionary by the name of Apollos came to Ephesus (18:24 to 19:1). However, his knowledge of Christianity was quite limited, and Priscilla and Aquila taught him more fully about Jesus. Apollos was an excellent orator, but his knowledge and experience had been inadequate. Having been more fully taught, he remained in Ephesus for a while and then left for Corinth.

Having completed his mission to the churches he had earlier established, Paul finally proceeded to Ephesus (19:1-20). At long last he intended to have a significant block of time to minister there. Ephesus was the capital of the Roman province of Asia and was the most significant city of the entire region of Asia Minor. It was also the fourth largest city in the Roman Empire, being exceeded in size only by Rome, Alexandria, and Syrian Antioch. Paul's visit there is one more evidence of his ongoing strategy of trying to win the cities for Christ and letting them become the centers for evangelizing their regions.

In Ephesus, Paul's mission was once again begun by a ministry in the Jewish synagogue, where he continued to preach for three months. At first he apparently found a friendly reception, as well as some disciples, although some of them had been improperly trained. He set about trying to correct the weaknesses in the experience of the disciples as well as trying to win new converts.

However, as usual, Paul's ministry finally aroused opposition on the part of the leaders of the synagogue. Finally forced to depart from the synagogue, Paul apparently rented a meeting place and carried on his mission for another two years. A measure of the significance Paul placed upon Ephesus is the fact that he stayed there longer than in any other city of his missionary travels.

In Ephesus, Paul had two major confrontations with opponents other than those from among the synagogue leaders. Ephesus had become a center of magic and sorcery. In fact, this was such a characteristic of Ephesus that books dealing with magic were generally called "Ephesian writings." At first, thinking Paul to be one of them, those who practiced these arts sought to copy some of his miracles. However, they quickly learned that his was a higher power, and many practitioners of these magic arts become converts (vv. 11-20).

In spite of the success of his mission in Ephesus, Paul knew that he had to move on. He was ultimately a missionary and church starter, not a pastor. He wanted to go back to the churches he had started on the Macedonian peninsula and eventually make his way to the very center of the empire, the city of Rome itself (vv. 21-22). During his stay in Ephesus, Paul obviously had contact with some of the churches he had started throughout the empire, receiving messages and messengers from them and sending letters and messengers to them.

Again, if our calculations have been at all accurate, Paul should have arrived in Ephesus in the late fall or early winter of A.D. 54. Twenty-seven months later would place him in the early part of A.D. 57. Although he sent two of his disciples, Timothy and Erastus, on ahead, he still stayed behind for a few more months. Paul's motive for sending others instead of going himself apparently was due to the fact that he had an ongoing and major conflict with the church at Corinth. However, his need for communicating with them was so great that he sent his disciples across the Aegean at the earliest possible moment the season would have allowed.

During the time when he remained behind in Ephesus, Paul had his second major confrontation. This was brought about by the fact that the major temple of the Ephesians was devoted to Diana (or Artemis). The temple dedicated to her was known as one of the seven wonders of the world. Paul's ministry had apparently been so successful that sales of the silver idols of Diana had fallen off, creating a business slump. As a consequence, the people of Ephesus were aroused by a silversmith named Demetrius (vv. 23-41). A riot ensued which lasted for hours before it was finally quelled by the leaders of the city. It is quite likely that the atmosphere of the empire under Nero set the stage for such a riot. It is also likely that his excesses in rendering judgments against officials who displeased him led to the eagerness of the Ephesian officials to quell the riot as quickly as possible.

After the riot had been ended, Paul decided to leave Ephesus and continue his journey. He probably felt that his continued presence in the city would constantly agitate his enemies so his departure might provide a time of peace for the disciples there. Furthermore, as always, the opportunities which were before him beckoned. Paul had his last meeting with the disciples in Ephesus and then set out for Macedonia (20:1).

Mission to Macedonia

We have few details of Paul's mission to Macedonia and Greece. He spent three months in Greece during this part of his trip (vv. 1-6). This probably was spent primarily if not entirely with the disciples at Corinth. In order to arrive there, Paul had traveled through Macedonia and most likely had visited the congregations which he had started on his earlier mission to that region. We are told that he gave "them much encouragement" (v. 2). It is therefore highly unlikely that he would have arrived in Corinth earlier than the latter part of A.D. 57 and therefore spent the winter there.

When Paul was ready to depart from Corinth, he wanted to sail for Syria from Cenchrea, Corinth's seaport. However, since this would still have been somewhat early for such a long sea journey and also he had discovered a plot against his life, he turned back northward for an overland journey. The plot against him must have involved someone on the ship, making it appear that his death had been an accident of the sea.

As he journeyed northward toward Philippi, he was accompanied by a large number of friends and fellow workers. These may initially have been for protection. They were apparently sent across the sea to Troas while he remained behind at Philippi for the Feast of Unleavened Bread. He finally set sail for Troas in April, A.D. 58.

Journey to Jerusalem

Spending a week in Troas, Paul once again set about proclaiming his faith. His companions then set sail, while Paul journeyed overland to Assos, where he intended to rejoin them. Luke's record of their sea voyage down the coast is quite detailed, indicating that he was probably along on this part of the trip (vv. 13-16). Paul was seeking to arrive in Jerusalem for the Feast of Pentecost, which occurred fifty days after Passover. Therefore he did not stop at Ephesus but sent word for the Ephesian elders to meet him on the coast (vv. 17-38).

Paul's message to the Ephesian elders was obviously one of farewell. He sought to strengthen the church to face the troubles which he was sure were yet to come. He also sought to help them realize what he had really sought to do among them. After a tearful farewell, Paul and his companions sailed again, proceeding on their way to Jerusalem.

Again, Luke gives a detailed account of that final voyage to Jerusalem (21:1-15). They continued on board what was apparently a small coaster, a ship which stayed close to the land, until they arrived at Patara. This city was the most important seaport of the Roman province of Lycia. There they were able to board an ocean-going ship which set out across the Mediterranean. This part of the voyage carried them within sight of Cyprus. We can only wonder if Paul's thoughts were at all turned toward Barnabas and Mark as he sailed on by. Eventually they arrived at Tyre and Ptolemais, where they left the ship and continued their journey to Jerusalem overland.

Paul seems to have been quite aware all along that this was his last missionary voyage. At the same time, when he and his followers had arrived at Caesarea, this was confirmed when he was confronted by a prophet who foretold Paul's arrest in Jerusalem. His disciples tried to turn him aside, but he steadfastly proceeded to the goal which he had set for himself.

From a human standpoint, we see that Paul had come to the

conviction that this was what he must do. On more than one occasion in his life, Paul had fled from danger in order to carry on
with his ministry. This time he marched toward his destiny with
no turning aside. To this end he led his companions on to Jerusalem, apparently arriving there at the Feast of Pentecost in June
A.D. 58.

Trials in Judea

Arrest in Jerusalem

Assuming that Paul arrived in Jerusalem just before the celebration of Pentecost, the city would most likely have been thronged
with Jewish pilgrims. These would have come not only from Judea
and Galilee, but from centers of Judaism throughout the empire.
Accommodations would have been very difficult for Paul and his
companions to find, but they were housed by one of the early disciples named Mnason (v. 15).

Paul brought with him offerings for the Jerusalem church which
he had raised in Macedonia and Corinth (2 Cor. 8:1-7; 9:1-4). The
church at Jerusalem had apparently been undergoing difficult
times which had become known throughout the Christian communities of the empire. We can be sure that these offerings from
other churches were gratefully received. However, when Paul made
his report to the elders of the church in Jerusalem, James pointed
out to him that both his presence and ministry were an embarrass-
ment to the Jerusalem congregation (Acts 21:17-26).

The throngs of people who had come to Jerusalem at that time
had obviously brought reports of Paul's activities. Many Jewish
Christians were still disturbed over the fact that Paul was not re-
quiring his converts to become Jews. Lest there be any trouble
with them, James asked Paul to demonstrate that he was still a
loyal Jew by performing a charitable work by paying the vows of
four impoverished men who were fulfilling their Nazirite vows.
This he readily agreed to do. Both by act and word, Paul had consistently shown that he never wished to use his freedom in a manner which might cause him to become a stumbling block to the
faith of others.

However, near the end of his stay in Jerusalem, some of the citizens accused him of having brought Gentiles into the temple precincts (vv. 27-36). This charge was leveled apparently because he

had been seen with Greeks in the city. To the Jews, the charge made against Paul was extremely serious, and anyone who had done such a thing deserved to die by stoning.

Because of the large throngs in Jerusalem and their volatility at festival occasions, Roman troops were always brought into the city at such times. They were quartered in the Antonia, which was a fortress adjacent to the temple itself. As the riot concerning Paul broke out, soldiers were quickly dispatched to restore the peace. In the meantime, Paul had been dragged out of the temple and surely beaten by the throngs attacking him.

In order to restore the peace, the Roman troops seized Paul and bodily carried him to their fortress. Two features perhaps made this riot significant from the standpoint of the Romans. First, the mismanagement of the procurator, Felix, had led to the rapid growth of the Zealots and their fanatical branch, the *sicarii*. Thus any outbreak had to be dealt with quickly and authoritatively. Second, a religious fanatic from Egypt had recently gathered a large group of followers together. Suspecting them of treason, Felix had crushed their movement with brutality, even though their leader had escaped.

The Roman tribune, Claudius Lysias, who was in Jerusalem, assumed that this new riot was tied up with these earlier problems. In fact, he apparently assumed that Paul was the leader of the religious movement with which Felix had dealt so summarily until he discovered that Paul could speak Greek (vv. 37-39). Deciding that Paul was not involved with any of the rebellious causes, the tribune allowed Paul to address the crowd. Things began to calm down until Paul spoke of his mission to the Gentiles, and then the crowd broke into a renewed uproar, refusing to listen any further (21:40 to 22:23).

The Romans then carried Paul into the Antonia, where they began to scourge him, seeking to gain information through torture (22:24-29). At this point, Paul appealed to his Roman citizenship, and he was delivered from the scourging thereby. Once again, we see just how highly prized the official Roman citizenship was.

The Hearing in Jerusalem

Probably because of Paul's Roman citizenship, the tribune called for a public hearing of the charges against Paul. The high priest and Sanhedrin gathered to hear the case, thus indicating just how significant the Jewish leaders considered this case to be (22:30 to 23:10).

After a brief confrontation with the high priest, Paul began to make his defense before the court. Quickly recognizing that the court was divided between Pharisees and Sadducees, he immediately identified himself as a Pharisee. Then, playing on a basic issue which divided the two parties, he began to speak of the resurrection. At this point the members of the court became so hostile toward one another that the hearing was ended, and Paul was returned to the Antonia.

It was at this point that the *sicarii* decided to take a hand. Seeing how the situation had developed, they laid a plot to assassinate Paul (23:12-35). Paul, however, was warned by his nephew of this plot and through him warned the Roman tribune. Deciding that the entire situation had gotten out of control, Paul was transported under the cover of darkness to the Roman headquarters in Caesarea.

Once again we can see just how much the Romans feared the Zealot assassins and how seriously they took the whole situation in that an armed guard of two hundred men escorted Paul along the way. It was that Paul was once again taken before a Roman court for judgment. Felix, the procurator, had Paul held until his accusers arrived and a formal trial could be held.

The Trial Before Felix

Paul had two hearings before Felix. The first was a formal, open trial, and the second was more or less a private hearing before the governor alone (24:1-27). In the first trial, Felix heard both the accusers and accused but put off judgment until the Roman tribune arrived to give his report of what had transpired.

One of the more intriguing features of the confrontation is Luke's statement that "Felix . . . [had] a rather accurate knowledge of the Way" (v. 22). This would have been expected of an effective Roman administrator, but Felix had shown himself to be somewhat less than effective in administering his province. It is possible that there had been enough conflict between the Jews and Christians in Jerusalem that even Felix had been forced to learn something of the issues which divided them.

On the other hand, the very fact that Felix put off making a decision reveals just how uncertain he was of his position. The uncertainties which Nero had brought to the empire had led greater men than Felix to try to avoid making decisions which might influence larger circles of the empire.

Felix's private hearing with Paul was also quite fascinating. Drusilla, the wife of Felix and daughter of Agrippa I, was a Jew. When Felix first saw her, he was so smitten by her beauty that he stole her from her husband and persuaded her to marry him. When Paul was brought before this couple, rather than defending himself, he dealt with their problem, speaking of "justice and self-control and future judgment" (v. 25).

A more powerful man might have had Paul executed on the spot, but Felix was too weak and insecure to do that. On the other hand, he was such a moral cripple that he had Paul returned to prison in the hope that some of Paul's friends might eventually pay a bribe for his freedom. This policy may have been adopted by Felix after he had heard of the large sum of money Paul had brought from his mission churches to the church at Jerusalem.

In the meantime, Paul was brought before the Roman governor frequently for further conversations. However, he was also kept in prison in a vain attempt to appease the Jewish leaders. After two years, Nero recalled Felix and sent Porcius Festus to succeed him as procurator of Judea.

The Trial Before Festus

One of the first things a new Roman administrator did upon assuming office was attempt to dispose of all the business which had been held over by his predecessor. This was certainly the policy adopted by Festus (25:1-12). Immediately upon his arrival in Jerusalem, the Jewish leaders sought to have Paul's case brought to judgment but in Jerusalem. They hoped to be able to assassinate Paul along the way. However, Festus refused to grant this request, calling for Paul's new trial to be held at the official residence in Caesarea.

When Paul was brought before Festus, he was given a chance to defend himself. By this time realizing just how much the Jews hated Paul, Festus sought to win their favor and support by suggesting that Paul return to Jerusalem for a trial. At this point Paul appealed his case to Caesar, a right held by every Roman citizen. Paul, sadly, had been forced to appeal to Caesar since he had failed to get the justice due him from the Roman procurators, but it was going to be an expensive process. The expenses of getting to Rome had to be borne by Paul who was no longer able to work, since he was a prisoner. He obviously had confidence that his friends and the churches he had started would rise to the occasion. It appeared that the mater was settled, insofar as Festus was concerned.

The Hearing Before Agrippa

While Paul was awaiting his transfer to Rome, King Agrippa II and his wife, Bernice, arrived in Caesarea to welcome the new procurator. Since Agrippa was a Jew, he was intrigued by the report of Paul's case and asked for an opportunity to examine him (25:13 to 26:32). Such a hearing bordered on being illegal since Paul had already appealed to Caesar. Festus sought to justify it by using it as an excuse to formulate the official charges to be transmitted to Rome.

According to Luke, at this time Paul preached one of the more masterful sermons with which he was ever credited. Festus' reaction to the message was to adjudge that Paul was insane. Agrippa II, on the other hand, realized what Paul was about. He recognized that Paul was trying to lead the king to accept his faith. Both rulers, however, appeared to have agreed that Paul could have been set free if he had not made his appeal to Caesar. The tragedy of the situation was that it was the Romans' failure to treat Paul with justice that had made his appeal necessary. So it was that after two years imprisonment at Caesarea, Paul finally set sail for Rome in the late summer of A.D. 60.

Trials at Sea

When Paul at last set sail for Rome, it must have been with mixed feelings. He had longed to go to Rome with the message of Jesus. The fact that he was at last going there must have given him a feeling of joy. At the same time, he was going as a prisoner. He and the friends he had left behind knew that there was a good chance that they would never see one another again. This would have produced significant sorrow and grief.

Paul set forth on this new stage of his life accompanied by two friends. One was Aristarchus, a companion from Macedonia, and the other was the author of the "we" sections of Acts, usually understood as being Luke, the beloved physician. In addition, Paul was accompanied by a Roman centurion and some other prisoners (27:1). The other prisoners may have included some who, like Paul, were appealing their case to Caesar. Others, particularly in the time of Nero, were probably being sent to fight with the gladiators or wild animals in Nero's famous contests.

The fact that they set sail in a ship of Adramyttium reveals that they had been unable to find a ship going all the way to Rome (vv. 2-5). Adramyttium was a major harbor of Mysia, located on the northern shore of the Aegean Sea. Thus this ship would have been a coaster, making frequent stops along the way. They obviously hoped to meet with a ship bound for Rome somewhere along the way.

Sure enough at Myra in Lycia they found an Alexandrian ship bound for Rome (vv. 6-8). Being a ship of Alexandria probably means that it was laden with grain and bound for the markets of Rome. Since most of Rome's grain came from Egypt and ships normally found such trips difficult during the winter, grain prices rose sharply in Rome during the winter months. It was risky to try to make such a voyage at such a time, but if it could be done safely, the financial rewards were great.

This particular voyage was late in the sailing season and the ship and its passengers had great difficulty with the journey. They paused briefly at Fair Havens on the southern shore of Crete. The time is given as after the fast, meaning after Yom Kippur, the Day of Atonement. Paul warned against setting forth again, but they chose to do so anyhow (27:9 to 28:1). They set forth with a fair wind which soon turned into a violent winter storm. After two weeks of drifting out of control and doing everything possible to save the ship, they finally foundered on the coast of Malta. The people on board were saved, but the ship was a total loss.

The survivors of the shipwreck were welcomed and treated with hospitality by the inhabitants of the island (28:2-13). They remained there three months, waiting for the winter season to end. During that time, Paul engaged himself in ministry to the people of Malta.

Eventually, Paul and the others who were with him set sail in another Alexandrian grain ship bound for Rome. The figurehead of that ship was Castor and Pollux, the Twin Brothers. Since there was a pagan festival honoring those two in late January, the ship's owner might have taken that as a good omen and set sail soon afterwards. This would have put Paul and his companions back on the sea again late January or early February A.D. 61. Sure enough, good fortune was with them and they landed at Puteoli, the seaport nearest to Rome, shortly thereafter.

Rome at Last!

When they arrived at Puteoli in the early spring of A.D. 61, Paul was welcomed by a community of Christians and remained with them seven days. Following the shipwreck, Paul was apparently given a great deal of freedom by the Roman centurion. Following his visit there, Paul was escorted up the Campanium Way to the Appian Way and followed it into Rome (vv. 14-16). We can only imagine the emotions which filled Paul as he arrived at the center of the empire, the place to which he had thought of coming ever since he had become a Christian.

Although Paul was officially a prisoner, he was allowed to rent his own home and remain there with a soldier to guard him, essentially under house arrest. During that time, although he was not free to leave, he had free access to those who would come to him (vv. 17-31).

For at least two years Paul remained there, waiting for his hearing before Nero. He was able to share his faith with the Christians of Rome as well as with any who would come to visit him.

We have no way of knowing what happened to Paul after that. This is just as it should be. The focus was not the journey of Paul to Rome but the journey of the gospel to Rome. Some traditions would indicate that Paul was freed by Nero and made his long hoped for mission to Spain. Following this, according to other traditions, he again came to Rome, where he was imprisoned and executed along with Simon Peter by the edict of the insane emperor who had declared himself to be a god. However, even though we don't know about Paul, we do know about the gospel. It was carried forth from Rome to the ends of the earth.

27
Outreach in Other Directions

If all one did was read the Book of Acts, the first and major impression gained would be that the mission efforts of the early churches were almost wholly confined to the work of Paul and his fellow laborers. No question exists but that the missionary work of Paul and his companions appears to have been the beginning of the first intentional attempt to carry the gospel to the ends of the earth. On the other hand, evidence both within and without the Bible clearly reveals that many other churches and Christians soon became involved in the work of carrying the good news of Jesus to those who had never heard.

These efforts at spreading the gospel were at first apparently sporadic and somewhat disorganized. Further, the missionary activities included inreach as well as outreach. By this, I mean that the Christians did attempt to share the good news both with those who lived near or around the Christian communities as well as with those who were in cities and lands where Christians had not yet gone.

In seeking to study these efforts, we need to realize that we are often dealing with hints, rumors, and traditions rather than with an abundance of clear-cut evidence. At the same time, the clues and hints which we are able to find do give us a picture of churches and individual Christians who were far more involved in carrying the good news of Jesus to others than we might suppose after our first superficial studies. (In considering the following areas of expansion, we need to recognize that each of these are not mutually exclusive.)

Initial Outreach

As we noted earlier, on the day of Pentecost when the Holy Spirit descended upon the disciples, Jerusalem was crowded with pilgrims from all over the ancient world. These pilgrims would have been primarily Jews who were accompanied by a smattering of proselytes and so-called "devout" Gentiles. The latter were "god-fearers" who were in varying degrees of commitment to the faith of Judaism and the God of the Jews. Luke reports that among them were "Parthians and Medes and Elamites and residents of Mesopotamia, Judea and Cappadocia, Pontus and Asia, Phrygia and Pamphylia, Egypt and the parts of Libya belonging to Cyrene, and visitors from Rome, both Jews and proselytes, Cretans and Arabians" (Acts 2:9-11).

At the end of that first day of proclamation, three thousand converts had been added to the number of disciples by conversion and baptism. It is quite likely, though by no means certain, that Luke had put together his list of the various nations who were represented in Jerusalem from those who were among the converts. Other converts from these pilgrims were apparently added to the number of the disciples in subsequent days.

When the festival was over, although some of these new converts possibly remained with the church in Jerusalem, many of them surely returned home. In so doing, they would have carried their faith and knowledge, limited though it probably was, home with them. Upon arriving home, these new converts must surely have shared their faith with friends and family.

Thus we can conclude with legitimate justification that the end result of Pentecost for the Christian church was that numerous churches or communities of believers were begun throughout the empire. Their existence went unrecorded in history. Their subsequent influence is known only to God. We know little or nothing about most of them, but the first halting steps of the church's expansion must be dated to that first period of proclamation and outreach. The disciples were simply telling their story to those who were around them, but those who were around them must have carried it to the frontiers of the empire.

In addition, Jerusalem was both a center of worship for Judaism and commerce for that part of the empire. Pilgrims and travelers from all across the empire would have been in and out of Jerusalem on a fairly continual basis. Such people must surely have heard the disciples' proclamation, and some surely accepted it. An illustration of this may be seen in the experience of the Ethiopian eunuch (8:27-38). Again, some of the many people who passed in and out of Jerusalem in those early days must have become Christians and carried their faith back to their homes. However, no evidence exists to prove this. Our best educated guess must simply be that some expansion of the Christian community had to have occurred in those early days of witness in Jerusalem.

Beyond this, we also know that the persecution of the Christians in Jerusalem also forced many of them to flee to other parts of the land. Paul reported to King Agrippa II that the end result of this was that they were scattered to "foreign cities" (26:11). In fact, the church at Damascus had become significant enough for him to journey there in an attempt to persecute the Christians (9:1-2). Beyond this, we discover early churches in the regions of Galilee, Samaria, Phoenicia, and Cyprus, as well as in the specific cities of Lydda, Joppa, Caesarea, and Antioch (9:31-32,36; 10:1; 11:19). Once again, we are forced to conclude that there was a significant, if unintentional, expansion of communities of Christians throughout these early days. In all fairness, in considering the missionary expansion of the early church, we must not ignore these.

In Judaism

Technically speaking, the outreach of Christianity into the synagogues of Judaism is not really foreign missions. All of the first Christians were Jews and thus were, at least nominally, adherents of Judaism. Thus the mission of the early Christians to Judaism was actually a mission to friends, neighbors, and family members. However, we often have a tendency to forget that there was such an outreach at all.

Part if not all of the reason for our underestimating the importance of the expansion of Christianity into the realms of Judaism may actually stem from the mission efforts of Paul. In most cases, we have seen that Paul began his ministry in new communities by first seeking out fellow Jews in the local synagogue. However, we have also noted that almost always such a mission on his part quickly led to opposition and to the rejection of both his message and himself.

Because of the fairly regular Jewish rejection of Paul and his message, many interpreters seem to assume that this was characteristic of Judaism as a whole. This is really quite far from the truth. When Paul returned to Jerusalem following his third missionary journey, James said to him: "'You see, brother, how many thousands there are among the Jews to those who have believed'" (21:20). We are forced to conclude then that the mission of the Christian community to the community of Judaism was both widespread and effective. It is particularly noteworthy that this was so at the same time that Paul had been involved in his mission to the Gentiles.

In Rome

Throughout his ministry, Paul had longed to carry his message to Rome, the capital of the empire. Yet long before he arrived, a Christian community had been born and was apparently thriving. We have no way of knowing who first carried the good news of Jesus to the center of the empire. One hint at least offers a possibility.

When Jesus was on His way to be crucified, He stumbled under the weight of the cross. At that point, the Roman soldiers compelled a bystander to carry it for him. The one who was so forced is identified as "Simon of Cyrene, . . . the father of Alexander and Rufus" (Mark 15:21). This was a most unusual form of identification, as a man was almost always identified by who his father was, not by who his sons were. The only possible reason for making this kind of identification would be if the sons were well-known to the audience.

According to tradition, which appears to be well-grounded, the Gospel of Mark was written from Rome. Is it possible that these two men were leaders of the church in Rome. Clearly one of them was because Paul's letter to the church in Rome urged, "Greet Rufus, eminent in the Lord" (Rom. 16:13). It is at least possible that the message of Jesus had been carried to Rome by the businessman from Cyrene and his two sons—Simon, Alexander, and Rufus.

We know that in A.D. 49 and 50 there were riots among the Jewish community in Rome over one "Chrestus." While we cannot prove this, it appears to be likely that this was a reference to Christ and that the riots stemmed from the evangelization of Jews by Christians. It would appear that there was a Christian church in Rome by at least that time.

When Paul arrived in Corinth on his second missionary journey, he found Priscilla and Aquila there (Acts 18:1-2). They were clearly Christians who were refugees from Rome who had been driven out under Claudius' order of expulsion.

Furthermore, when Paul was in prison in Rome, he wrote a letter to the church at Philippi. In his final greetings, he wrote, "All the saints greet you, especially those of Caesar's household" (Phil. 4:22). This would indicate that at the time of Paul's imprisonment a rather large congregation of Christians were active in Rome. Further, some of those Christians were actually servants in the household of Nero himself. What hardy Christians they were!

Thus we can conclude that Rome had a strong church fairly early in the New Testament era. We do not know by whom it was started. We do not know when it was started. What we do know is that it was started and its members were active in living and sharing their faith.

In Alexandria and Africa

All we really know about Christianity in north Africa is that quite soon after the end of the New Testament era there were a number of relatively important churches scattered along the Mediterranean coast of Africa. No real tradition exists as to when they were started or by whom.

The one thing we do know about African Christianity is that before Paul arrived in Ephesus on his third missionary journey, a missionary by the name of Apollos had arrived there from Alexandria (Acts 18:24-26). He was a Jew who was proclaiming the things of the Lord. He was lacking a full understanding of the gospel, so Priscilla and Aquila took him aside and sought to teach him those things of the faith which he did not know.

All that we know of Apollos' background is summed up in the assertion that he was a Jew from Alexandria. We have seen that there was a large Jewish community in Alexandria which had undergone intense persecution from the Gentiles of the city. Obviously, some among that community had become Christians.

Christianity might possibly have been carried back to Alexandria after Pentecost. Some of the Jerusalem Christians might also have carried the gospel to Alexandria as a result of merchants' journeying, direct missionary activity, or the persecutions of the Sanhedrin. Suffice it to say that a Christian community was in existence in Alexandria by at least the early A.D. fifties and possibly even earlier.

We should also acknowledge that at least at the beginning the church of Alexandria was to some extent apparently not quite in the mainstream of the New Testament faith. This was certainly true of this most famous representative, Apollos. However, if Apollos was representative of Alexandrian Christianity, somewhere along the line other missionaries came to Alexandria and helped them as well. It is even possible that Apollos returned to his home base. The end result was that the churches which later spread throughout north Africa, probably from Alexandria, were to become some of the more vital and vibrant of the ancient world. However, no evidence appears to exist that the gospel was carried southward in Africa for a number of centuries. This was probably due to the great desert barriers which kept civilization essentially confined to the northern coastal areas.

In Cyprus

As usual, we have no way of knowing when or how the gospel first reached out into the Mediterranean and its influence was felt on the island of Cyprus. We do know that Barnabas was a wealthy Cypriot who became a part of the Jerusalem church (4:36). He was a landowner in Jerusalem. We have no way of knowing whether or not he was a Christian before he left Cyprus. If he were, then Christianity would have reached that island very early, probably as a result of Pentecost.

On the other hand, Paul and Barnabas started their first missionary activity there (13:4-13). This clearly shows Barnabas' concern for his homeland. It also probably indicates either that Christianity had not reached that island or its influence there was quite limited.

While we have no reference to any church being started by Paul and Barnabas while they were on Cyprus, it is not unlikely that one was. This is particularly so since that was Paul's missionary strategy for all the rest of his career. On the other hand, since Paul regularly revisited the churches which he started, the fact that he never went back to Cyprus may be evidence that his initial efforts did not result in a church being formed. This becomes even more likely since he passed so near to Cyprus at the end of his third missionary journey and did not stop (21:3).

What we do know is that Barnabas and John Mark did return there when Barnabas and Paul went in separate directions at the beginning of the apostle's second missionary journey (15:39).

Again, we have no way of knowing what kind of success they enjoyed there, since they are not mentioned in the rest of Luke's record in Acts. However, when Paul arrived in Palestine at the end of his final missionary journey, he was accompanied to Jerusalem by several disciples, one of whom was from Cyprus (21:16). Thus we conclude that it is likely that by A.D. 58 there had been some success in Christianity's spread to this major island in the Mediterranean.

In India and the Far East

When we turn from the Mediterranean world to those regions of the Far East—India, China, and Japan—we have even less information concerning the spread of Christianity. However, as one would expect just from looking at a map, the earliest Christians of Japan and China had traditions that the gospel came to them from India. That would only be logical. We have no way of knowing when the gospel reached the Far East, but we know that it was there at least within four or five centuries after the death of Jesus. Christians may have reached there earlier, but we have no record of it. At the same time, we must acknowledge that we have few records from that region during this period of history.

India is a somewhat different situation. When the first missionaries of whom we have any record reached India several centuries after the death of Jesus, they were amazed to find that there were Christian churches already on the scene. No record exists which indicates when or by whom those churches were started. On the other hand, these churches do have the tradition that they were started by the missionary efforts of the apostle Thomas. In fact, the churches actually called themselves the Mar-Thoma churches.

We cannot verify the accuracy of that tradition. However, given the name and the tradition, we have no great reason for doubting it. It is fascinating to consider that, even while Luke was following the missionary activities of Paul as he carried the gospel to the center of the Roman empire, Thomas may have been moving eastward at the same time. Whether or not the tradition is true, it is obvious that some Christians within the Roman Empire had moved outside of the borders of the empire carrying the gospel of Jesus on to the east.

In Britain and Spain

The final areas of expansion for the Christian communities of the New Testament era which need to be examined are those to the north and west of Rome. When the first Christian missionaries of record arrived in Britain, they found Christian churches already on the scene. Once again, the origin of these churches, like those of India, is clouded in obscurity. It is possible that some Roman soldier who had been converted carried the gospel with him on his military assignment.

An ancient tradition, however, claims that Joseph of Arimathea made his way to England and established churches there following the resurrection of Jesus. This tradition appears to be far less believable than the Thomas tradition of India. On the other hand, we have no other explanation. At the very least, some Christian(s) from the early days of the church did carry the gospel into Britain.

On the other hand, while we cannot claim that the Joseph tradition explaining the origin of the British Christianity is likely, it is certainly not impossible. He was a man of means, and either his business affairs or sense of mission could have carried him to that far-off isle.

No evidence exists as to the geographic route which was followed by whatever missionary first carried the gospel to Britain. To go by sea would have been unlikely but not impossible. Yet if the missionary journey was made overland through the regions of the Roman province of Gaul, either no churches were established in those regions or they died out.

To the west of Rome lay Spain. We know that Paul had wanted to make a missionary journey to Spain after he had visited Rome (Rom. 15:23-24,28). However, all that we are told of the end of the life of the great apostle was that he arrived in Rome and lived there in prison for two years (Acts 28:30). An ancient tradition claims that Paul was executed in Rome during the persecution of Nero in A.D. 64. If this date of his death is correct, then he was most likely released from prison after a hearing in A.D. 63. If he had been condemned at that time, his execution would certainly not have been postponed for more than a year.

However, if Paul was freed in A.D. 63, this leaves at least a full year of his life unaccounted for. Either he remained in Rome for this period or made his planned journey to Spain. We have no way of knowing which. Although our historical records are silent concerning this period, ancient tradition claims that Paul did visit Spain. This same tradition also claims that churches were started in Spain by James, the brother of Jesus. Although we do not know for certain, I like to think that Paul did get to go to Spain, returning to Rome just at the time of Nero's persecution, when he was put to death.

28
Summary

The splash which is made when a stone is thrown into a pool of water is easy to see. It is sudden and makes a significant disturbance upon the face of the water, catching the attention of all who are standing by. On the other hand, the aftereffects of such a splash are much harder to see, becoming ever more difficult to follow the farther away we get from the point of the splash. The same effects are seen throughout history. Major events are easily seen, and their immediate consequences are fairly easily observed and evaluated. This is clearly true of the events which make up the history of the New Testament era.

The splash was the resurrection of Jesus or, in a larger sense, His entire life. However, the consequences of that splash, analogous to the spreading ripples, are more difficult to see the farther away we get from the actual event itself. At the same time, in a very real sense it is the spreading ripples which have altered history, as the effects of the splash are felt by the common people throughout the world of that era and this.

This section of our study began with the decision made by the church at Antioch in Syria to send missionaries. Paul and Barnabas were selected under the leadership of God's Holy Spirit to carry the effect of the "splash" of Jesus' resurrection into the world. As we noted at the beginning of this section, a hurried and superficial reading of the Book of Acts leads us to suppose that the work of these two men was the major missionary enterprise in the first century by the church of Jesus Christ.

However, a more careful reading of this document reveals that many other people were also involved in this missionary effort. Among these are the efforts of the friends and companions of Paul, as well as the later efforts of Barnabas. To these we must add the work of Apollo from Alexandria and Priscilla and Aquila from Rome. In addition to these we find the unnamed persons who carried the gospel to those places where Paul found Christians and churches upon his first visits.

In addition to these bits and pieces of information from Acts, we can also enlarge our picture of the missionary activities of some of those early Christians as we come across hint after hint in the letters of Paul and in the General Epistles of the New Testament. This picture of expansionist activity is even further enlarged when we begin to examine nonbiblical traditions and other hints from writers and historians of the era.

The point to all of this is that sometime shortly after the resurrection of Jesus, the gospel message began to spread throughout the ancient world. However, in about A.D. 45 a conscious effort seems to have begun with the purpose of carrying the good news of Jesus to the ends of the empire. It appears from the evidence that this was the time when the Christians and churches became intentionally missionary. These efforts changed the pattern of the churches forever and made a transforming difference in the lives of those who heard and accepted the message. From this time forth the churches of the New Testament became a force with which to be reckoned by the Roman Empire and its official representatives, wherever they might have been.

We must also note, however, that the real impact of the New Testament missionaries and their proclamation cannot be measured either by their impact upon Rome or the effects within the lives of those who were the missionaries. History must be evaluated by what happens to the common people of the world. It is here that the most significant feature of the early church must be seen and measured. Unfortunately, we do not have the records by which we can measure this. We can only see faint shadows on the stage of history which represent the people involved in Christianity, but the world was never the same.

Contrary to the initial impression of the Book of Acts, as we have shown, from a historian's standpoint the expansion of the early church is not just the story of Paul and his companions, however significant that may have been. The expansion of the early churches is the story of those persons scattered throughout the world who dared to believe the message which they had heard.

By the end of this era, Christians were clearly found at the center of the empire. Far more significantly, Christians were also found at the edges of the empire. Perhaps of most significance is the fact that they were even found beyond the borders of the empire. Christians carried their good news to places where Romans had not dared to tread. The sphere of Christian influence was far more widely spread than was that of Rome.

This has always been the story. For all of the church's periods of withdrawal and weakness, Christians have still consistently gone beyond the borders of nation, culture, and race to share their message of Jesus. Thus, in a very real sense the history of the New Testament era is still going on. The ripples sent forth by the splash of the resurrection are still spreading to the edges of recorded time.

Part 6
Conclusion: The Lord God Omnipotent Reigneth

The final book of the New Testament draws to a close with a vision of all the saints and the heavenly court joining in a shout of triumph as they proclaim: "Alleluia: for the Lord God omnipotent reigneth" (Rev. 19:6, KJV). Clearly, the future which was envisioned by the human author of that triumphal book is beyond the purview of a historian of the New Testament era. To be even more precise, that future is beyond the purview of any historian.

In all honesty, however, a New Testament historian must recognize that the vision of that future was itself a part of the New Testament era, produced by those who lived in it and enshrined by those who looked beyond it. In the light of the significance which this hope had upon the development of the New Testament community and its faith, we should at least give a parting glance at that hope and the faith which produced it.

Throughout this book, we have been giving our major attention to the history of the New Testament era rather than to the faith of the New Testament. This was certainly not due to the fact that this faith was (or is) unimportant. To the contrary, the New Testament faith is the reason for the existence of the New Testament and therefore for this book itself.

Throughout the writing of this book, I have sought to place the faith of the New Testament against its cultural, geographic, and historical background. Thus this background has been the focus of attention. On the other hand, it is quite possible to study the history of the New Testament era without ever considering the fact that the New Testament is a book of faith. Such an approach would be a gross error. The faith of the New Testament writers and people is what makes their history significant and what colors their interpretation and understanding of that history. Therefore, this has been noted throughout the book.

At the same time, in drawing this book to a conclusion we also need to give consideration to the fact that while the early Christians were clearly in the world and can only fully be understood in terms of the world in which they lived, they did not consider themselves to be *only* of this world. To the contrary, they considered themselves to be citizens of two worlds. This belief significantly affected the way they approached the world in which they lived.

Further, we really cannot understand the New Testament Christians without understanding this "two world" aspect of their faith. In simple terms, for them this world was not all there was. Further, for those of us who follow after them, this belief is a part of our faith. Thus to try to understand the history of those early Christians without understanding their faith is just as impossible as trying to understand their faith without trying to understand their history.

In its simplest form, the faith of the New Testament was set forth in Peter's sermon on the day of Pentecost. There he proclaimed to the people of Jerusalem,

> Men of Israel, hear these words: Jesus of Nazareth, a man attested to you by God with mighty works and wonders and signs which God did through him in your midst, . . . this Jesus . . . you crucified . . . This Jesus God raised up, and of that we are all witnesses. Being therefore exalted at the right hand of God, and having received from the Father the promise of the Holy Spirit, he has poured out this which you see and hear. God has made him both Lord and Christ, this Jesus whom you crucified (Acts 2:22-23,32-33,36).

The faith of these early Christians quickly developed all sorts of additional dimensions and clarifications, as can be seen from the Book of Acts or from the Epistles. Its essence always seems to have been that *Jesus died, was buried and resurrected, and is Lord.* It is the sovereign lordship of the resurrected Jesus which appears to be the central focus of the New Testament. Thus any attempt to understand the history of these people aside from this belief is a task doomed to failure. This faith was what made them what they were. If we do not approach the understanding of their history from this standpoint, we are doomed to failure from the beginning.

They believed that Jesus is Lord. Therefore they had to surrender themselves to Him as servants.

They believed that Jesus is Lord. Therefore they had to seek to do what was His purpose and not their own.

They believed that Jesus is Lord. Therefore they had to tell others of what He had done on their behalf and what he expected from them in response.

They believed that Jesus is Lord. Therefore their view of the world was wholly colored by its reaction to and reception of that lordship.

They believed that Jesus is Lord. Therefore their hope for life beyond this world was based upon the conviction that He was Lord beyond the grave.

They believed that Jesus is Lord. Therefore their ultimate hope was shaped by the conviction that His lordship would finally be realized throughout all the universe as well as in this world and the one which was to come.

The early Christians' belief in the lordship of Jesus shaped their relations with Judaism as well as with the other world religions with which they came in contact. This belief also determined the limits to which they would go in obeying others' authority, whether political or religious. Quite early in the history of the church, Peter and John said to the Sanhedrin, "Whether it is right in the sight of God to listen to you rather than to God, you must judge" (Acts 4:19). They remembered Jesus Himself admonished His followers, "Render to Caesar the things that are Caesar's, and to God the things that are God's" (Mark 12:17; cf. Matt. 22:21; Luke 20:25).

Further, His followers remembered that Jesus did not in any way dispute Pilate's claim to have power over Him: "Do you not know that I have power to release you, and power to crucify you?" (John 19:10). But Jesus' actions plainly showed that, while He was submissive to Pilate's authority, He served a higher authority and was moved by a higher allegiance.

Jesus' example was clearly understood by His followers at this point. Thus Paul later admonished those living in the very heart of the empire, "Let every person be subject to the governing authorities" (Rom. 13:1). Paul also showed both by percept and example that being subject to the governing authorities was always understood in the light of his prior subjection to the Lord Jesus. Because of this he endured the punishments of Rome rather than disavow his ultimate commitment to the Lord Jesus.

As we have already noted, the faith of the early Christians rapidly grew beyond the simple assertion of the lordship of Jesus. The very pressure of life as it was made this necessary. Thus their growing faith added other central statements to it. These were related to the organization of the communities which they established, to the implications of the lordship of Jesus to every aspect of their lives, and to their obligation to share the news of God's salvation with all people everywhere. These also related to drawing the distinctions between their faith and that of all the religions which existed alongside of them in the Roman Empire, including Judaism, their parent faith.

Two things stood out in the process of the development of the larger circle of beliefs to which the early Christians held. First, they developed these larger areas of faith under the leadership of the Lord Jesus and derived from their belief in that lordship. Second, the development of that larger faith was not without its problems and disagreements.

The Jerusalem Council which is described in Acts 15 was called because a major disagreement grew between Gentile Christians and Jewish Christians as to the basic definition of what being a Christian entailed. When the decision of the council was finally reached, although an official pronouncement was made, there was neither unanimous agreement with it nor acquiescence to it.

In addition, both the Book of Acts and the Epistles of Paul show numerous places where various Christian communities or people within those communities disagreed with one another as to the nuances or essences of their faith. Many of Paul's Epistles were written precisely because of these differences. For example, 1 Corinthians dealt with disagreements both within the church and between the church and Paul about allegiances (1:12; 3:4-6), marriage (7:1ff), celibacy (7:25ff), food sacrificed to idols (8:1ff), the freedom of believers (10:23ff), propriety in worship (11:2ff), the Lord's Supper (11:17ff), spiritual gifts (12:1ff), the nature of the church (12:12ff), orderly worship (14:26ff), and the nature of both Jesus' resurrection and ours (15:1ff).

Thus the New Testament developed as a book of faith, not as a book of history. Though it reflects history, it is a faith statement. We turn to it for an understanding of Christian faith. However, all we can really learn about the historical details of the life of Jesus and early Christian history are also found in its pages. We take, as we have done in this book, the direct historical statements and the many historical hints and seek to place them within the context of what we know about the ancient world in which it developed. Oftentimes all we know about events is what is recorded in the Book. Sometimes all we know is what we find in non-New Testament sources. Most of the time the historian is fitting the two records into one another. However, to do this without seeing that the New Testament was primarily a faith pronouncement is to fail to do it properly. The New Testament proclaims a faith which was both set and developed in history, not a history which produced a faith. It begins and ends with a proclamation of the lordship of Jesus.

A record of the genealogy of Jesus Christ the son of David, the son of Abraham: Abraham was the father of . . . Joseph, the husband of Mary, of whom was born Jesus, who is called Christ (Matt. 1:1-2,16, NIV).

Alleluia: for the Lord God omnipotent reigneth (Rev. 19:6, KJV).

BIBLIOGRAPHY

Aharoni, Yohanan. *The Land of the Bible*. Rev. ed. Philadelphia: The Westminster Press, 1979.

Baly, Denis. *The Geography of the Bible*. New York: Harper and Brothers, 1957.

Barclay, William. *The Gospel of Luke*. Philadelphia: The Westminster Press, 1956.

Barclay, William, ed. *The Bible and History*. London: Lutterworth Press, 1968.

Barr, David L. *New Testament Story*. Belmont: Wadsworth Publishing Co., 1987.

Beasley-Murray, George R. *Word Biblical Themes: John*. Dallas: Word Publishing, 1989.

Bevan, Edwyn. *Jerusalem under the High Priests*. London: Edward Arnold Ltd., 1958.

Blomberg, Craig. *The Historical Reliability of the Gospels*. Downers Grove: Inter-Varsity Press, 1987.

Briggs, R. C. *Interpreting the New Testament Today*. Nashville: Abingdon Press, 1973.

Bruce, F. F. *Israel and the Nations*. Exeter: The Paternoster Press, 1975.

_____. *The Time Is Fulfilled*. Exeter: The Paternoster Press, 1978.

Caird, G. B. *The Apostolic Age*. London: Gerald Duckworth and Co. Ltd., 1955.

_____. *Paul's Letters from Prison*. Oxford: The University Press, 1976.

Cate, Robert L. *A History of the Bible Lands in the Interbiblical Period*. Nashville: Broadman Press, 1989.

_____. *These Sought a Country: A History of Israel in Old Testament Times*. Nashville: Broadman Press, 1985.

Cornfeld, Gaalyah. *Archaeology of the Bible: Book by Book*. San Francisco: Harper and Row, 1976.

Daniel-Rops, Henri. *Daily Life in Palestine at the Time of Christ*. Translated by Patrick O'Brian. London: Weidenfeld and Nicholson, 1962.

Davies, Philip R. *Qumran*. Guilford: Lutterworth Press, 1982.

Ellison, H. L. *From Babylon to Bethlehem*. Exeter: The Paternoster Press, 1976.

Filson, Floyd V. *A New Testament History*. London: SCM Press, 1964.

Finegan, Jack. *Handbook of Biblical Chronology*. Princeton: Princeton University Press, 1964.

Foakes-Jackson, F. J. *Josephus and the Jews*. London: SPCK, 1930.

Forster, Werner. *Palestinian Judaism in New Testament Times*. Translated by G. E. Harris. London: Oliver and Boyd, 1964.

Gasque, W. Ward and Ralph P. Martin, eds. *Apostolic History and the Gospel*. Exeter: The Paternoster Press, 1970.

Goodwin, Frank J. *A Harmony of the Life of St. Paul*. Grand Rapids: Baker Book House, 1951.

Grollenberg. L. H. *Atlas of the Bible*. Translated and edited by Joyce M. H. Reid and H. H. Rowley. London: Thomas Nelson and Sons, Ltd., 1958.

Harrop, Clayton. *History of the New Testament in Plain Language*. Waco: Word Books, 1984.

Hengel, Martin. *Acts and the History of Earliest Christianity*. Translated by John Bowden. London: SCM Press, 1979.

_____. *Jews, Greeks, and Barbarians*. London: SCM Press, 1980.

Hopkins. I. W. J. *Jerusalem: A Study in Urban Geography*. Grand Rapids: Baker Book House, 1970.

Jagersma, H. *A History of Israel from Alexander the Great to Bar Kochba*. London: SCM Press, 1985.

Jones, A. H. M. *The Herods of Judea*. Oxford: Clarendon Press, 1938.

Kenyon, Kathleen M. *The Bible and Recent Archaeology*. Rev. ed. Atlanta: John Knox Press, 1987.

Kraeling, Emil G. *I Have Kept the Faith: The Life of the Apostle Paul*. New York: Rand McNally and Co., 1965.

Leaney, A. R. C. *The Jewish and Christian World: 200 B.C. to A.D. 200*. Cambridge: Cambridge University Press, 1984.

Lohse, Eduard. *The First Christians*. Translated by M. Eugene Boring. Philadephia: Fortress Press, 1983.

_____. *The New Testament Environment*. Translated by John E. Steely. Nashville: Abingdon Press, 1976.

Malina, Bruce J. *The New Testament World*. Atlanta: John Knox Press, 1981.

Martin, Ralph P. *New Testament Foundations*. 2 vols. Exeter: The Paternoster Press, 1975, 1978.

May, Herbert G., ed. *Oxford Bible Atlas*. 3d ed. New York: Oxford University Press, 1984.

McCullough, W. Stewart. *The History and Literature of the Palestinian Jews from Cyprus to Herod*. Toronto: University of Toronto Press, 1975.

Meyers, Eric M. and James F. Strange. *Archaeology, the Rabbis and Early Christianity*. London: SCM Press, 1981.

Neill, Stephen. *Jesus Through Many Eyes*. Philadelphia: Fortress Press, 1976.

Perowne, Stewart. *The Political Background of the New Testament*. London: Hodder, 1958.

Ramsay, William M. *St. Paul the Traveller and the Roman Citizen*. Grand Rapids: Baker Book House, 1982.

Reicke, Bo. *The New Testament Era: The World of the Bible from 500 B.C. to A.D. 100*. Translated by David E. Green. Philadelphia: Fortress Press, 1964.

Robinson, John A. T. *Redating the New Testament*. London: SCM Press, 1976.

Russell, D. S. *Between the Testaments*. London: SCM Press, 1960.

_____. *From Early Judaism to Early Church*. London: SCM Press, 1986.

Sanders, E. P. *Jesus and Judaism*. London: SCM Press, 1985.

Schurer, Emil. *The History of the Jewish People in the Age of Jesus Christ (175 B.C.-A.D. 135)*. 3 vols. Revised by Geza Vermes and Fergus Millar. Edinburgh: T. and T. Clark Ltd., 1973-86.

Sherwin-White, A. N. *Roman Society and Roman Law in the New Testament*. Oxford: Clarendon Press, 1963.

Stalker, James. *The Life of Jesus Christ*. New York: Fleming H. Revell Co., 1912.

Stauffer, Ethelbert. *Jesus and His Story*. Translated by Richard and Clara Winston. New York: Alfred A. Knopf, 1960.

Stone, Michael Edward. *Scriptures, Sects, and Visions*. Philadephia: Fortress Press, 1980.

Tidball, Derek. *The Social Context of the New Testament*. Grand Rapids: Academie Books, 1984.

Vardaman, Jerry. "Jesus' Life: A New Chronology," *Biblical Illustrator,* Winter 1985, 12-18.

Vermes, Geza. *The Dead Sea Scrolls: Qumran in Perspective*. London: Collins, 1977.

White, Reginald E. O. *The Stranger of Galilee*. Grand Rapids: Wm. B. Eerdmans Publishing Co., 1960.

SCRIPTURE INDEX